BUILDING PEDAGOGUES

BUILDING PEDAGOGUES

*White Practicing Teachers and the
Struggle for Antiracist Work in Schools*

Zachary A. Casey and Shannon K. McManimon

Published by State University of New York Press, Albany

© 2020 State University of New York

All rights reserved

No part of this book may be used or reproduced in any manner whatsoever without written permission. No part of this book may be stored in a retrieval system or transmitted in any form or by any means including electronic, electrostatic, magnetic tape, mechanical, photocopying, recording, or otherwise without the prior permission in writing of the publisher.

For information, contact State University of New York Press, Albany, NY
www.sunypress.edu

Library of Congress Cataloging-in-Publication Data

Names: Casey, Zachary A., 1985– author. | McManimon, Shannon (Shannon K.), author.
Title: Building pedagogues : white practicing teachers and the struggle for antiracist work in schools / Zachary A. Casey and Shannon K. McManimon.
Description: Albany : State University of New York Press, [2020] | Includes bibliographical references and index.
Identifiers: LCCN 2019043528 | ISBN 9781438479750 (hardcover : alk. paper) | ISBN 9781438479743 (pbk. : alk. paper) | ISBN 9781438479767 (ebook)
Subjects: LCSH: Multicultural education—United States. | Culturally relevant pedagogy—United States. | Anti-racism—Study and teaching—United States. | Race awareness—Study and teaching—United States. | Teachers, White—Training of—United States.
Classification: LCC LC1099.3 .C376 2020 | DDC 370.117—dc23
LC record available at https://lccn.loc.gov/2019043528

10 9 8 7 6 5 4 3 2 1

*For the teachers in RaceWork,
whose work and commitment are an inspiration
to those who seek racial justice, in schools and out*

Contents

Acknowledgments		ix
Introduction: Who We Are Becoming		1
Chapter 1	What We Read	23
Chapter 2	What We Did	45

Part 1
The Personal

Chapter 3	Fears	67
Chapter 4	Personal Change	85

Part 2
The Local

Chapter 5	Relationships	107
Chapter 6	Tensions: Conflicts with Colleagues in Three Movements	125

Part 3
The Structural

Chapter 7	White Privilege	147

| Chapter 8 | Seeing and Getting "It" | 163 |

The Work

Chapter 9	Approaches and Beliefs	179
Chapter 10	For the Future of Antiracist Work with Practicing Teachers: From Professional Development to Critical Teacher Learning	195
Appendixes		215
References		223
Index		233

Acknowledgments

The authors would like to thank our partners, Elyse Wigen and Jesse Roberts, our parents Paul and Teresa Casey and Don and Valerie McManimon, the Midwest Critical Whiteness Collective, and especially Tim Lensmire for years of support, love, and guidance in this work. Both Jane Joyner and Michael McCanless were dedicated research assistants who, with their contributions and insights, helped move this work forward. We would also like to thank the many practitioners, students, teachers, scholars, and activists we have worked with on questions of whiteness, racial identities, and white supremacy over the past decade. All that we learned with you and from you has made this book possible.

Portions of this project have appeared previously, though not in the same format or depth, in McManimon, S. K., & Casey, Z. A. (2018). (Re)Beginning and becoming with white practicing teachers: Antiracism and professional development with white practicing teachers. *Teaching Education*, 29(4), 395–406, as well as in Casey, Z. A., & McManimon, S. K. (2018). Uneasy racial "experts": White teachers and antiracist action. In S. K. McManimon, Z. A. Casey, & C. Berchini (Eds.), *Whiteness at the table: Antiracism, racism, and identity in education* (pp. 77–92). Lanham, MD: Lexington Books.

Introduction

Who We Are Becoming

One fall Saturday morning in Minnesota, a group of white teachers and two white teacher educators spent 3 hours together in a basement classroom of a university teacher education building. As we were wrapping up, one teacher, Angela, with tears in her eyes, asked why she had not had access to the information we had presented in either her teacher education program or her more than 2 decades of practice. Like most of the teachers in the room that morning, Angela had been to many diversity and equity trainings and professional development (PD) sessions—and often felt frustrated. In the following 2 years, our collective work would help her, particularly in interacting with other white teachers in her building. She explained the second month that she "came back because I *had* to—well, not had to, but need to. I felt really empowered . . . I need to do something that is head-heavy, nourishing, educational."

This book attempts an impossibility: to analyze and share what happened in and as a result of this 2-year PD seminar—RaceWork—for white practicing teachers. This impossibility arises out of three complications: (1) We (Zac and Shannon) were simultaneously *facilitating* the group as we were *researching* it; (2) as scholars and teacher educators, we are simultaneously proud of our work with this group yet wish to remain scholarly and critical of antiracist pedagogies (including our own) with practicing teachers; and (3) as scholars, teachers, and people in relationships with these eight teachers, we are well aware that we can never completely rid ourselves of the possibility of committing violence in writing about our work, whether through omission, our own interpretation, or the ways in which we share—or don't share—these stories. In other words, in many ways we are too close to this group, to this "data," to write from a position of disinterested-objective academician. And so we have made the writerly decision to suspend such demands of academic writing. We also state upfront that we are writing from a place of love and the utmost respect, gratitude, and awe for these eight teachers.

We want to tell you, the reader, what happened when we broke the mold of professional development focused on race and racism for white practicing teachers. We want to tell you how we organized our sessions, and why we read what we read and did what we did. We want to tell you about the incredible antiracist practices these teachers enacted in their own school settings. We also want to tell you about the complications, difficulties, and failures of our collective work. Finally, we want to tell you what we think others can learn from our group about combatting white supremacy in schools.[1]

Before we can proceed to the stories and analyses of RaceWork, we need to set the scene a bit more explicitly, because, as Nicole, one of the participating teachers, wrote at the end of our first of 2 years together, we need to "remember [that] nothing is free of context." In this introductory chapter, after these contexts, we write about RaceWork's origins, our goals, and introduce key terms necessary to situate our work and that of the eight RaceWork teachers. Last, we outline the chapters that follow and explain the title of this book. First, we explain our contexts of time, space, and who we are as white people that led us toward building antiracist pedagogues in Minnesota in 2012.

Contexts: Time, Space, and (White) Community

We wrote this book in 2017 and 2018, a time that feels extraordinarily different racially from when we started RaceWork, in 2012. In 2012, we were nearing the end of Barack Obama's first term as the first Black (and nonwhite) president of the United States.[2] His election, in 2008, had been

---

[1] "White supremacy" here should be understood as analogous with the term "systemic or structural racism." By white supremacy we mean the overarching racialized system of belonging, value, and worth that has resulted in peoples of European descent in the United States occupying positions of power and superiority over those seen as nonwhite and peoples of color. White supremacy signals the primary logic of racialized exploitation, genocide, conquest, and settler colonialism that animates our contemporary social reality. We detail our own conception of white supremacy in greater detail in chapter 1.

[2] It is worth noting that President Barack Obama was born to a white mother and Black father. However, given the legacies of "one-drop" laws and practices to protect the interests of white elites, and the ways in which white supremacy continues to distort and limit possibilities for racial configurations that do not neatly

widely lauded as a sign that we, in the United States, were "postracial," "proving" that meritocracy works in this country, that no matter one's racial identity, anyone can aspire to and be elected to the highest office. Of course, this assertion itself was highly racialized—with many more white people asserting a postracial stance than people of color or Indigenous people. And often, white people who talked about a postracial society took an explicitly "colorblind" stance—it is not "necessary," or even polite, to acknowledge race and the legacies of racial oppression. (We say much more about "colorblindness" in Chapter 1.)

In the years that followed, though, the lie of a supposed postracial society continued to be challenged overtly, just as it had always been in communities of color. High-profile killings of Black people—Sandra Bland, Michael Brown, Philando Castile, Eric Garner, Freddie Gray, Aiyana Jones, Trayvon Martin, Tamir Rice, Walter Scott (and too many more)—by police, while in police custody, or extra-judicially, along with the frequent legal exoneration of those involved, led to the creation of the international but decentralized movement Black Lives Matter in 2013. Social media brought us news nearly daily of racialized oppression. It became less and less weird for us (Shannon and Zac) to get blank or quizzical looks when we told people that we were critical whiteness scholars. More white people seemed to be aware—as people of color and Indigenous people have always had to be—that "white" is also a racial identity. In 2016, for instance, the white hip hop duo Macklemore & Ryan Lewis released a song (featuring Jamila Woods) called "White Privilege II." Later that year, Donald Trump was elected by the electoral college to the presidency after explicitly courting white voters who were upset about assertions that the United States was not now nor had it ever been a white nation, despite resources and power being disproportionately concentrated in white hands. In other words, to start this book, we want to point out that conversations about race have shifted over the last decade—even as they've largely stayed the same.

Also important to know are the spatial contexts in which this PD work occurred: What is now known as the Twin Cities of Minnesota (Minneapolis and St. Paul) occupies Dakota and Anishanabek land and is home to many Indigenous peoples. In recent centuries, Minnesota has had a reputation as a white space, populated by people of Scandinavian descent. But the Twin Cities are home to incredibly diverse groups of peoples—and as someone once said, our diversity is more diverse than in

---

map on to binaristic or census-based racial and ethnic classifications, Obama was and continues to be interpolated not as mixed race or "half-white" but as Black. Our reference here intends to situate the very different racio-political moments we are navigating in this work: professional development in the Obama years, written about in the Trumpocene.

many places. For instance, the St. Paul area is home to one of the world's largest Hmong populations, who immigrated there after the 1960s/1970s war in southeast Asia (Vietnam and Laos). The area is also home to one of the world's largest Somali diasporas, with between 40,000 and 80,000 people of Somali descent. While still majority white, the area is home to a wide range of people of many racial and ethnic identities, including American Indians. Yet as in other metropolitan areas across the country, neighborhoods—and thus schools—are quite often segregated. And as in other cities, regentrification has also meant that many residents of color are being pushed out of urban areas and into suburban schools and neighborhoods. But despite our "diverse diversity," most white people in the area aren't any better at talking about this—and particularly about what it means to be white.

In the first episode of their *Code Switch* podcast, Meraji and Demby (2016) assert that we're really, really bad at talking about what it means to be white in the United States. Demby said that part of this difficulty and discomfort is that

> We've had this reflexive habit of talking about what's normal or what's default in American politics in ways that are really, really just about white people in white culture. But we're not really used to talking about white people directly as their own identity group . . . It's like whiteness is everywhere and invisible all at once. So trying to put your hands around it is like trying to hold on to air.

It was this simultaneous invisible-everywhereness that we, as two white people, wanted to address with other white people and specifically with white people teaching in public schools. This was our responsibility, following Darder (2011), who wrote,

> There must be an active commitment by those from the dominant culture to work in their own communities and to challenge forms of injustice that result from racism, classism, sexism, homophobia, disablism, and other forms of institutional oppression, for all forms of oppression are inextricably linked to the overarching consequences of a political economy that chews up our hearts to feed the fat royal beast of capital. (p. 90)

Our explicitly acknowledged identities as white people who needed to address white supremacy are thus the third context of our work: We believe that white supremacy is, at its heart and soul, a white people's problem enacted on the bodies and communities of peoples of color, but one that is also destructive to white people. Rather than leaving attempts to dismantle it solely to people of color, we, as white people, must also do the work. We are committed politically to a praxis premised on the idea that it is our particular responsibility to do this work with white teachers and students.

Origins of RaceWork:
Who We Are and What We Decided to Try

In 2009, both of us, Zac and Shannon, moved to Minnesota to begin the Culture and Teaching doctoral program (a specialization within the Department of Curriculum and Instruction at the University of Minnesota), wanting to study and act on race and racism—and, in particular, white racial identity. We met at the first day of orientation; soon we were having weekly conversations about our new lives in Minnesota. Within a month, we participated in the first meeting of the newly created Midwest Critical Whiteness Collective (MCWC), a non-university-based research group of academics, educators, practitioners, and activists. Over the next years, MCWC took on a serious study of McIntosh's (1988) groundbreaking writing on white privilege, talking, presenting, and publishing on our work.

As doctoral students, drawing on knowledges we had arrived with and were further developing through MCWC and other spaces, we (Shannon and Zac) spoke and presented at a number of conferences for practitioners and educational researchers. These talks were so well received that we found ourselves repeatedly invited to give similar versions to other groups in other settings. Excited to share our work with others, we always agreed to speak with whomever would have us, never asking for compensation. We spoke in college courses, to student groups, to teaching assistants and university instructors, and to academics. A common theme emerged across these settings: Almost everyone wished that they had either learned more about the history of white supremacy and white racial identity in their formal educations or that they could engage in such study longer than the hour or two we were able to spend with them.

During these years, Zac organized a small group of practicing teachers who had taken various courses with him and wished to continue meaningful conversations about race and difference. Dubbing themselves the White Anti-Oppressive Teacher Support Group, the five members met once a month for 6 months during the 2011–2012 school year. While Zac sent a chapter or two to read between each session, meetings were largely about story sharing and, well, supporting one another. As each teacher worked in a different school and district, the group served as a sounding board and as a place for teachers to not feel as isolated as they often did. Still, the group was primarily social and cathartic, rather than explicitly intentional around building capacity for anti-oppressive work in classrooms and schools. The group met to help one another feel better about the daunting and dehumanizing realities of our institutions, but it became clear that we needed to do more. These teachers wanted more: not just to talk, but to figure out *what to do*.

At the same time, Shannon was conducting research for our teacher education program by interviewing principals and teachers at local area partner schools. Many of these educators spoke about the changing racial demographics of their schools or racialized disparities; they were looking for tools and resources to equip teachers. Some had hired PD organizations to do this work.

We also saw these needs in the courses we taught and recognized them in our own histories. For Shannon, a decade spent doing antiracism work with adults had been a—probably *the*—compelling factor in going back to school; her experiences working with white adults in their 50s, 60s, and 70s led her to ask why we weren't more frequently doing this work in public schools. Animated by commitments to combatting white supremacy and by the experience outlined here, we, Zac and Shannon, believed that such work would never achieve its full transformative power if white people were not more explicitly figured as antiracist actors. Again, white supremacy is a white problem, and white people must explicitly oppose and dismantle it if we are to ever overcome its devastation and dehumanization.

We talked about all of this frequently. We shared stories—our own and others—of white educators getting stuck trying to do antiracist work. We were struck by the chasm we felt between academic research or analyses of race and racism and the professional development and teacher education curricula we had experienced, curricula that also dominated the social justice/activism circles in which Shannon had worked prior to moving to Minneapolis. Such programs rely almost exclusively—or at minimum begin with or are premised—on white privilege frameworks. (See Chapter 7 for a more detailed discussion.) While these programs can often support educators who have spent little to no time considering the ways in which their work is culpable in maintaining the oppressive status quo, they often result in a kind of "dead end" for participants who have been engaged in such work for a more extended period of time. That is, white privilege frameworks tend to be circular: The object is to help white people understand their relative privilege. Such consciousness is supposed to lead to antiracist actions, although this is almost never elaborated, resulting in participants sharing sentiments along the lines of "OK, I get that I have privilege, and I can recognize privilege, but what should I *do*?"

This is, of course, tied in with what Charlie, a teacher introduced later in this chapter, reminded us often: "Teachers want the checklist." In other words, many teachers desire explicit strategies, checklists, and instructions, yet explicit instruction around classroom procedures is rejected by most culturally relevant or sustaining and multicultural pedagogies. If we tell a teacher exactly what to do, we foreclose possibilities for engaged learning with the *actual* students who inhabit our classrooms. As Ladson-Billings (2006b), teaching in an undergraduate teacher education course, told her students,

> Even if we could tell you how to do it, I would not want us to tell you how to do it. . . . The reason I would not tell you what to do is that you would probably do it! . . . In other words, you would probably do exactly what I told you to do without any deep thought or critical analysis. You would do what I said regardless of the students in the classroom, their ages, their abilities, and their need for whatever it is I proposed. (p. 39)

Social justice–oriented PD tends to do the same, even as teachers often report feeling stifled by a lack of concrete suggestions. Arguing that "we can't tell you what to do, because then you would do it" feels like an easy-out to many practitioners. It feels overly academic, possibly even condescending.

Concomitantly, many teachers have experienced PD that feels overtly infantilizing, that positions teachers as if they don't know or understand anything about their students or contexts. These PD experiences tend to feature an expert from somewhere else, who hasn't spent a day in their school, yet knows everything that's wrong with it and how to fix it, providing solutions or formulas.

Because of such challenges, both of us had previously shied away from PD as a meaningful way for us to engage educators or teacher candidates in antiracist work.[3] But we thought we could try something different. Our research and presentations on the history of white racial identities and storytelling as antiracist praxis taught us that there was a great desire for opportunities to get smarter about race and structural racism. Our work with practicing teachers, in the support group and in partnership schools,

---

3. We prefer the term "teacher candidates" to "pre-professional," "preservice," or "future" teachers. This move is intentional, as we understand the work of teaching and becoming as always ongoing. Rather than making our teacher education a preparation for the future, we are motivated by Dewey's (1897/2010) maxim that "education, therefore, is a process of living and not a preparation for future living" (p. 22).

taught us the limits of most professional development for antiracism. The teachers we were working with wanted more: more engagement, more time to dig into this work, and more support to take risks and to create more antiracist classrooms and schools. Our study and writing with the Midwest Critical Whiteness Collective taught us that we cannot be content with the most widely cited and read account of white privilege as if such an account were the *only* way of engaging white people in understanding white supremacy (see Lensmire et al., 2013). A new project was taking shape, built out of our work as teachers, researchers, and facilitators. In the spring of 2012, we were ready to start something more formal, more official, than the various talks and discussion groups we had been a part of until then. We decided to call it RaceWork.

RaceWork Goals

We wanted RaceWork to be different from what we had experienced. We wanted to center praxis—critical reflection and action—and to create a space that honored the experiences and expertises of teachers. We also wanted to put our academic work into practice—to engage white practicing teachers, based on our interpretations and syntheses of critical whiteness studies and critical pedagogy literatures. We wanted to emphasize the materiality of racism and antiracism, rather than a too-frequent emphasis on rhetoric. We wanted to engage antiracism as a way of being. As living out our commitments is terribly trying and fraught with difficulty and isolation that often override our collaborative impulses, we decided to build a group based on a simple organizing principle: Rather than grouping around subject matter, grade level, or geography, we recruited, via email, white practicing teachers who were committed to working to combat structural racism in schools and classrooms. We sent this invitation to teachers and administrators in groups we had contact with, such as from the districts Shannon had been interviewing or the White Anti-Oppressive Teacher Support Group Zac was meeting with; we encouraged forwarding the invitation as well. We initially planned to offer a 1-year PD experience. And then something amazing happened: We actually *did it*. We started with the idea that we would spend a year together, but at the end of that 1st year, all eight RaceWork teachers asked if we could continue working together the next year. So, we did.

Our work had three aims: first, to develop and enact a meaningful PD experience for practicing teachers focusing on their own white racial identities and the ways in which these racial identities impact and influence their teaching practice; second, to empower teachers to undertake structural, antiracist change in their classrooms and schools; and third, to research this experience. While these three objectives are explored throughout this book, we briefly detail them below.

PD Focusing on White Racial Identities and Legacies of White Supremacy in Schools

Our primary goal was for teachers to experience meaningful racial equity PD. We began with a premise that teachers, like all people, are intellectuals (a la Gramsci, 1971) and that in many ways, it is not possible to do the extraordinarily challenging work of antiracism without deep historical and theoretical understandings—or at least that these nuanced concepts provide grounding for the moments when the work feels impossible or insurmountable. We thus created an intellectually grounded curriculum to engage teachers in understanding the ongoing legacy of structural racism in schools and society. We knew that our PD group would need a serious understanding not only of the history of white supremacy, but of how that history has acted upon, and continues to act upon, schools and schooling. Too often, white people learn the history of racism as a series of events from the past, as something that society as a whole has "gotten over"—as in the "postracial America" examples mentioned above. While our early work focused on the history of white supremacy and white racial identity, we were careful to make connections to the present realities of schools and classrooms, analyzing the ways in which white supremacist aims and projects are taken up in schools. Teachers connected these to their own contemporary experiences.

This also meant working with these practicing white teachers to develop a rich and nuanced understanding of ourselves as racialized white actors in our own teaching contexts. As critical whiteness scholars, we have seen that too often the emphasis on understanding privilege belies the more complex and nuanced identities of white people. No one is reducible solely to their racial identity; we are never *just* our race, as our identities are made up of thousands upon thousands of commitments, positionalities, determinations, performances, behaviors, and habits. As we move in social space, our identities are figured primarily from two vantage points: our own internal sense of self and the way(s) we are interpolated by others. Thus, regardless of my own self-identity, I am always also simultaneously figured along various schema by those who are interacting with me. White identity has meaning only within the current structural nature of white supremacy and how it constitutes particular subjectivities. To appear white in social space is to be read within a series of codes and norms. We thus worked to understand how each of us and our families became white, the origins of white racial identity in the United States, and the complexities surrounding white antiracist positionalities.

Enacting Structural, Antiracist Change in Classrooms and Schools

These knowledges (and reflection on them) are not, by themselves, enough—or, as Patel (2016) has argued, we wanted our research (and teaching) to focus on *material* changes, not changes solely in words. Thus, our second goal was to work with teachers to collaboratively develop and then implement structural, antiracist change in their classrooms and schools so as to address our first and most critical commitment as teachers: the well-being and learning of our students. We sought to make explicit the ways in which increasing dialogue and engagement with issues of race and structural racism are central to the development of sociopolitical and critical consciousness with students. We wanted teachers to be able to improve learning outcomes for their students through antiracist pedagogical strategies, to forge new connections and relationships that supported students and their families in robust ways, and/or to engage in critical dialogue on race with their students and colleagues.

Here, of course, we bump into the problem of not telling teachers "what to do." Thus, we entered this PD with no preexistent strategies or checklists for RaceWork teachers to follow. Rather, we would work collectively, over time, to support teachers in developing their own antiracist, uniquely contextual, and situated pedagogical interventions in their schools, classrooms, or districts. Importantly, we approached this work with a commitment to *sustaining* engagement with white supremacy and antiracist pedagogies. Rather than a single day, or even a series of days in a workshop, we wanted to build iteratively and scaffold ways that teachers' work in schools could combat white supremacy, thus rejecting the fly-in-fly-out model of professional development with prepackaged lessons and strategies.

Over our time together, the eight teachers who joined us in RaceWork designed and tried out their own antiracist changes. From the beginning, we were careful to delineate what we meant by antiracist. For instance, we asked teachers not to focus on the overcoded concept of "academic achievement" tied to standardized test scores. Our goal was never just to raise the test scores or grades of students of color, but to develop antiracist ways in which to engage students in culturally relevant and sustaining ways, to self-appropriate learning, to create knowledge. We built from the premise that all of our students, in all of our classrooms, possess a wealth of knowledge and expertise on their own lived experiences that can be built upon in each and every course. We must mobilize students' "funds of knowledge" (González, Moll, & Amanti, 2005) to help them connect what they already know to course content and curriculum. At the same time, we acknowledged we should not reduce antiracist pedagogies merely to "good teaching," understanding that "teaching well" is not enough to eliminate white supremacy from our classrooms. We wanted to avoid making the mistake of reducing structural oppressions to the level of individual social actors.

Last, we acknowledged that while talk is not enough, we must get better at talking. For instance, while often ashamed to admit it, many white teachers find parents and students of color intimidating. They worry that they will "misspeak" or "offend" and as a result often resort to silence and omission. RaceWork teachers had very different experiences and feelings regarding interactions with parents and students of color. Some felt comfortable interacting with students, but not with parents, some felt fully confident in interacting with people of color across various ages, and some felt stunted in all of their interactions with people of color. Importantly, we emphasized the ways in which our antiracist pedagogical work must be *with* others, not *for* others.

Research

Our final goal was to research this process, both contributing to the research literature on work for social change within schools and asking teachers to engage in their own forms of research in action. We wanted our work, and everything that we learned with and from these teachers, to support ongoing efforts in educational research, professional development, and teacher education. We thus embedded the data collection (for more about data collection and analysis see Appendix B) that animates what we share in this book. We have shared some of the results of this work at professional conferences; this book represents the culmination of our research and our pedagogy in RaceWork. Importantly, we work to center the teachers and their interventions, struggles, and reflections. This book is not so much about *how* we engaged RaceWork as facilitators, but rather about what teachers took from their work with us, and what we learned from and with them in the process. *Building Pedagogues*, then, is not primarily about *us*, but rather about the work and learning of RaceWork teachers and what happened in their classrooms and schools—where antiracist changes are most needed.

Contexts: Key Terms and Participating Teachers

These goals provided context for our work and practices together. Also important was building a shared understanding of what we were working on and toward; often we assume a shared understanding without actually doing the work of clarification. While emphasizing the materiality of racism and antiracism, we also know that language is powerful and that our words have dramatic and important consequences for racial justice work. The more explicit we can be about what we mean and why we are making our discoursal choices, the more space is opened up for antiracism that goes beyond (just) language. Thus, before introducing the eight RaceWork teachers, we outline some key terms that provide additional contexts for our approaches to antiracist work with white teachers.

White Supremacy and Structural Oppression

Perhaps the most important concept in RaceWork, white supremacy refers to "an historically based, institutionally perpetuated system of exploitation and oppression of continents, nations, and peoples of color by [elite] white peoples and nations . . . for the purposes of maintaining and defending a system of wealth, power, and privilege" (Challenging White Supremacy Workshop). Rather than "racism," white supremacy functions to name the cause of racialized oppression (whiteness), includes people of color as participating in systems of oppression (e.g., buying goods made by people who are oppressed for the benefit of cheaper costs for those with more relative privilege), and focuses on the structural and historical nature of oppression as it impacts people's lives.

White supremacy is structural and systemic. Discussions of racism sometimes focus on individual acts of meanness or bigotry rather than on the larger social forces that operate more directly on the life chances of actual people. While individual racist acts or beliefs must be challenged, some of the acts most harmful to people of color take place without intended malice. Racism is bigger than any individual actor, which is why the term "white supremacy" accomplishes so much in terms of its explanatory power for the focus of our antiracist work.

Pedagogy/Pedagogical

Pedagogy, in its simplest form, is the art of teaching. But pedagogy is more complex than that. Freire (1998) has written that a pedagogue is an educator "who has a political understanding of the task of teaching" (p. 57). All teaching and learning are inherently political, enmeshed with competing claims of justice and injustice, right and wrong, and these claims are often hidden and depoliticized. To approach a problem or theory pedagogically is to privilege the learner and ask the critical question, "what is this teaching?" Pedagogy can then be understood as intentional, political, student-centered teaching (Casey, 2016).

To approach antiracism pedagogically means not to seek to "call out" moments of individual racism, but rather to approach all people as having valuable knowledge with which they can work to build more critical stances on issues of racial equity. It also means that we understand that antiracist dispositions, given our current state of institutionalized white supremacy, require work to learn; different folks will want and need different things and will need different amounts of time to engage in this work.

White/Black Focus of Race in the United States

Some people wonder why discussions of race and racism in the United States frequently center on Black–white racial dynamics and history. It is important to remind ourselves and others why this is so: Because whiteness was literally invented in opposition to Blackness. As Morrison (1993) put it, "Nothing highlighted freedom—if it did not in fact create it—like slavery" (p. 38). In what is now the United States, "whiteness" was invented in colonial Virginia to distinguish slave/servants of European descent from those of African descent in the hopes of creating a false sense of solidarity along racial lines between the white elite land/slave holders and white servants/slaves. This was done out of fear on the part of white elites, who believed that people of African descent and European descent might unite to overthrow their oppressors. This same practice—pitting poor and otherwise marginalized white and Black people (and other peoples of color and Indigenous peoples) against one another—continues to this very day, as we'll discuss in Chapter 1.

Privilege/White Privilege

One way that this happens is through white privilege, a term that refers to the unearned advantages that come with having white skin or a white racial identity in a white supremacist society, such as being able to shop in a store without being suspected of shoplifting, usually being able to talk with a person of one's own race when asking to speak with "the person in charge," not having to serve as a representative of one's race, and not having to educate one's children about structural racism for their own safety. But privilege is always relative. We are all complex actors; no one is reducible *solely* to their privilege (or solely to their racial identity). Additionally (and probably more importantly), privilege is not the *cause* of racism and white supremacy, but an *effect*, of the true cause: oppression. We discuss this much further in chapters to come.

Intersectionality

To help understand the complexity of our identities, we turned to intersectionality, a concept drawn from Crenshaw (1989) and Critical Black

Feminism: We can never fully understand one system of oppression without understanding how other systems of oppression impact and inform it—how they intersect. For Crenshaw, her experience of oppression as a woman is racialized, as a Black woman; her experience of oppression as a person of color is gendered, as a woman. To treat either as distinct would be to ignore core components of our lived reality. Often, sources of resistance to conversations about race and racism are the ways in which other systems of oppression and forms of identity are ignored.

RaceWork Teachers

We—Shannon and Zac—have already introduced ourselves. Now we will introduce each of the eight teachers (although their names are pseudonyms) in RaceWork that you will meet in this book.

Amelia works in an urban high school as a chemistry and physical sciences teacher. At the time of RaceWork, she was in her 6th and 7th years of teaching. Amelia grew up in North Dakota and attended university in Minnesota. She has worked in the same district, one of the largest and most ethnically and racially diverse districts in the state, throughout her teaching career. The majority of students at her school are people of color and qualify for free or reduced-price lunch. Like all of the teachers in RaceWork, the majority of her colleagues are white. Amelia's district had contracted with a number of PD programs centered on white privilege and antiracism in recent years, resulting in many teachers feeling "attacked" and creating a pervasive sense of fear around issues of race and racism throughout the district. Amelia's first school was closed due to district enrollment shifts; thus, while she had already been teaching for 5 years before beginning at her current school, her status as a "new" teacher to the building was a significant source of trepidation.

Angela was the only teacher in our group who had been teaching for more than 2 decades. Stationed in Spain after enlisting in the Navy, she became fluent in Spanish before being discharged and attending university in Wisconsin. She became dual-certified in Spanish Education and in English Language Learning, before teaching for 6 months in Japan. Following this, she moved to the Twin Cities area and began working in a Catholic elementary school. Feeling stifled by the religious demands placed on her, she left this position after a year to move to a suburban district as an English Learner (EL) specialist. Her work with ELs and their families "continued to open my eyes to ways of life that are unique and different than middle-class white people, white people that I grew up with," she told us early in our work together. Angela has been in the same district, working in two elementary schools, ever since. She was in her 23rd year of teaching when she began RaceWork. Due to a series of family crises, Angela was able to attend only one session during our 2nd year together. She remained a critically important figure in the group, however, with other members regularly referencing her in discussions and reflections. Angela has been a vocal proponent for greater attention and services for English Learners in her district, to the extent that she reported that others in her district saw her as a "broken record" when it came to issues of equity and justice. She worried other teachers would not be able to "hear" her, that because she had been so vocal in the past, and because of who she was, the messenger, others would not take her input seriously.

Charlie works in an immediate suburban school as a 3rd- and 4th-grade teacher.[4] She was in her 4th and 5th years of teaching while participating in RaceWork. Charlie's school is comprised primarily of working-class communities of color, particularly African American, Eastern African, East Asian, and Latinx. Over 80% of the district's students qualify for free or reduced-price lunch. Charlie lived outside of the United States for most of her childhood and served in the Peace Corps after graduating from a university in Minnesota. Charlie had been the chair of her school's equity team for a year prior to beginning RaceWork and has remained in this leadership capacity ever since. She is seen in her building as an equity leader; this status has often been a source of conflict for her, particularly with more veteran white teachers.

Lisa was in her 3rd and 4th years of teaching during her time in RaceWork. She works as a French teacher in a racially and economically diverse immediate suburban district, in a combination middle and high school. Lisa attended university in Wisconsin and Vermont before beginning her teaching career in her home state of Minnesota. Of the group members, Lisa had spent the least amount of time formally engaged in professional development or teacher education around issues of race and racism. Her work with us focused nearly as much on her relationships with her family—particularly her father, who expressed deep-seated resentments against people of color and the community Lisa taught in, comprised almost entirely of peoples of color—as it did with her relationships with her students. Lisa's engagement with us saw her grow both in independence from her family and in her confidence as an educator.

Morgan works in a suburban elementary school as a 5th-grade teacher. During her time in RaceWork, she was in her 5th and 6th years

---

4. By "immediate suburban" we mean communities immediately adjacent to either St. Paul or Minneapolis. As we discuss throughout subsequent chapters, many of the schools in historically "white" neighborhoods and communities are increasingly attended by more students of color.

of teaching. Morgan began her career in an all-white rural school hours from the Twin Cities, not far from where she completed her undergraduate degree. After 1 year at the school, she moved to the district she herself had attended, becoming a teacher at the same school she went to in her elementary years. In fact, she was hired by the same principal who worked there when she was a student. The district has experienced a greater than 40% increase in the number of students of color it serves in recent years. Despite this significant shift in demographics, most teachers in Morgan's school and district have resisted learning about race and white supremacy as it impacts their work, believing that such concerns are not relevant for them in their still majority-white area. Feeling "young" and being positioned that way by senior teachers who knew her as an elementary schooler was a significant point of tension for Morgan.

Nicole was in her 4th and 5th years of teaching while participating in RaceWork. Nicole's mother has been a teacher for more than 20 years and served as a model for her of what a teacher committed to social justice ought to do. After attending university in Wisconsin, Nicole began her teaching career at a suburban high school in her home state of Minnesota. Her year at the school was characterized by intense racial conflicts between students, who maintained rigid hierarchies around racialized friend groups, with Black, white, and Latinx students self-segregating and resisting efforts to combat racial tensions. Following this, Nicole moved to a rural school district in a small college town, commuting from the suburbs each day. She worked for 2 years in the alternative high school before taking a full-time English teacher position at the mainstream high school. In this rural, predominantly white context, Latinx students disproportionately live in low-income housing with their families who work in agriculture-related industries. Her school is comprised of a majority of white, middle-class students, many of whom have parents with advanced college degrees, and a small but significant number of students from immigrant families of color. Nicole struggled to help her colleagues understand that while the majority of their students are highly successful, students of color were being stifled and undermined through a lack of engagement of their needs by teachers and staff.

Sarah was in her 1st and 2nd years as Dean of Students for an immediate suburban middle school. After completing her undergraduate degree in Minnesota, she began her teaching journey working in the same private elementary school she had attended. She taught 2nd grade for 3 years, before moving to her current district as a middle school science teacher, as she was dissatisfied working in the homogenous environment of her first school. She was in the classroom in her middle school for 9 years, serving primarily as a life science teacher for 6th grade. As Dean,

Sarah was responsible for student discipline and for standardized testing. Her district, similar to Morgan's, has rapidly increasing numbers of students of color and students qualifying for free or reduced-price lunch. Sarah was struck over the course of her first year as Dean by the frequency and consistency of students who were referred to her by the same teacher multiple times. Taking a restorative justice approach, by the end of the school year immediately following her time in RaceWork, Sarah had led her school to more than a 50% decrease in student referrals and suspensions. Despite this success, Sarah regularly finds herself in conflict with other administrators over policies and procedures regarding student discipline. She is currently pursuing her principal licensure.

Veronica works in an exurban district as a high school social studies teacher. She was in her 8th and 9th years of teaching while participating in RaceWork. Veronica's school is one of the most highly regarded public schools in the state, regularly earning awards and accolades for academic performance, as well as boasting nearly universal high school graduation and college acceptance rates. After attending a private, Christian undergraduate college in Minnesota, she began working at her current school just 10 days after college graduation and has been there ever since. While Veronica's school is overwhelmingly white (over 90%), she has worked for years to build more antiracist capacities with both students and colleagues. By her 2nd year of work with us, Veronica came to be positioned as a building "expert" on issues of race and social justice, a status she was deeply uncomfortable with, believing that her upbringing as Christian and conservative conflicted with such a mantle. While she has led and organized a number of activities and workshops for students and teachers, she remains uncomfortable with the "bubble" that her school community creates and maintains for itself.

Outline of Chapters

The five sections of *Building Pedagogues* explore the work of these eight teachers in their time with us. Following this Introduction in which we have introduced RaceWork and its concepts and participating teachers, Chapter 1 explores what we read: the written texts that animated our work and how we sequenced them. This chapter situates our work in scholarship on whiteness and outlines our tripartite approach to white supremacy: simultaneous work against white supremacy at the level of the personal, the local, the structural. It discusses what we as a group read about antiracist action, language, and approaches. Chapter 2 explores what we did together as a group, starting with our understandings of the classroom and pedagogy and including our articulation of white supremacy. We then move to stories and analysis of RaceWork and the antiracist praxis of these eight white teachers, organized in a way that follows the tripartite structure we engaged of thinking on the personal, local, and structural levels.

This work starts in Part 1 of this book, about the personal, our own mental terrain. Chapter 3 explores fears, whereas Chapter 4 looks at personal change. Fear is one reason white people fail to engage in antiracism; we must explicitly address our fears to avoid getting stuck in them. Chapter 3 explores four fears RaceWork teachers confronted: getting it wrong, not doing enough, harming existing relationships, and being called racist. The chapter argues that we can mobilize these fears as a productive part of antiracist praxis. To address these fears also means undertaking personal change. Chapter 4 thus unpacks ways in which RaceWork teachers experienced personal change, specifically in terms of their growing sociopolitical consciousness and racial fluency.

Part 2 is about the local: those spaces immediately around us over which we have some influence. At the level of the Local, we are intimately involved with other people. Thus, Chapter 5 is concerned with relationships and, specifically, how RaceWork teachers worked to center antiracism in their relationships with each other, with their students, with their students' families, and with like-minded others. It argues that building these pedagogical relationships—and thus an antiracist community—is critical to our work. But this is not easy. Chapter 6 is thus about the tensions RaceWork teachers experienced in doing antiracist work in their buildings, particularly due to liberal individualist conceptions of racism. It details the costs of doing antiracist work in schools, as RaceWork teachers were blamed for calling attention to white supremacy, as they stuck up for students, and as their institutions reproduced white supremacy.

The two chapters of Part 3 deal with the structural: Chapter 7 on white privilege and Chapter 8 on the conundrum of seeing and getting "it." White privilege is the most common approach to dealing with structural racism in PD contexts. But how does this get taken up in schools? Chapter 7 works to (re)define white privilege, exploring how white privilege was both a powerful way of naming RaceWork teachers' own racialized experiences as well as a structural barrier to engaging their colleagues more robustly in antiracist work. Chapter 8 explores how white supremacy was conceptualized through a common phrase RaceWork teachers used: "getting it." "Getting it" (or not) stood in for ways in which other teachers did (or did not) connect the personal and local with the structural: how they came to a process of "reading racially." We also argue here that "getting it" can never just be about words, but must also be about materially enacting antiracism.

The final section of the book ("The Work") offers some unfinished and tentative conclusions for doing the ongoing work. Through examples from each teacher, Chapter 9 details the complex and unique approaches and beliefs RaceWork teachers took as they persisted in their antiracist convictions and actions, enacting antiracism through both doing and being. RaceWork teachers resisted both their own and their colleagues' desires for the simplicity of checklists and strategies. Chapter 10 offers our thoughts on the future of antiracist PD, or what might better be called *critical teacher learning*. RaceWork is a model for antiracist professional development and ongoing teacher education—in other words, critical teacher learning. Yet it is in many ways paradoxical and unreplicable. That is, we do not suggest a rigid set of steps to follow for antiracist PD, because it would lead to the "Yes, but how do we do it?" conundrum that Ladson-Billings (2006) cited in relationship to culturally relevant pedagogy: This work—and, by extension, this book—cannot be prescriptive nor center "best practices" as if such practices can be applied and effective in any professional development context. Thus, we conclude by asserting that we must continually reinvent antiracist teacher learning and enactment with and for teachers grounded in local considerations of contexts and pedagogical specificity.

Last, although MCWC continues, and both of us work with other white people (as white professors in education programs—Shannon in New York and Zac in Tennessee) to better understand our own racialized identities and work for antiracist change in schools, classrooms, and communities, we note here that we too are unfinished.

Building Pedagogues: Nouns and Verbs

As highlighted in the final chapter of this book, we are never finished. This echoes the title of this chapter, an introduction to "Who We Are Becoming." Our work is always unfinished and ongoing; we are always in the mess that centuries of white supremacy have wrought. Further, there are limits on our antiracist work, including the structural (e.g., teachers often have less power than administrators or policymakers, and we are always embedded in larger systems), the interpersonal (such as relationships we already have or assume we have), and the personal (e.g., our own fears).

And yet, our collective work strengthened us as teachers and as antiracist actors. We spent 2 years building our pedagogical selves together as co-learners and co-teachers. In this case, "building" functions as a verb: We engaged in the work of transforming ourselves, our identities, and our classroom and school spaces. RaceWork teachers were *doing* the work as they (and we) were becoming antiracist actors. In the process, RaceWork teachers were positioned as racial experts—they were their building's (as a noun) "expert" pedagogues on issues related to race and antiracism, even when they resisted this title or explicitly acknowledged its complications. Our book title thus names the shift RaceWork teachers made as they collectively found themselves in leadership positions for the first time based on their antiracist engagement. "Building pedagogues" reflects our broader pedagogical project—in both RaceWork and our current teaching—of supporting teachers to, themselves, be(come) teacher educators for other teachers in their buildings.

Building Pedagogues thus has two intertwined meanings. It contextualizes antiracist work in the locale of the schools and districts—the buildings—in which we work. And it emphasizes that this work is ongoing—building is an active labor. Antiracism cannot be passive; if we are not continually building community, ideas, and antiracist identities, we are implicitly endorsing our white supremacist status quo. The community that we built in RaceWork was a space that honored our experiences and expertises and emphasized learning—not just planning—together. We built, in other words, a collective that learned together. We centered our lived experiences (such as family and classroom stories), coupling them with sophisticated theoretical and historical work that did not simplify or call upon stereotyped tropes of race or whiteness. While this work was ultimately about enacting antiracism in our buildings for the sake of student learning, it started with us as educators who are always in the process of becoming.

To close this chapter, as the facilitators of RaceWork and the writers of this book, Zac and Shannon recognize that we have the power to frame RaceWork for you, the reader. And so, before turning to what we read together in the next chapter, we share some of what RaceWork teachers anonymously reported about our work together. At the end of the 1st year, one teacher said that RaceWork had provided "an approach to a huge, scary problem in an unscary, manageable way." Another said that because of RaceWork, "I have had a lot more conversations with others but it has totally changed (in a good way) how I teach and talk to students." A third said that she realized her "incredible power in my classroom to make change and impact students" and another that she is "not alone in my struggles with race issues in my school district." Teachers found solidarity with each other and were supported in having tough conversations, "giving us the resource of each other," even when it was hard or felt overwhelming. At the end of the 2nd year, a teacher reported that "this has completely changed how I teach in my classroom and how I view policies in my school" and another that "it has dramatically changed my approach to curriculum and families/students of color. It has helped me to have conversations with staff members."

From these anonymous written comments, we are validated in our assertions that RaceWork has been and continues to be about all 10 of us becoming building pedagogues. This writing—and the reading of it—continue this work.

CHAPTER 1

What We Read

In March of our 1st year together in RaceWork, the 10 of us (eight teachers and two teacher educators) read a piece by Ladson-Billings. In the conversation about institutionalized racism that followed, Veronica referred to

> this idea of talking about the problem a lot without actually doing anything about the problem—no action. There's a lot of thought, a lot of processing by a few people. But the problem seems so *big*, just like the national debt, that how can you ever deal with it? You can put band-aids on stuff, but you don't want to make it *worse*. But I see a *lot* of programs band-aiding things or talking about how to bandage, like a first-aid class, without ever doing anything.

Veronica was commenting both on what she'd seen in her own school—echoed by other teachers—and on the national conversation on racialized disparities and outcomes in U.S. public schools. We didn't want to be just a bandage or a first-aid class. In RaceWork, we wanted to think, to talk, *and* to do something, both together and in our own schools and classrooms.

And the 10 of us were attempting to *be* something together—to build our pedagogical knowledges and skills in response to the immense challenge of white supremacy and to *be* antiracist teachers with and for other people in our buildings. One of the ways we approached doing and being together was to gather around texts and to explore their meaning in our lives and work.

In talking about RaceWork, over the years we (Shannon and Zac) have been frequently asked about our curriculum. We thus start here, in Chapter 1, with what we read—the written texts that animated our monthly

RaceWork sessions.[1] The two of us chose readings to provide multiple opportunities for entry into study about race and white supremacy; this nonformulaic approach to texts that provide multiple theories or contexts for understanding race and white supremacy was purposeful, allowing each teacher to find stories/theories/texts that explain race and white supremacy for themselves—and then to use those to teach (with) others. We included historical texts, psychological accounts, poetry, short stories, educational literature, practical applications, and more.

This chapter thus functions as a kind of literature review of how we (Zac and Shannon) approached our work and the ways our group collectively attempted to make RaceWork more than just talking about band-aids, more than a first-aid class. We first outline our tripartite approach to whiteness and white supremacy (structural; local contexts of schools; personal contexts of white racial identities). We then describe the texts that supported this model, followed by what we read about antiracist action, language, and approaches.

RaceWork's Tripartite Model

Our emergent practices (more in Chapter 2) meant that we chose texts (particularly for year 2) as they became important for the group, but we knew from the beginning that we wanted to build a curriculum around two ideas: (1) praxis (reflection and action in equal measure to change the world) and (2) a tripartite model that encouraged multiple entry points. While we were very clear that white supremacy is both structural and individual (as C. Wright Mills [1959] wrote, "Neither the life of an individual nor the history of a society can be understood without understanding both" [p. 3]), we had both been part of antiracism trainings in which rigid adherence to a particular understanding was deemed necessary. This hadn't worked for us. Further, we both had texts that had been particularly instructive for us personally, sometimes shared and sometimes not. We thus built a curriculum using critical whiteness studies and reflexive practice on white racial identities as the center, beginning with a nuanced historical and cultural exploration of white racial identities and meanings in a society beset with structural racism (e.g., Roediger, 2007; Thandeka, 2006) that then would

---

1. We note here that this chapter is not an exhaustive literature review of critical whiteness studies or critical race theory; instead, it is a summary of the texts that the 10 of us read together that also provides a conceptual overview of RaceWork. As we limited the amount of reading we did together, it leaves out a number of foundational scholars (e.g., Delgado & Stafancic, 1997; Du Bois, 1920/1999; Harris, 1993; Sleeter, 1996, 2016).

guide teachers in incorporating and embedding reflexive practice in their classrooms. We chose texts based on our own reading, both personal and academic. We kept the readings short and provided a variety, drawing on different disciplines and genres. We called our design a tripartite model.

Personal	Local	Structural
Our perspectives, histories, biases, cultural practices, identities, etc.	The spaces in which we work and live, those areas where we have (some degree of) control over elements of others' lives (e.g., the classroom)	The larger systems that regulate, limit, and shape the personal and the local; those things that are "bigger than us"

Too often we (as educators or activists) create a binary or dualism in our conceptions of antiracist work: There's the personal work I need to do for myself and then all the big work that happens outside, with others. In many ways, such a positioning sets up two unhealthy consequences: we think of our work to learn more as an end in itself, often as the prerequisite to doing "real" antiracist work, and we think of acting on the outside world as too big to ever make a difference (only ever band-aids), because "what can I do, as just one person, about this immense structure of white supremacy?" To avoid such tendencies, in RaceWork we worked with a different vision, or metaphor, for organizing the ways we understand antiracist work and the possibilities for antiracist practice in our lives. It is a way of breaking out of the inside/outside or me/them dichotomies that stifle so many sincere desires for antiracist change.

We can think of ourselves and our identities on three levels: the personal, the local, and the structural.[2] The personal is what happens in our heads: what we think, how we understand ourselves, who we are, and what our commitments are. For work in white antiracism, we might explore our family histories to better understand how our family came to be white. In the personal, we spend time thinking through our own lives and positionality—who am I and what can I do *for me* that works on the side of antiracism? This work is important, but of course limited because of the responsibility to do such work on our own.

The local is often left unconsidered in antiracism; because white supremacy is so much larger than our own limited experiences, we don't often think of ways in which we can actually take action in the immediate contexts around us. To find the local level, we need to ask where in our

---

2. For another way of conceptualizing oppression through multiple dimensions (individual, institutional, social/cultural), see Hardiman, Jackson, and Griffin (2013).

lives our desires and responsibilities have actual, material consequences for the lives of others. These are the spaces between the personal and the structural, ones in which we have some form of power over others. These local spaces are often part of larger structures, encountered in personally specific and contextual ways. As teachers, the local is often our classroom: What can we do in this space, where we have some control over expectations and practices, to work on the side of antiracism? As teachers, for instance, our expectations are used as criteria for understanding our students. We have some control over others' lives as teachers, which makes the classroom a critical site of action for antiracism. It is limited, in that we only have power over so much, but those areas in which our will is held up as the standard create opportunities for us to engage in and live out our antiracist desires.

The final remaining level is the structural. While the structural impacts the other two, we have more agency and control over the personal and local than we do over the structural. We can make choices about how to organize our own thoughts and beliefs about who we are and how we came to be who we are (personal), and we can make choices about how we want to organize those areas of our lives where we have (degrees of) control over the lives of others (local). The structural creates the limits of possibility in and for the other two levels. The structural level is school level, district level, and even bigger phenomena. The structural are those pieces that seemingly no one living has actually created; yet we still live in them. To engage in antiracism at the structural level is in some ways the most difficult, yet also the most imperative because of the conditioning quality of the structural on the personal and the local. Taking action at the level of entire school buildings, districts, and states takes coordination and collaboration. But it also needs personal and local grounding to stay meaningful for those engaged in the work.

Thus, focusing on only one level, even if it were the structural, would have the negative consequence of deemphasizing the ways in which *all three levels* are continually acting on us, and that we are acting on. We need all three, at the same time, to be clear on our own aims and aspirations, the limits and possibilities of our local practice, and how these experiences can inform our work to transform the larger structures that negatively impact life chances for the vast majority of humanity.

In RaceWork, we very intentionally began with the structural: the history of whiteness and how it has been constructed over time, through law, policy, economics, practices, beliefs, science, and so on. We did so because whiteness (and race) is bigger than any of us individually. This is in contrast to many other approaches to race and white supremacy, which often start with the personal, asking people to consider their personal beliefs and experiences or having white people think about the privileges they have experienced or inherited because they were/are white. Over and over, we had seen challenges to this approach, watching white people get defensive or write themselves out of the story of whiteness because of gender, social class, sexuality, religion, or other identities that complicated overdetermined notions of privilege. We, however, wanted to emphasize that we cannot write ourselves out of whiteness, regardless of the unique ways in which our experiences, identities, and positionalities situate us. Further, we wanted to emphasize the intentionality of the creation of race as a social construct that has been used to divide people. We also wanted to be clear that the effects and ongoing legacies that are with us today are hundreds of years in the making—even when their creation has been obscured. Starting with the social, legal, political, and economic construction of race over time enables us to understand that whiteness is both theoretically and historically constructed and that this construction is with us today on multiple levels. We then turned to schools as one place where white supremacy has been institutionalized, and then we examined the personal level: white racial identity, both its larger construction and what it looks like in each of our lives.

Our first 4 months were spent in this historical and theoretical overview; during the second half of the year we examined schools, with a particular focus on action and how theories about learning and anti-oppression could assist us in this work. For coherence, this chapter groups texts together in a more linear fashion than we together read them; broadly speaking, while we approached our work in this manner, we also moved between texts and levels more frequently, drawing connections and introducing ideas that we took up in greater detail later on.

The 2nd year, we chose texts from month to month, based on teachers' interests. They included having conversations about race with colleagues, intersectionality, antiracist school policy, specific activities in schools and classrooms, and language to talk about race in schools. We also read from local newspapers about antiracism initiatives.

Texts Supporting RaceWork's Tripartite Approach

While there was constant motion between the structural, the local, and the personal, we focused the texts in our first semester together in that order. (See Appendix A for topics and the reading list.) Working with white people, we focused specifically on whiteness, although whiteness, of course, cannot be discussed outside the larger contexts of race. We began by building a critical foundation for our work together.

Whiteness as Structural: Theoretical and Historical Constructions

At the top of the syllabus we put together for our 1st year is a James Baldwin quote from his letter to his nephew: White people "are, in effect, still trapped in a history which they do not understand; and until they understand it, they cannot be released from it" (1985/1962, p. 336). While the history we are often taught or learn is frequently white (in that it celebrates and centers the accomplishments of white people), we very rarely learn the history of *whiteness itself*. This is where we started. In other words, "race continues to shape both identities and institutions in significant ways," and it is not possible "to acknowledge or oppose *racism* without comprehending the sociohistorical context in which contexts of race are invoked" (Omi & Winant, 1994, p. vii).

We began with the assertion that the history of the United States can be read as a history of domination, with the nation founded on principles of European entitlement and capitalist accumulation. This new country was to generate immense wealth for European merchants and investors. While notions such as "freedom of speech" and "freedom of religion" were important founding principles, the majority of U.S. history has also featured the very rich taking advantage of those who are poor and middle class for their own benefit. This is how race was invented in the U.S. context: through laws, policies, and practices, based on religious and scientific beliefs of the time, deliberately constructed to separate people upon newly defined—and continuously shifting—racialized categories largely demarcated by phenotype and birth.

Whiteness, as a racialized category in the United States, was created to demarcate who could and could not be citizens and to differentiate between various people's positions in relationship to labor and wealth. We drew on extensive work detailing these processes from scholars such as Jacobson's (1998) *Whiteness of a Different Color*, Morrison's (1992) *Playing in the Dark*, Omi and Winant's (1994) *Racial Formation in the United States*, and Roediger's (2007) *The Wages of Whiteness*. (See Casey [2016] for more on this history; we detail our pedagogical approach to providing a conceptual history of whiteness in Chapter 2.) White people came to be white both through laws and through practices encouraging them to imagine themselves in contrast to other groups of people, specifically American Indians and enslaved African Americans. Whiteness was imagined as a contrast to negative characteristics (e.g., "lazy" or "uncivilized" American Indians) or positionalities (e.g., enslavement) attributed to other groups; while the majority of people beginning to conceptualize themselves as white led difficult lives, at least they could conceptualize themselves—whether morally or relationally—as better than other racialized groups.

Supremacy—superiority—became associated with whiteness—and science (see, for instance, Saini, 2019; Watkins, 2001) and laws were created to justify this position. Morrison (1992), importantly, argued that whiteness cannot be understood without real and imagined (e.g., literary) conceptions of enslavement—freedom and what it meant for white people was defined in relation to *non*freedom, to enslavement.

The meanings of whiteness, and who was/is included in this categorization, have shifted over time. In both legal and social processes, various groups of people were identified or sought to identify themselves as "not Black" or as further distanced from Blackness—and thus closer to or as white. Examining the history of groups such as Irish Americans, who in the 19th century were envisioned in the popular U.S. imaginary as analogous with Blacks, or court cases, such as those of Takao Ozawa (1922) or Bhagat Singh Thind (1923) who petitioned for U.S. citizenship (which was restricted to "free white persons" until 1952), demonstrate that whiteness as we conceive of it today has not always been composed in the same way. In other words, "whiteness is able to accommodate, or make certain compromises, in order to maintain its ideological hegemony" (Leonardo, 2009, p. 129).

The first reading we asked teachers to engage was Lipsitz's 1995 article, "The Possessive Investment in Whiteness." In the second paragraph, Lipsitz wrote:

> Whiteness is everywhere in American culture, but it is very hard to see. . . . As the unmarked category against which difference is constructed, whiteness never has to speak its name, never has to acknowledge its role as an organizing principle in social and cultural relations. (p. 369)

Lipsitz detailed how whiteness is more than a series of individualized prejudices, but a defining category for life in the United States, emerging out of enslavement, segregation, genocide, colonialism, and displacement: "A fictive identity of 'whiteness' appeared in law as an abstraction, and it became actualized in everyday life in many ways" (p. 370). This fiction-turned-reality served to unite peoples of various European ethnicities, creating a new white identity out of disparate cultures, languages, and religious backgrounds, with both cultural and social causes *and* consequences. In other words, this created identity had, and continues to have, material consequences—a "possessive investment." Lipsitz's article provided examples of the different ways that racism has shaped U.S. history and served social and economic purposes, for instance, the racism embedded in the Federal Housing Act of 1934 and subsequent "urban renewal" projects and discrimination in housing loans (familiar due to the housing bubble collapse of 2008 and the exposure of racialized predatory lending practices—the past is never just the past).

Lipsitz's article detailed very specific practices and their consequences. While reading about racialized environmental pollution in Houston, Texas, in the 1990s may seem far removed from white teachers in Minnesota in 2012, we read this article because we agree with Lipsitz (1995): "Because they are ignorant of even the recent history of the possessive investment in whiteness—generated by slavery and segregation but augmented by social democratic reform—Americans produce largely cultural explanations for structural social problems" (p. 379), blaming people of color for problems that are societal and based in valuing white lives over those of people of color and Indigenous peoples. Like Lipsitz, we wanted to set up our work together by being explicit that we, as white people, can work to counter white supremacy only if we have some understanding of the long patterns of historical, economic, political, and legal discrimination and violence.

Whiteness Institutionalized in Schools: White Supremacy and/as Structural Racism in Education

Lipsitz's examples of housing set us up to talk about how whiteness and white supremacy have been and continue to be embedded in public education: Schools have historically been neighborhood-based, funded through property taxes, and we live in segregated neighborhoods. In other words, white supremacy is institutionalized—but it is also localized in our schools and classrooms (and in our personal identities; see the next section). We approached thinking about race in schools from multiple perspectives: first, thinking about the purposes of education and what this means for both white students and students of color in a racialized society through reading Jansen (2008) and Baldwin (1963), thinking about teachers' roles through reading Milner (2003), and putting these into larger political and policy contexts through reading Leonardo (2009).

Before we met in January 2013 (our 2nd semester working together), we read Jansen's (2008) lecture "Bearing Whiteness: A Pedagogy of Compassion in a Time of Troubles." Writing from South Africa only 14 years after the first universal elections and in a time of violence, rapid inflation, and fragile democracy, Jansen described a lack of historical accounting, of young people's "racial knowledge without racial power" (p. 11). Jansen, the first Black Dean at an historically white university, had spent years immersed in the lives of white students, spending time with them, their families, and their communities. He had seen that they were "decent, idealistic and committed to their country" yet "carry within them the seeds of bitter knowledge that, left unchallenged, can easily germinate into the most vile and vicious racial attacks" (p. 13). This troubled—and troubling—knowledge of racial exclusivity, supremacy, and victimization is transmitted through the family, the church, the school, cultural organizations, and peers. Transformation of a violently racialized society, Jansen argued, "means recognizing that the students are not the enemy and that as teachers and leaders in schools and universities, we have failed white youth by not interrupting their troubled knowledge" (p. 14), including not examining "what counts as worth teaching and learning and knowing in the first place" (p. 14).

Jansen focused on white supremacy as a relational problem, arguing that its resolution must also be relational. Through several moving stories, he wrote of his personal learning to move *toward* white people, who in many ways were his enemy, responsible for Black oppression and disenfranchisement. In interactions with white South Africans, he came to see that they too, like himself, were broken—that racialized and other systems that keep us apart also break us as humans. All of us, regardless of racial identity, must move out of our comfort zones. From our different positionalities, we must "bear whiteness"—and transform it. Formal education, then, requires a pedagogical reciprocity in which people move toward each other, recognizing our likenesses and engaging in dialogue.

We also read Baldwin's (1963) "Talk to Teachers." Like Jansen, Baldwin's piece was originally given as a lecture in a time of upheaval in the racial order of society. He too questioned what was and wasn't being taught—and what this meant for white people and for people of color (although he specifically wrote about Black people). Baldwin contended that the societal purpose of schooling is socialization—to educate us within a framework that perpetuates society. If society is white supremacist, then schools will be—and are—white supremacist. Yet, Baldwin also argued that the purpose of education is to enable a person to look at the world for themselves, "to ask questions of the university, and then learn to live with those questions" (p. 326), even though society discourages this kind of thinking as it ultimately leads to dismantling the injustices of that society. It is, he argued, the educated person's obligation "to examine society and try to change it and to fight it—at no matter what the risk. This is the only hope society has" (p. 326). Examining his own education as well as the education of Black children in the United States, Baldwin determined that we have been lied to and thus "what is upsetting the country is a sense of its own identity" (p. 329). He argued that curriculum needed to change, to present both an honest portrayal of the violence of structural racism and the contributions of people of color—and that this curriculum change is necessary both for children of color and for white children—for "liberating white people who know nothing about their own history" (p. 329). Speaking of what he would teach a Black child, Baldwin said,

> Just as American history is longer, larger, more various, more beautiful, and more terrible than anything anyone has ever said about it, so is the world larger, more daring, more beautiful and more terrible, but principally larger—and that it belongs to him. (p. 332)

We brought this understanding of our responsibilities as pedagogues to RaceWork and asked teachers to bring it also to their schools: to learn and to teach a more nuanced version of the world than is often available in textbooks, found in standardized tests, or reflected in school discipline policies or dress codes.

Or, for that matter, found in much of teacher education. That month, we also read an article by Milner (2003), in which he asserted that while scholars for a century have been arguing for the importance of teacher reflection, such reflection specifically on race or cultural contexts is seldom taught or practiced. Yet, he asserted, to dismiss race is to misunderstand who a person—student or teacher—is. Thus teachers must engage in racial reflection, such as journaling and critical racial dialogue, "as a way to uncover inconspicuous beliefs, perceptions, and experiences [and] to understand hidden values, dispositions, biases, and beliefs" (p. 175). Teachers must reflect on the "racial influences of their work" (p. 177), to better understand both their own practices and the contexts of their students and their experiences, thinking of experience as theory. This work is not complete without considering the political and policy contexts in which teachers work and students learn.

We then considered how whiteness is institutionalized in schools. Leonardo (2009) wrote that No Child Left Behind (NCLB, the law structuring public education at the time of RaceWork and still the basis of federal education policy today)

> is an example of color-blindness par excellence. NCLB's hidden referent of whiteness makes a casual pass at racial explanation that sidesteps race as a causal explanation for educational disparities. In this sense, NCLB is an "act of whiteness" and . . . a form of whiteness as policy. (p. 127)

NCLB, in other words, acknowledges the *symptoms* of the racialized order of the United States, but not the causes. It obscures the structural obstacles to equal (not to mention equitable) educational opportunity, dressed in a "language of tough love and sanctions" (p. 136). In other words: "pull yourselves up by your own school straps" (p. 138). This colorblind approach focuses on surface racial classifications—for instance, mandating that achievement data be disaggregated by race (as well as disability, class [as measured by free and reduced-price lunch], and English learning) because we as a nation must leave no child behind—but obscures social practices that lead to such differentials, such as labor market discrimination and lack of access to health care. In other words, NCLB recognizes race but misrecognizes racism (Leonardo, 2009). Yet as a national educational law and based in whiteness, NCLB also continues the project of constructing U.S. nationhood as white.

RaceWork teachers were all too familiar with the mandates that structured their teaching lives under laws such as No Child Left Behind (most of them having spent their entire teaching careers under NCLB). Having words and larger contexts to frame these policies was helpful. But it didn't necessarily change the day-to-day practices of their classrooms. For help here, we turned to several other readings, specifically examining the experiences of students of color in the white supremacist structure of schooling.

Delpit's (2006) work, specifically around the culture of power, has been instructive both for us as facilitators and for RaceWork teachers. Delpit argued the following:

1. Issues of power are enacted in classrooms.

2. There are codes or rules for participating in power; that is, there is a "culture of power."

3. The rules of the culture of power are a reflection of the rules of the culture of those who have power.

4. If you are not already a participant in the culture of power, being told explicitly the rules of that cultures makes acquiring power easier.

5. Those with power are frequently least aware of—or least willing to acknowledge—its existence. Those with less power are often most aware of its existence. (p. 24)

In a white supremacist society, in schools with whiteness as the unacknowledged referent, the culture of power *is* whiteness—and the language of power that of middle-class whiteness, with its emphasis on politeness and indirect language. (For instance, "Would you like to finish your homework?" stands in as a command that actually means "finish your work.") Drawing on examples from our own lives and teaching, we as a group talked about the ways whiteness has structured our communication and ways of carrying ourselves and instead advocated using our relative power to advocate for justice by being explicit in our language and about our expectations and rules. Delpit helped us to focus on paying close attention to the cultural context of every lesson and the ways in which structural racism, the "culture of power," is embedded in everything that happens in schools and classrooms.

Throughout our time together, we also looked at the work of other scholars and teachers. For instance, we talked about Carter's (2006, 2010) theorization of "cultural straddlers"—students of color who successfully navigated schools by maintaining their own racial identities while also working within the white culture of power. We talked about a piece by Valenzuela (2008), in which she wrote about the "soul wounds" that students of color inflict on each other, leading to internalized oppression—believing in the negative stereotypes about themselves. We read a chapter by a white teacher, Fecho (2004), about teaching in a predominantly African American school and his assertion that "so many of my early forays across cultural boundaries were what I would characterize as being either too subtle or too safe" (p. 19) and how he put students' stories into conversation with what he knew about schooling, about language, and about communities.

White Racial Identities

Whiteness is institutionalized in societal structures and in the structures of schooling, but it is also very personal. As 10 white people, we also needed to consider how each of us had become white—in our own lives and in our families' histories. We needed to understand ourselves as racialized white actors, to ask such questions as: How am I part of these histories, structures, and interactions? How do I see and read myself—and my personal identity—into the racialized world—while at the same time recognizing that whiteness is a part of but not my whole self? What does it mean to be white in the United States today, in a time and in spaces (including our schools) where the values of neoliberal capitalism are often paramount (even if hidden)? In the context of white supremacy, what is my personal identity and commitment?

Through what we read and the conversations we had, we worked to understand ourselves as racialized white actors as well as how a person became, becomes, and is continuing to become white. We approached this not as a stage theory (e.g., Helms, 1993), but as a social and historical process. In other words, we concur with Frankenberg (1993) that we as white people can simultaneously hold multiple discursive and material orientations toward whiteness and racialization. Frankenberg wrote:

> Whiteness changes over time and space. . . . it is a complexly constructed product of local, regional, national, and global relations, past and present. . . . And if whiteness varies spatially and temporally, it is also a relational category, one that is coconstructed with a range of other racial and cultural categories, with class and with gender. (p. 236)

Our work as white people, then, is to excavate these relations and processes in our own lives and locations, to fit ourselves into history—to personalize larger histories as the contexts for the history of one's own life. How did we get here (and who is the "we")? How did we come to read ourselves into the social construction of whiteness?

Certainly, as most white people are raised in white families (and often in disproportionately white communities), the sites of our early childhoods are sources of inquiry. We turned to the work of Thandeka (2006), who wrote in *Learning to Be White* of "the formation of racial identity as small but not inconsequential personal defeats" (p. 20). White people *learn* to be white as they come to understand what it means to fit into their community, adopting its dominant language, traditions, and customs. When white children, she argued, go outside the bounds of these traditions or customs, they are punished—abused, she named it—and must choose between the love of their families and remaining in the white community or going outside it, a choice that for a child is rarely actually a choice. For instance, a child may feel shame for violating some usually unspoken racialized rules, such as speaking with or about a person of color or asking questions about race. To compensate for shame—feeling bad for who one *is*—the child adopts white norms.

We also read about how white supremacist cultural norms are normalized, becoming standards that we live by, even when they are damaging to ourselves and our relationships. Okun (n.d.) wrote that "culture is powerful precisely because it so present and at the same time so very difficult to name or identify." These norms—such as perfectionism, a sense of urgency, defensiveness, an emphasis on quantity over quality, worship of the written word, progress as bigger and more—are deeply connected to the ways in which whiteness has been historically constructed—in opposition to racial and ethnic cultures with different values, such as a relationship to language or to time. Becoming white, then, is often about a relationship to how we understand the world and what we value.

Additionally, we read a number of texts about how different people came to understand the development of their own racialized identities. We read Zac's personal narrative (now in the first chapter of his book

A Pedagogy of Anticapitalist Antiracism [2016]) about discovering his great-great grandfather's obituary, who went "west from Boston to fight Indians." What did it mean, he asked, that he grew up on the west coast because his ancestor, whose last name he now carries, moved west specifically to kill Indians—to participate in genocide? Understanding what he did about history, Zac knew that in 19th-century Boston, people of Irish descent were not white, but were participants in the struggle to define what ethnic groups would be considered white. But upon moving west, Frank Casey was white—and so would be future generations with the same ethnic heritage, later reduced to a handful of food-based and religious practices, if that. Knowing this history makes possible an understanding of one's personal history—but also situates personal history in a larger context. As Zac wrote, "while I did not author this plan, I am here because of it." This acknowledgment is important. Chapter 2 details more about how we engaged teachers in exploring these stories.

Of course, the racialized process of becoming white differs from other racialized identity processes. We thus read other personal narratives, especially ones that complicate simple racial stories, such as examples from Thompson and Tyagi's (2006) edited volume of racial identity autobiographies *Names We Call Home*. We read Wong's (2002) poem "When I Was Growing Up," which begins with the words, "I know now that once I longed to be white" and details the ways in which whiteness was valued.

Perhaps most telling, though, was reading Morrison's short story "Recitatif." This story, about two girls, Twyla and Roberta, was, in Morrison's (1992) words, "an experiment in the removal of all racial codes from a narrative about two characters of different races for whom racial identity is crucial" (p. xi). The removal of racial codes in a story about race, class, gender, and family in the United States is upsetting for many readers. It calls into stark relief how racialized our worlds are, as we want to know: Who is white? Who is Black? How can we understand these characters if we do not know this? This question then forces us to ask: How can we understand ourselves in this racialized time and space if we do not, as white people, work to understand the racial codes and norms that we have learned and how these influence how we move and participate in the world?

Doing the Work

We read most of the texts above early in our time together, to set the contexts for our work—and, specifically, to provide the background for planning and taking antiracist action, knowing that the long history of racial construction and oppression is formidable. We did not assume that educating teachers on the realities of oppression in contemporary schooling would automatically lead to transformations in classroom practice; reflexive practice is impossible if practitioners have never had the space or language to reflect not only on the realities of racism, but also on their own racialized identities. These knowledges thus both contextualized and complicated the work, helping us all to understand the larger conversations and contexts in which we are explicitly and implicitly taking part. They provided language and theory in which to *do* antiracist work. But knowledge alone was not enough—we, individually and collectively, had to move to action grounded in those knowledges and also to discuss what might get in the way of this work. As facilitators, we grounded our work in what we believe about education, explicitly talked about coded languages of whiteness and discoursal strategies that don't always allow us to enact antiracism, and finally, read about enacting antiracist practices.

Anti-Oppressive Teaching and Learning

Our work, both in the "classroom" of our professional development, and what we did in between meetings in both personal and professional spaces, was grounded in understandings of critical pedagogy and anti-oppressive education. Our work as educators is not only teaching content, but "requires our involvement in and dedication to overcoming social injustice" (Freire, 1998, p. 58). Or, as Kumashiro (2002) wrote, "Educators have a responsibility to make schools into places that are for, and that attempt to teach, all their students. To fail to work against the various forms of oppression is to be complicit with them" (p. 37).

We also acknowledged that this is not the understanding of education that we have experienced, either as students ourselves, as students becoming teachers, or in schools as teachers ourselves. More frequently, the "common sense" understanding is that education is neutral, consisting of content presentation by the teacher and absorption by the student. Drawing on Kumashiro's (2002, 2009) work, we positioned ourselves as "against common sense" and asked what that meant for our beliefs and practices as teachers. This work is not easy, particularly when we are troubling the ways that we as teachers have often approached race and white supremacy:

> Perhaps we desire teaching and learning in ways that affirm and confirm our sense that *what we have come to believe is normal or commonsensical in society* is really the way things are and are supposed to be. . . . My point here is that perhaps we resist anti-oppressive practices because they trouble how we think

and feel about not only the Other but also ourselves. . . . Our desire to teach and learn about the Other in traditional ways is a desire to maintain some sense of identity and normalcy, and to affirm the belief that we are not contributing to oppression. . . . We resist learning what will disrupt the frameworks we traditionally use to make sense of the world and ourselves. (Kumashiro, 2002, p. 57)

Instead, Kumashiro argued, education must be about disrupting our common-sense notions, even when this throws us into crisis—crises that we often explored in together in RaceWork. Crisis thus becomes a necessary part of unlearning oppression; "Learning is about disruption and opening up to further learning, not closure and satisfaction" (Kumashiro, 2002, p. 43). This is true not only for the students in the P–12 classrooms of RaceWork teachers, but for all of us as learners as well. Kumashiro (2002) emphasized that there are multiple ways of approaching anti-oppressive education, each with benefits and drawbacks. This is important in light of the aforementioned desire for a checklist and also because we worked throughout our time together to provide multiple perspectives.

One common-sense notion that needs troubling is the relationship or distance between an educator and learners (explored in Chapter 5). As Freire (1998) wrote, "Our relationship with the learners demands that we respect them and demands equally that we be aware of the concrete conditions of their world, the conditions that shape them. To try to know the reality that our students live is a task that the educational practice imposes on us" (p. 58). As facilitators, we were thinking about this always in both the context of ourselves as educators facilitating professional development and all of us as educators in our own classrooms, from 3rd grade to university. We emphasized the centrality of knowing our students—including their personal and social racialized histories and identities. We approached learners in this professional development—white teachers—as agentic and capable learners, rather than as resistant racists.

Challenges to Enacting Antiracist Practices: Languages We Live

Examining whiteness and our beliefs about teaching enables us to closely interrogate whether our practices match our beliefs, as "an educational practice in which there is no coherent relationship between what educators say and what they do is a disaster" (Freire, 1998, p. 55). But we would be remiss if we did not also explicitly talk about challenges to enacting antiracist practices. Chapter 6 explores tensions RaceWork teachers experienced, while the sections below outline the readings that we used to situate these tensions throughout our time together. We begin here with challenges arising from dominant ideologies or languages used to discuss—or avoid discussing—race and white supremacy.

Colorblindness. Perhaps most glaring is the predominance of colorblind ideologies. Colorblind racism, according to Bonilla-Silva (2003), has been the dominant racial ideology since the late 1960s, explaining "contemporary racial inequality as the outcome of nonracial dynamics" (p. 2). According to colorblind ideologies, it is racist to even mention race—to see color. So we just aren't supposed to see or talk about it. Colorblind practices reinforce the racialized order of society. This obviously works for some people—especially affluent white people—more than others and further serves to obscure intersectional injustices. Not only does colorblindness often prevent meaningful conversations about race, but it leaves whiteness itself unexamined and thus unknowable to many white people (while glaringly obvious to people of color and Indigenous peoples). When teachers ignore the racial identities of their students, they both ignore what is often an important piece of identity and the structural barriers and relative privileges such identities make possible. For white teachers, colorblindness means not recognizing how race affects what we teach, how we teach, how we assess, and who is learning with us. As we have mentioned, this also coincided with talk of the "postracial era." Not only did we not have to see race—or so dominant discourses said—but a Black president, especially one elected twice, meant that we as a society had "moved past race." Of course, many people challenged this notion, but the idea of a postracial society was common enough that it sometimes seemed to have become common sense.

Colorblindness frequently plays out in rhetorical strategies—racially coded language that evades race. With the help of Bonilla-Silva (2003), Delpit (2006), Milner (2003), and others, we examined—and, unsurprisingly, readily identified in our lives and schools—this coded language that evades race or racialized histories (e.g., "my ancestors had to pull themselves up by their bootstraps too"; "the past is the past"); racial identities ("I don't even think of you as Black"; "some of my best friends are . . ."); or the consequences of living in a racialized world ("I want the same things for everyone else's kids as I do for mine"; "we have good intentions, so our choices are okay"). In these frameworks, acknowledging racial or ethnic backgrounds and how they impact one's experience of the world is at best "politically incorrect" and at worst racist or offensive. What this means is that many white people have little practice talking about race and thus much discomfort: "I, I, I don't mean, you know, but, those . . ."

White talk. This discomfort is alternatively called "white talk," a term McIntyre (1997) used in particular for the way white people have "controlled the discourse of whiteness so that they didn't have to shoulder responsibility for the racism that exists in our society *today*" (p. 45, emphasis in original). McIntyre (1997) defined white talk as "derailing the conversation, evading questions, dismissing counterarguments, withdrawing from the discussion, remaining silent, interrupting speakers and topics, and colluding with each other in creating a 'culture of niceness' that [make] it very difficult to 'read the white world'" (p. 46). For instance, white talk often positions race as a zero-sum game (e.g., if "they" gain, "we" will lose—as in debates about affirmative action that misunderstand both the practice and real-world consequences of these policies) or point out exceptionalities (e.g., look at Obama!)

White privilege. Elsewhere, in spaces not afraid to discuss race, the dominant discourse was (is) often that of white privilege.[3] White privilege discourse figured prominently in our work together. Nearly all RaceWork teachers had experiences with thinking about white privilege—some very helpful. So had Shannon and Zac—as mentioned in the Introduction, RaceWork coincided with years of discussion and writing through the Midwest Critical Whiteness Collective that culminated in "McIntosh as Synecdoche" (2013), a reference to our shared experience of McIntosh as often the only text or idea we had had about whiteness in PD or teacher education settings, effectively meaning that McIntosh's list of white privileges has come to stand in for any and all antiracist work with white people. The dominance of this discourse primes us, as white people especially, as racism detection devices, listening for times when other white people fail to acknowledge how whiteness privileges us. According to white privilege discourse, all white people are racist and must confess their racism as the primary action against racism (Lensmire et al., 2013; Thandeka, 1998). White privilege discourses, in attempts to help white people understand white as a race—and one with material and psychological consequences—often leave little room for nuance, for intersectional identity work, or for antiracist action that is more than acknowledging the privileges attending whiteness.

Colormuteness. While not always the case, discourses such as white privilege, in attempts to address historical silences and wrongs, simplify complex realities so that white people cannot use distancing or avoidance strategies. But sometimes this means that it is difficult to talk about the realities of race. Pollock (2004) called this phenomenon "colormute": we end up in race talk dilemmas when we simultaneously use and suppress race labels. For instance, although talking in racial terms can make race matter,

---

3. Another discourse that is less prominent now than in the past is that of "race treason": white people renouncing whiteness. We briefly discussed this in RaceWork; for more, see Chapter 5 in Casey (2016).

not talking in racial terms can make race matter, too. Often, discourses of "*all* students should be able to . . ." or "but *all* students deserve . . ." function to avoid race completely, resulting in colormute discussions about race that go nowhere. This leads many people to confusion and anxiety about racial (and racialized) labels, particularly as "race and racism have always been at root *about* evaluating people—about creating hierarchies and displacing responsibility for social 'problems' rather than simply describing 'difference'" (Pollock, 2004, p. 205).

Framing. Finally, the ways in which we talk about race also affect how we frame the impact of race on education. Perhaps the most-discussed way is in how we frame differentials between white students and students of color and Indigenous students in academic achievement (e.g., GPAs, test scores, course or track placement) and behavior (e.g., suspensions, referrals, participation). Most commonly, these differentials are referred to as an "achievement gap." This is indirect culture of power language, obscuring the origins and actual issues at hand. A different framing is an "opportunity gap" (see, e.g., Milner, 2010), which focuses on processes and contexts, rather than on the outcomes of individual students. This framing rejects colorblindness and context-neutral mindsets and practices, instead focusing on recognizing and shifting adults' low expectations and deficit mindsets in favor of their developing skills in working through cultural conflicts. "Opportunity gap" shifts the focus to the system itself, offering an ability to see that it is not students' faults or deficits, but problems with the system. Ladson-Billings (2006a) went even further, saying that we should rightly call these differentials the educational debt—referring to an accumulation over time of "historical, economic, sociopolitical, and moral decisions and policies that characterize our society" (p. 5) and result in inequities. In other words, whiteness—based in historical, economic, sociopolitical, and moral understandings, practices, and norms—has meant that students of color have had a different, and frequently unequal, educational experience for generations. Given that a debt is the sum of all deficits that have occurred over time, as educators—and especially as white educators—we have a lot of work to do, beginning with reframing white supremacy—and not students, families, and communities of color—as the problem.

Language (as) barrier. Antiracism work, in our experiences, depends a lot on language use. We have learned to listen for clues that someone "doesn't get it" or might be missing "the point." We are certainly not the first to point out that sometimes these practices get in the way of actually doing the work to challenge oppression and make links between forms of oppression. Thus, in RaceWork, we read two pieces specifically about this: Mayer's (1997) "Barriers to Organization between Anti-racist White People" and Thandeka's (1999) "Why Anti-Racism Will Fail." Mayer's piece challenged white people to "collaborate creatively, effectively, and responsibly without reliving" oppressive legacies (n.p.). Yet as white people, we enact many barriers to doing this, such as distancing ourselves from other white people (particularly in the wake of a racist incident), being self-righteous or judgmental, assuming that white spaces are monolithic, dividing white people into "good" and "bad," or seeing (or being seen) as an "exceptional other," the one truly "good" white person (Mayer).

Mayer argued that these barriers may result from tendencies toward dualistic thinking—a longing for simple answers and divisions. As a result, antiracism is also seen as dualistic: society is divided by racial identity (people of color/white people); people of color are the "experts" who give knowledge to white people, which white people need to "get." (We discuss "getting it" in Chapter 8.) Thandeka (1999) likewise critiqued the binary nature of the antiracist program of her church, specifically an authorized antiracism training workshop in which, she said, she learned that all whites are racists, no Blacks are racist (although they are prejudiced) because they lack institutional power, and that whites must confess their racism. Both Thandeka and Mayer argued that these dichotomies simplify complex issues and/or avoid discussions of intersectionality or social class. Both believe in the necessity of doing anti-oppressive work but also point out the ways in which this often falls short when we rely on dichotomies or, in the case of Thandeka, don't base our work in our moral (in her case, religious) beliefs. We read these articles because we too have seen these barriers; we wanted to be able to name them for ourselves and to challenge ourselves to always think complexly. As Darder (2011) wrote in another piece we read:

> I have come to a place where I can see no possibility of liberation unless we are willing to abandon worn-out traditional protocols and practices that continue to be informed by deceptive and twisted views of our humanity. Instead, we must embrace a politics that is grounded upon a willingness to challenge openly those values, attitudes, and practices within our schools and communities that perpetuate oppression, injustice, and human suffering. (pp. 81–82)

We have spent, both here and in RaceWork, much time discussing language because language structures so much of our interactions, as humans and as teachers. Talking about race is necessary, and white people need both practice in doing so and practice in naming and navigating what gets in the way. Our work with these authors, then, argued that we, as racialized people, especially those of us who are white, need to "ask provocative questions, navigate predictable debates, and talk more about talking" (Pollock, 2004, p. 221) because "we do not really see through our eyes or hear through our ears, but through our beliefs" (Delpit, 2006, p. 46) and thus "must learn to be vulnerable enough to allow our world to turn upside down in order to allow the realities of others to edge themselves into our consciousness" (Delpit, 2006, p. 47).

Enacting Antiracist Practices

In the 2nd half of our 1st year together and throughout the 2nd year, we focused more on action. Our aim was to enact antiracism: not just to resist actively supporting structures and practices of white supremacy, nor to be nonracist, but to counter, in word and deed, white supremacy. We thus read examples of the difficult and never-ending work of enacting antiracist practices and pedagogies with colleagues, with students, and through policy. We read texts on institutionalizing antiracist policies (Gillborn, 2008), on engaging colleagues in conversation (Briscoe, Arriaza, & Henze, 2009; McIntyre, 2008), and on other practices (Pollock, 2008). For instance, we read a chapter on "critical language awareness" (Briscoe et al., 2009) for specific help on more effective ways of addressing the unjust language practices above. This was particularly important as more than one of us in the room had faced the problem of being the "broken record" on race—our colleagues knew that we would bring it up and had their own strategies for dismissing us. Briscoe and colleagues wrote about connecting before correcting, interrupting with grace, thoughtful inaction, modeling, and more—giving concrete practices for working with colleagues. We also read Horton and Freire's (1990) discussion about the problem of "expertise" (detailed in Chapter 3). At the conclusion of our 1st year together, each teacher chose a copy of an edited volume that they thought would be most useful to them as they worked to enact antiracism in their local contexts: Grineski, Landsman, and Simmons's (2013) *Talking about Race* or Pollock's (2008) *Everyday Antiracism*.

We remained careful to place this work in the contexts of what it meant for us as white people, participants in the culture of power who must actively reject what Darder (2011) named "an arrogant refusal to acknowledge the limitations of one's subject position as a dominant cultural being" (p. 83). We were specifically engaging this work as white people, working with other white people, but also in collaboration. Our position echoed that of Darder, whom we quote at length here:

> In a society like that of the United States, enacting a politics of liberation is next to impossible unless we come to terms with the tremendous power inherent in our ability to act and engage

collectively as consciously grounded cultural beings . . . we must know who we are within the contexts of American [sic] society and the conditions that have shaped our histories. This also requires an acknowledgement of the fundamental strengths and limitations of our social locations, with respect to our ability to know and transform the world. In so doing, we can come closer to understanding the cultural knowledge and histories that inform our ideas, while also recognizing that to know one another as comrades we must be involved in ongoing dialogue and political labor together. (p. 88)

To conclude this chapter, reading was an important practice for us in RaceWork. Discussions that drew on our shared reading were rich and rewarding, always supplemented with stories from our own lives. We practiced *being* together in ways that centered our commitments to equity and social justice, to teaching and learning *with* each other. What we *did*, together and separately, was just as important. As Darder (2011) argued, while reading and words are important, we need "the intimacy of solidarity that emerges from our mutual emancipatory labor . . . in the realm of human encounters in the flesh" (p. 88). We take up what we did—our labor together, building on our labor with others in our individual schools and communities—in Chapter 2.

CHAPTER 2

What We Did

The story of RaceWork can be told in many ways. In Chapter 1, we told the story through what we read. Here is another:

Us: Dear Advisor (we shared a doctoral advisor, Tim Lensmire): We want to do a PD class for white practicing teachers.

TIM: Okay. Let's try to get some money.

We tried. We submitted grants. None came through.

Us: Okay. So let's do it anyway. Will we get in trouble?

TIM: No.

Us: Okay. So let's go.

Being the somewhat naïve—yet engaged—graduate students that we were, we weren't quite aware of *all* the rules we were breaking. Some, of course, we were deliberate about breaking, such as decentering white privilege discourse or grouping solely around a shared antiracist commitment rather than school, content area, or grade level. Another was centering the teaching lives of the people in the room.

In this chapter we explore our own texts—our lived experiences and stories of engaging in RaceWork. What we did together, the shared work of RaceWork, builds on two understandings that we brought to this professional development: our understanding of the classroom (broadly defined) as a learning space, and an articulation of white supremacy as the oppression against which we were struggling. Our first day, we shared these quotations:

> Learning is a place where paradise can be created. The classroom, with all of its limitations, remains a location of possibility. In that field of possibility we have the opportunity to labor for freedom, to demand of ourselves and our comrades, an openness of mind and heart that allows us to face reality even as we collectively imagine ways to move beyond boundaries, to transgress. (hooks, 1994, p. 207)

We also defined our common adversary not as racism, an overcoded word, but as white supremacy: "An historically based, institutionally perpetuated system of exploitation and oppression of continents, nations, and peoples of color by white peoples and nations . . . for the purposes of maintaining and defending a system of wealth, power, and privilege" (Challenging White Supremacy Workshop).

Using a specially designed curriculum based on both the lived experiences (such as family and classroom stories) of teachers and sophisticated theoretical and historical work that did not simplify or call upon stereotyped tropes of race or whiteness, our goal with RaceWork was to intentionally sequence learning experiences for white teachers around race and white supremacy over an extended period, providing time, space, and language to reflect on historical, institutional, and structural racism and the roles schools and teachers play in both perpetuating and combating racism. We wanted white teachers to develop a rich and nuanced understanding of themselves as racialized actors and to understand the ongoing legacy of structural racism in schools and society. But our end goal was not solely knowledge; we wanted to create a space on which practitioners could draw to collaboratively develop and implement pedagogical strategies that engaged others in their buildings in meaningful dialog and action on race, structural racism, and academic success. Ultimately, our work was about student learning and community connections. In this chapter we share our pedagogical orientation (doing PD differently, facilitating a critical pedagogical space) and outline what we actually did together, including the research study. We then detail what we learned and enacted together and individually in Chapters 3 through 10.

Pedagogical Orientation

As facilitators, we approached RaceWork with explicit attention to the relationality of pedagogy. This meant centering relationships not only among people, but working to integrate the content of our professional development, our pedagogy (how we set up our teaching and learning time together), and ourselves (our identities as white people and as teachers in Minnesota in the early 21st century). We intended our space to provide both theoretical and emotional support systems for teachers doing the difficult work of challenging white supremacy.

Doing PD Differently

This meant doing professional development (PD) or out-of-formal-school education differently. Teachers are required to do PD—and not infrequently it is the source of consternation and griping. Mandated by districts or buildings, PD may be one-size-fits-all (and thus not relevant to a teacher's actual students, subject matter, etc.), passive "sit-and-get," or not seen as immediately practicable or implementable (the "what to do on Monday" problem). Too often, a certain logic pervades PD (as well as teacher education and P–12 schooling more broadly) that might best be described as "Do as I say, not as I do." That is, the practices being modeled are often incongruent with the content being taught or engaged. Of course, a similar problem presents itself in much school-based learning: It is not relevant to learners' lives and thus not engaging or relational.

We have sat impatiently through many such training sessions. We also had experiences of such work on race and racial injustice. For example, Shannon remembers attending versions of "Racism 101" over and over, filling out worksheets: "Racism = _____ + _____" (correct answer: prejudice + power). While well intended, these trainings left no room for the nuances of her life and living situation; any attempts to ask questions or to complicate the narrative were met with "you're trying to wriggle out of your responsibility as a white person." Certainly, many people leading these trainings are drawing on decades of experience and responding to common defense mechanisms and barriers. But there was no space for nuance or options; any nuance or option set up antagonism. This is a monologic and banking pedagogy—the opposite of a problem-posing and dialogic pedagogy.

We had looked at or experienced other models, such as work drawing on Tatum's (1997) *Why Are All The Black Kids Sitting Together in the Cafeteria?*, Howard's (2006) *We Can't Teach What We Don't Know*, Wise's (2008) *White Like Me*, and other related materials. Two common models for this work are Beyond Diversity, based on Singleton and Linton's book *Courageous Conversations* (2006), and McIntosh and Style's "Seeking Educational Equity and Diversity" (SEED). Beyond Diversity aims to "break silence," especially around the intersection of race and achievement, by "provid[ing] the content and process for educators to grapple personally with race as a critical sociopolitical construct . . . [toward] a transformed racial philosophy that guides their policy analysis, institutional restructuring, and instructional practice reform" (pp. xv–xvi). Led by outside trainers, the Courageous Conversations program sets up a process with agreements for interracial dialogue aimed at everyone's participation and at sustaining and deepening conversation even (and especially) when it is uncomfortable, to move toward understanding and action. SEED is a peer-led process in which educators meet monthly to explore intersectional oppressions in the context of local school climate, curricula, and teaching methods; the aim is to assist educators in understanding and valuing their own voices so they can better value those of their diverse students.

There is much to commend in such models. They advocate a common language so that we can be clear on what we are addressing; they situate racism and other oppressions as both individual and institutional. Through reflection prompts and work on self-understanding, they position a commitment to action as a moral imperative. Yet, in our experience (and, we learned later, the experiences of many RaceWork teachers), these PD sessions had limitations: They were prescriptive, presumed a deficit view of teachers, centered stage models of racial identity development or white privilege, used banking-type pedagogies, or were led by trainers who didn't understand the unique contexts of schools in the area and the racialized identities of local students. (For instance, when looking at the experiences of students of color in Twin Cities schools, it is imperative to distinguish between African American and Somali students, not lump them together as Black students, or to distinguish among Hmong, Indian American, and Korean American students, not just "Asian American students.") As with Shannon's experience, in the end, many of these other models—or at least how they were commonly implemented in schools—seemed to stop with Racism 101, or maybe 102—with an implicit stance that knowledge would be the solution: *"Now that you know that racism is so embedded in our schooling institutions, we will fix the achievement gap."*

We wanted to do PD differently, to intentionally align our content and pedagogy, to focus on praxis, to be emergent to fit the needs of learners (rather than one-size-fits-all or prescriptive), to provide multiple theories and contexts, to emphasize the self-appropriation of knowledge, and to learn collectively. We were explicit about our beliefs about learning and about schooling, about what education should and can look like. Intentionally, we never called our PD experience "class," although RaceWork teachers did over and over, in writing (e.g., Nicole's notes were labeled "Race Class") and in conversation. To us, this demonstrated both that we had been explicit about our pedagogical stances and that these teachers were serious in their commitments to learning and relationships to each other. In other words, we wanted to do critical professional development, PD in which teachers are engaged as "politically aware individuals who have a stake in teaching and transforming society" (Kohli, Picower, Martinez, & Ortiz, 2015, p. 9) and have "space for complex reflections on their role in the reproduction or resistance of inequality" (Kohli, 2010, p. 41).[1] In RaceWork, we built a space together that, while maintaining many qualities of a "course," worked not only to cover the material and subject area of antiracism, but to put it into practice at the same time.

Facilitating a Critical Pedagogical Space

We base our work in critical pedagogy (e.g., Freire, 2000; hooks, 1994; Kincheloe, 2008), asking ourselves and students to question and understand systems of domination and oppression and, working together, to envision and enact more just ways of being and living. Freire (2000) called this "praxis"—action and reflection in equal measure in order to transform the world. A critical pedagogical stance also requires positioning students— here, RaceWork teachers—as agentic learners, rather than deficient learners about multiculturalism (Lowenstein, 2009) or the ways Shannon had been treated as a learner in Racism 101 PD. Indeed, Kumashiro (2009) wrote, "oppression can also result from who we allow students to be" (p. 23).

We did not want to replicate these ways of being, but instead made explicit our belief that all learners (including us as facilitators) bring to a learning space many kinds of knowledges. The classroom is always a space of "dispersed, shifting, and contradictory contexts of knowing" (Ellsworth, 1989, p. 322). Acknowledging this openly, we shared our belief that the classroom should be a space in which we collectively make sense of the world, which requires acknowledging what we already know (including that which may be untrue) and building from there, examining the contexts of our lives and learning. Learning is thus about transformation; in RaceWork, we positioned schooling as a primary site for this transformation.

---

1. Kohli, Picower, Martinez, and Ortiz (2015) wrote about this kind of PD, drawing on three case studies of grassroots PD. In each, "teachers were engaged in a cooperative dialectical process, there was strong emphasis on unity amongst participants around their social justice goals, the structure was organized through shared power between teachers and organizers, and teacher and student needs were centered using a practice of cultural synthesis" (p. 7). For another example, see Navarro (2018). Kohli (2019) also notes, in writing about critical professional development for teachers of color, that because this work offers teachers agency as well as ways of responding to intersectional oppressions, schools or districts may not support it and thus "CPD often exists outside the bounds of institutions and thus, is seldom formally recognized as teacher development" (p. 41).

As educators, we share Rogers's (1989/1957) assertion: "I have come to feel that the only learning which significantly influences behavior is self-discovered, self-appropriated learning" (p. 302). Learning that is meaningful is what we internalize and personalize so that it becomes a part of who we are and what we do (behavior), rather than mere facts to be memorized. A transparent pedagogy aligned with the content under study is how such learning can be made possible. We cannot make antiracism into a separate body of knowledge from who we as facilitators are or from who learners are; the challenge is to make antiracist dispositions a part of who we are, not simply things we know the right answer to. Of course, this is perhaps easier written about than practiced.

Learning can be—perhaps needs to be—uncomfortable; teaching and learning are spaces of unpredictability. As both students and teachers, we both desire and resist these types of learning spaces: "What and how students learn is influenced by a desire to relearn only certain things, especially only certain ways of making sense of the world, as well as by a resistance to learning other things, especially things that reveal the problematic nature of prior knowledge" (Kumashiro, 2009, p. 26). We cannot predict how learning will or will not proceed. When our content is race and white supremacy, discomfort and unknowing are even more heightened. This is not, however, a bad thing. We referred often to Kumashiro's (2009) ideas:

> What is unethical is an approach to teaching and learning that does not involve crisis. Learning is not a comforting process that merely repeats or affirms what students have already learned. Learning is a disarming process that allows students to escape the uncritical, complacent repetition of their prior knowledge and actions. Learning is a disorienting process that raises questions about what was already learned and what has yet to be learned. Learning involves *looking beyond* what students already know, what teachers already know, and what both are only now coming to know. (p. 32, emphasis in original)

As facilitators, both in this space and in our other classrooms, we recognize the need for teaching to be emergent: participant-driven and participant-centered. Certainly, we provided direction and parameters: We set a framework (the tripartite model), chose readings, and set up activities. But we also started with only a very broad sketch—more or less the tripartite model. Only after the first few meetings did we sketch out a curriculum for the rest of our 1st year together, as opposed to a model in which we had/owned the content and asked teachers to fill in the blanks. As facilitators, we met after each meeting to debrief and to start planning the next session, based on what we'd heard and seen—and most importantly, what these teachers were telling us they needed. This meant that sometimes we threw out what we had planned, or planned to do something that wouldn't have been our personal choice or priority. We once heard how Paulo Freire discussed centering the people's needs, especially as learners: If they tell you that what they need is motor scooters, then you find a way to get motor scooters—even if motor scooters were the last things you would have anticipated as the greatest community need. Taking him seriously, we tried to tailor to the needs of the people in the room, adjusting after each session (and almost always *during* each session as well).

Our broad goal at the beginning was antiracist praxis; we would collaboratively set goals for what we would do together and in our own pedagogical spaces; we would channel our knowledges into personal goals (the idea of consciousness-raising into action). As facilitators, we provided tools, through readings, discussions, activities, and *being* together, that scaffolded and enabled teachers to ask questions, to figure something out for themselves or their spaces, to try something, to report on how it went, and then to do it all over again. In other words, we asked them (and us) to reflect and to act—to read, study, theorize, tell stories, act, reflect. In our estimation, this is critical pedagogy.

We also were transparent with our pedagogy. A traditional vision of a teacher is premised on knowing, on being an expert—and often this position is abused in authoritarian ways. We can think of, for instance, that most critical and recurrent question from (so-called) "resistant" students: Why do we have to do this? A transparent pedagogy works to answer this question before it is asked; it seeks to contextualize all lessons and activities from a coherent operating logic that is made explicit for the benefit of those participating. In other words, we owe it to anyone we are working with to explain *why* we are asking them to do what we are asking them to do, and to do so in ways that make sense based on what we (and they) are worried about and trying to live out. "Because I said so" is not transparent, but rather quite the opposite—it doesn't explain why. "Because you need this when you get to next year's grade" is not transparent, because it reduces the question of relevance to a temporal argument about futures rather than the lived experience and expertise of participants. A transparent pedagogy is thus a concrete practice of putting front and center in our teaching what we are worried about and why we are worried about it. When we don't do this in antiracist contexts, we run the risk of not helping participants find their own ways into the material—of making antiracism into something that is not accessible or possible for everyone.

We could not have done this without an explicit commitment to personal relationships. This began with us as facilitators. As mentioned in the Introduction, we had met at the orientation to our graduate program, and that day, over beers on Shannon's porch, we began what is now a decade-long dialogue on critical pedagogy and whiteness. We both had experience facilitating challenging conversations and spaces around race. In RaceWork, we were intentional and explicit about co-teaching and modeling collaboration, while also drawing on our individual strengths and knowledges. Part of our planning involved reflecting on who we were being, in this respect, and what we each might bring into the PD space.

Much more important than this, though, was the sense of group accountability and collaborative relationships that these teachers built with each other (see McManimon & Casey, 2018, for other examples; see also Navarro, 2018, for an example of a teacher inquiry group as a "community of transformative praxis"). While some teachers asked for and received professional development credits necessary for maintaining their teacher licensure, there were no other external motivations associated with this PD—no grades, no public kudos from building or district leaders. Yet teachers kept showing up—and requested to keep showing up for a 2nd year. Of course, there was important learning happening here. And as facilitators, we shared knowledges, both book and lived. But in interviews, RaceWork teachers talked mostly about how they were accountable to each other, how they wanted to show up for and with each other and to share what they were working on. They read between sessions ("homework") not because we as facilitators assigned papers or reading reflections on them, but because they wanted to be able to talk with their peers. They wanted to use the space to reflect on how what they had tried in their classrooms went well or didn't.

Very quickly, storysharing (see McManimon, 2018) became central to our work together. We knew we needed to work through our lived stories of whiteness and race, for "the fiction of our lives—how we conceive our histories by heart—can sometimes provide a truth far greater than any telling of a tale frozen to the facts" (Moraga, 2000, p. 4). Further, as Hampl (1999) wrote, "A story, we sense, is the only possible habitation for the burden of our witnessing" (p. 18). We knew that there is power in knowing where we come from and in knowing how our personal identities impact what happens in classrooms.

At our very first session, we all shared stories, drawing on Silko's (1977) words that for the original inhabitants of this land, stories "are all we have, you see,/all we have to fight off/illness and death./You don't have anything/if you don't have the stories./Their evil is mighty/but it can't stand up to our stories" (p. 2). The stories we wanted our group to collectively share, Shannon stated, would not be about recentering white-ness, reinforcing that racism is (only) the problem of people of color, or advocating race treason for white people. Instead, we wanted to share our stories as white people: how we were attempting to work against white supremacy and in the interests of our students. In other words, our stories would likely not be heroic or mythical, but instead based in a belief that there are far more antiracist white people and antiracist white stories than are commonly known and that storytelling as a pedagogical project can lead to further antiracist action on the part of white people. These stories, Shannon told us that first day, matter because we construct ourselves through (telling) stories; these stories (can) illustrate the structural nature of white supremacy, critique white as normal, standard, or good, examine power and what is at stake for whom, and take away silence around white supremacy. These stories, in short, can allow us to construct different selves. We intentionally welcomed our *own* stories, while also acknowledging that stories in and of themselves can reify certain lives, reinscribe oppression, or turn classrooms into therapy spaces. By several months into RaceWork, we usually had to stop our opening storysharing after about an hour or it would have taken our entire time together. This storysharing reflected our pedagogical approach—emergent, flexible, unpredictable—and shaped how we were with each other.

This was not always easy. Ellsworth (1997) reminded us that "pedagogy as a social relationship is very close in. It gets right in there—in your brain, your body, your heart, in your sense of self, of the world, of others, and of possibilities and impossibilities in all those realms" (p. 6). As facilitators, we struggled with when to support and when to push or confront, when to cut off processing time that teachers sorely need, when to redirect attention to make the most of everyone's contributions. We also celebrated each other—sharing photos of "RaceWork babies" (multiple teachers had children over our 2 years together) and giving gifts to each other. The last day of RaceWork, amid tears and hugs, we all stood around, no one wanting to be the first to leave our sacred and shared space.

This extraordinary sense of group accountability and collaborative relationships had also been facilitated by the space, both physical and ontological. As we do in our formal classrooms, we (Zac and Shannon) made sure that we all knew each other, starting with our names and something fun or interesting about ourselves. In contrast to many formal classrooms (where sometimes the bodies outnumber the spaces for them to sit), we were a small group. We could really get to know each other, to know each other's stories and even, vicariously, some of our students. Further, each of the teachers came from a different school, even from a different district. This had two important consequences: Teachers did not worry that what they said would be shared with people in their building or district—they could take risks and also share what was really hard, such as conflicts with colleagues. Second, teachers saw that the racism and white supremacy that they identified in their buildings was not occurring in just their space, their district—it was pervasive, across districts that were outwardly quite different from each other. As facilitators, we were careful to emphasize the absence of easy answers for the challenges that we face and to acknowledge that we, especially as white people, simultaneously perpetuate and combat white supremacy. We challenged the pervasive idea of "safe space," knowing that white people often call for safety as a way to avoid being uncomfortable or sitting with emotion. This work is not safe, but we can be brave in attempting it, in sharing our ideas, resources, and struggles. (See Arao & Clemens, 2013, for a discussion of safe vs. brave spaces.)

Physically, we met in the basement of a university education building, a space in which half of RaceWork teachers had taken a graduate class with Zac and in which Shannon and Zac both taught. This physical location—and our prior and current experiences in it—shaped both accountability and relationships, from the very first day when Sarah recommended that other teachers trust Zac and where we were going, even when it seemed to counter their prior experiences, and Angela's comment that coming back to the space after months away was "coming home."

What We Did Together

As stated in Chapter 1, we knew from the beginning that as facilitators we would draw on a tripartite curriculum model: the structural, the local, and the personal, operating both independently and always together. Beginning with a comprehensive history of whiteness in the United States, we made whiteness the primary object of consideration. We all explored our own racial identities and the meanings we attribute to being white in a society beset with structural racism and the ongoing legacies of white supremacy. After developing a language and a means of understanding ourselves as racialized actors and how structural racism is embedded in schools and society, each teacher developed and implemented their own unique and specific pedagogical intervention.

Our goal as facilitators was to empower these white teachers to do the terribly difficult work of combating racism in their classrooms, informed by research on anti-oppressive education and by their own research into their lives as white people and as teachers committed to young people and to more equitable school experiences for students. Of course, we also write this believing that pedagogy, "when it 'works,' is unrepeatable and cannot be copied, sold, or exchanged—it's 'worthless' to the economy of educational accountability" (Ellsworth, 1997, p. 17). We began this process on our very first day together, by jointly setting goals and asking RaceWork teachers what they wanted from the space and what they were thinking, wondering about, or hoping for in their school or classroom.

Pacing: Big Picture

Often, educational work around social justice and equity asks learners to start with the personal: to identify their own experiences, biases, identities, and positionalities. This is vitally important work. But we had frequently seen it not go well; white people have many defensive mechanisms to resist this work (see, e.g., Okun, n.d.), and such work can easily become solipsistic. Given our own experiences as well as academic backgrounds, as facilitators we decided to flip this: to start with the structural. We cannot fully understand ourselves (the personal) without knowing how our selves came to be, what the larger patterns and histories are that shaped the spaces into which we were born and in which we now live. (Marx [1963/1852] wrote: People "make their own history, but they do not make it as they please; they do not make it under self-selected circumstances, but under circumstances existing already, given and transmitted from the past.") Without understanding these circumstances, our efforts for change—whether of self or of structures—are likely to fall short.

Work in classrooms and in research is nearly never as tidy as the ways that we must portray it on the two-dimensional page, without space or relationships to contextualize it. While we moved continuously between action and reflection and between the levels of our tripartite model, our pacing roughly fell into four segments, aligning with school semesters (see chart below): (1) structural overview, both theoretical and historical, to situate whiteness and white racial identities; (2) exploring whiteness in our own contexts, schools, and practices; (3) examining how to do this work: what it might look like and how to have conversations around antiracism; and (4) what it means to continuously do this work in our own settings and how what we know and have done positions us as both expert and beginner. Our 1st year thoroughly explored the three levels—structural, local, and personal—and asked each teacher to engage in action based on these knowledges; we reflected together throughout. We asked teachers to identify potential projects (action) that they could take in each of the three levels and then, later, to choose one as a focus. While the first half of the year focused on learning, the second half shifted toward helping teachers do work in their buildings, particularly as "building experts" around race. This also was a way of acknowledging that RaceWork, as a formal group, was going to end, so each teacher needed to find ways to make this work their own.

But then it didn't end. Unanimously, and individually in interviews with us, each teacher asked if we could continue our work together. Our 2nd year was more practice-based, taking up specific questions on which they had gotten stuck, namely, how to work with colleagues and how to address the problem of being named an expert while knowing that one is always beginning this work again and again. At the end of this 2nd year, one teacher anonymously wrote that this year "was more focused on action rather than history. I liked having the opportunity to experiment with my knowledge." Another wrote that this year was "less instructive—[Zac and Shannon] made an effective and purposeful move to us owning our own projects and actions."

Fall 2012	Spring 2013	Fall 2013	Spring 2013
Theoretical & historical overview of race (including whiteness) & structural racism: U.S. → schools → lives (white racial identities)	Whiteness in our own contexts and schools (what it means) → goal setting and inquiring into our practices/contexts	Models and conversations about antiracism	Being an expert and being a beginner: antiracist work in our own contexts

[Note: Should this be Spring 2014?]

These rough divisions were supported through readings (see Chapter 1) and through the activities and conversations we engaged in together. As our process was emergent, we returned to where teachers asked us to go or went in different directions than we might have originally intended.

Pacing: Individual Sessions

Each month, RaceWork invited process-oriented engagement and conscientization with antiracist ideas and practices. Each 3-hour RaceWork session generally included check-ins and a mixture of small-group and large-group activities and conversations. As facilitators, we asked teachers to *do* something with what they had read for each session and to report on what they had done in their school or classroom since we last met. In other words, we asked something of them. This was not passive participation. Our activities were experiential, both to actively involve all of us and to model different pedagogical activities that teachers could use in their own settings (and to include discussion of such activities). We set up a structure but made this a space for discussion and disagreement. In the sections that follow we provide examples of how we did this.

Facilitator-led instruction. While we carefully acknowledged the experiences and knowledges of those in the room, we also drew on our knowledges as critical scholars. In our first session, after everyone introduced themselves and we talked about the purpose of the space, Zac presented a history of legalized white supremacy in what is now the United States, starting with colonial laws about enslavement and including legal challenges over the association of U.S. citizenship with whiteness. This presentation heavily emphasized the construction of whiteness through both laws and practices, especially focusing on economic bases and on social interactions. In the following months, we attempted, through both such instruction and through varied readings, to offer different avenues for racial understandings to become deep and personal, knowing this is always a process. What has most moved Shannon, for instance, has been personal experiences coupled with the work of activists, scholars, and writers like Okun and Baldwin. We argued that each of us needs to find our own way into this work, finding languages that speak to and with us and ways of pedagogically connecting self and family and community. This is especially important because this work is hard, and we will face common responses of colorblindness, defensiveness, distancing ("my family didn't own slaves"). Readings could help.

Discussion of readings. Every time teachers read something between our sessions, we asked them to do something together with the reading at the next RaceWork session. Sometimes we provided discussion questions for small groups. For instance, questions related to Lipsitz's (1995) "The Possessive Investment in Whiteness" included the following: "Share one or two examples of systemic racism that stood out to you; talk about differences or similarities in what you choose. Also generate a short list of examples of systemic racism you've experienced or noticed in the schools and communities in which you've lived and taught. Write these on the board, and be prepared to explain why your examples show evidence of structural racism/white supremacy." This type of activity not only asked teachers to understand what they had read and to apply their learning, but positioned them as intellectual agents. It opened spaces for us to collectively discuss questions such as the distinction between "racist" and "racism." In our 2nd year, when much of our work revolved around working with other people in our respective buildings, we drew on Horton and Freire's (1990) insistence on the need to start with the knowledges that people already possess, to discuss: "What are the knowledges that our colleagues already bring with them to this work? Where does this knowledge fall short? What kinds of approaches can we take to scaffold up the antiracist work of others in our buildings?"

These conversations encouraged us to take both the readings and each other seriously. We collectively created a space for white people to practice talking about whiteness and white supremacy—to get more sophisticated in our understanding, in our discourses, and in our listening. We argued that getting better at talking was getting better at teaching, but that this was hard work, both because of our own inexperience and fear and because of other peoples' responses. We acknowledged that there is frequently tension between what can be perceived as "language police" and getting better at having racialized conversations. In other words, we were working to learn to be pedagogical in these conversations. There are very rarely easy answers or one correct way to go about this; each month thus became a practice space for all of us.

Activities. Learning is not just intellectual, but also embodied. We thus built in activities that engaged bodies as well as minds. In the second session (the same one in which we discussed Lipsitz's article), we used Boal's (1985) image theatre. This was a pedagogical move: Schooling disciplines our bodies as well as our minds. White supremacy does the same. To counter this immense system of oppression, we might need to struggle bodily with it. We gave two small groups this task: "Talk briefly about your reaction to our first 1.5 sessions, paying particular attention to the concreteness of white supremacy—its structural nature (Lipsitz, 1995). Then, with your bodies, create a frozen tableau illustrating your discussion; give the tableau a title that is a question." Each group shared their image; the other group commented on what they saw. The power of this activity is that the commenting group often succinctly names both what the image group was attempting to portray and more—our bodies show more than our words do and provide enhanced meaning and emotion. The images of both groups pointed to the challenges of antiracist work: that it makes us feel isolated, that we don't always know what we are fighting against, and that we can feel stuck, or as one teacher succinctly summarized: "trapped, system, barriers."

After discussion in the large group, small groups returned to their images. As white people, we are historical actors in a structure that is way bigger than us, but that was also set up by people. So, we asked: How do we work together to change this? If the original images portray the actuality of white supremacy today, how do we change this reality to a different one? In other words, how do we change, in Boal's language, from spectators to spect-actors? In the second images the teachers created, the spect-actors looked at each other or in a common direction rather than away from each other; there seemed to be a sense of leadership, although tension persisted. These embodied images and discussion on them encapsulated what we knew from readings and from our lives and in our bodies.

To practice addressing how white supremacy and racialized communication play out on the local level, at another session, we role-played a PTA meeting to discuss the "achievement gap." Each of us had a role (including Shannon as school board superintendent and Zac as PTA president). In our roles, we mingled and had informal conversations, with the goal of thinking about who we would sit by in the actual PTA meeting and how we would respond to others. Our debrief included both how we racialized and responded to racialized language as well as how we felt about what happened. We practiced skills in understanding, working through, and transcending cultural conflicts, particularly practicing denormalizing whiteness and Eurocentric cultural ideologies.

Sometimes our activities involved "homework." For instance, over the winter break the 1st year, we challenged teachers to talk with their families to see if they had family stories/histories of how they became white or memories of learning race or racism at home. Each person brought in family stories of racialized violence, silence, and loss—such as community members dressing up as KKK members for Halloween, homeschooling or moving to avoid going to public schools that were predominantly students of color (even as this was never explicitly stated), and loss of home languages, such as German. Angela, for instance, shared that her family didn't think of themselves as white until they moved to the United States and were thrown together with other white people—that her family knew this history, but didn't know how whiteness structured the losses the family incurred (e.g., language and customs) and also the violences they committed (e.g., leaving a hospital when ill because of a refusal to be touched by Black hospital staff).

Not all activities always went well. Sometimes activities we thought would be meaningful fell flat. For instance, Zac and Shannon had spent a lot of time thinking about and discussing how white privilege pedagogy requires white people to confess their whiteness and how these confessions can trigger guilt and inaction. We set up a narrative activity around this idea. While this had been meaningful for us, the activity clearly didn't work for RaceWork teachers. We thus reinvented and reworked activities for the specific needs and desires of the teachers we were working with.

Action. In February of our 1st year together, teachers identified projects on which they wanted to work—what Fecho (2004) called teacher researchable moments. Our first work with these was collective, asking: (1) What else do we need to know/what information do we need? and (2) If the teacher did this, how would she know the impact? We then asked teachers to try something and to bring back these stories to the next session, recognizing that non-events could also be a story. In March, we asked the following questions: What is the project asking of me as a teacher, of students, of larger structures? What action steps will I take over the next 2 months? What reflecting will I do? We asked teachers to choose readings that would help them in their projects. Stories of these projects are shared in Chapters 3 through 9.

RaceWork teachers identified for themselves how they would know their impact: when more and more people in their buildings—staff and students—asked questions about texts, news, and so on from a place of curiosity, seeking, and problematizing; when relationships based in reciprocity, respect, and honesty were strengthened; when it became easier and more natural to reflect more often and when students participated in this reflection; when they had information to support arguments and conversations; when antiracism became part of the work of the classroom; when there were changes in data (behavior, grades); when problem-solving conversations became a consistent norm; and when they had small communities of support and reflection in their buildings.

Talking about race. From our very first session, one of the shared goals of RaceWork teachers was to get better at talking; we articulated this as working at being pedagogical, needing both more sophisticated discourse as well as practice in engaging others without being the language police. We pointed out that every time RaceWork met, we were practicing talking about race and that the practice we were doing together was likely visible to other people even if not to RaceWork teachers themselves. By the end of the 1st year, Morgan reported: "I feel much more confident . . . I think a lot of that confidence came from being able to 'practice' talking about race in a safe environment." Likewise, Angela said, "I use words and talk about concepts with much greater ease than before. I no longer walk on egg shells when talking about race . . . I am not afraid to talk about something that they [students, particularly of color] live every day. They return with comments that light up my heart." But RaceWork teachers also asked for more practice.

Thus, for much of our 2nd year we focused on the practical issue of talking about race. In the 1st year, teachers tried something. Often, they stumbled through talking about their work, particularly in their school settings. This is, of course, a common problem: As white people, we are often uncomfortable talking about race, so we don't do it, which creates a cyclical pattern. Or, we jump into critiquing others for their language use or practices or point out their deficiencies. We thus wanted to work on comfort with communicating about race, to challenge our own discomfort and question the often-unspoken rules of racialized communication, which lead to racism without racists (Bonilla-Silva, 2003), to carrying out oppression without the intention of being an oppressor. Instead, we wanted to focus on transformation, to transform resistance into relevance in the service of students and communities. As Charlie said, prior to RaceWork, "I felt 'stuck'—didn't know how to have the conversations."

Thus, in October of our 2nd year, we generated examples of challenging conversations we had encountered, including setting, participants, roles, and background. The pairs that generated these then switched scenarios with another pair. We fish-bowled these conversations. The pair took on the roles provided; they could call a time-out if they got stuck or other group members could tap in to take on the role of someone in the conversation if they had ideas. In the large-group discussion that followed, we discussed strategies we had heard (e.g., those identified by Briscoe et al. [2009], the reading for the day) as well as how it felt to be in the different roles. We focused in particular on the question: How could I (or you) have said something differently so that I (or you) would promote a more just situation or resolution? We recognized ways in which language can get us stuck, such as through binaries (e.g., insider/outsider, good/bad, right/wrong), classifications, hierarchies, exclusions, or presumptions.

Two months later, in December, we had three guests of color in our class: a new secondary ESL teacher, a PhD student who had been a math teacher, and an assistant principal in a local elementary school. While Race-Work teachers acknowledged the benefits of talking in an all-white group, they also wanted to talk with teachers of color. Shannon and Zac approached this with some trepidation, cognizant of the many ways in which this could go wrong, including ongoing violence against these teachers of color and positioning them as racial experts (above and beyond their expertise on their own experiences). These guests started with their own experiences and learning, such as getting a school to change its family–teacher conferences because they had been scheduled over Muslim holidays (in a school with many Somali students), the assertion that "students of color are loved at home and should be loved at school," or that relevance is based not as much on content as on connection to students' lived realities.

Shaped by questions and listening. Over the course of the 2 years, our time together became less formal, less facilitated by Zac and Shannon and more by the group. In the beginning, Shannon and Zac did more direct instruction, providing theoretical language and frameworks so that teachers could analyze and theorize their own experiences. But we also both implicitly and explicitly modeled and emphasized the importance of listening and of asking questions.

The first formal activity we asked teachers to participate in was a listening activity. In pairs, they took turns telling race stories. We provided prompts, but the instruction was that person A would talk, uninterrupted, for 5 minutes about race, followed by person B talking, uninterrupted, for 5 minutes. The purpose was to listen and speak from the heart—to tell our own stories of race. We knew from past experiences that this was a challenge for many white people. We took this risk because we wanted to establish the seriousness of our work together. This required risk—both for us and for these teachers—but it also created possibility:

> Openness of mind and heart creates the possibility of being touched by the other, transformed by the other, even as one maintains a healthy sense of criticality. It is within a community of others that the self is challenged and transformed, that we are taken "out of ourselves," that the sense of self-certainty might be challenged and shattered. (Yancy, 2009, p. 35)

But this also had a larger purpose, for as Macedo and Freire (1998) wrote: "The sharing of experiences must always be understood within a social praxis that entails both reflection and political action. In short, it must always involve a political project with the objective of dismantling oppressive structures and mechanisms" (p. xiv). We did this at our first session by pairing this listening activity with Zac's presentation of the history of white supremacy mentioned above.

On many occasions, we asked teachers what questions they had and shaped our sessions around those questions. Listening to these questions directed both our reading choices and our pedagogical choices. As facilitators, we took them very seriously and asked ourselves to "ponder ferociously" (Mayer) what they meant for our teaching and our lives.

Co-teaching: Modeling collaboration. Another important approach that we took to RaceWork was in co-teaching, in which we modeled collaboration as white people, both as teachers and researchers. We shared responsibilities for facilitating, for planning, for conducting interviews, and for writing. We were explicit about this, naming that we had different roles that drew on our different strengths and knowledges. We also talked about our own struggles, fears, mistakes, and difficulties listening, modeling speaking from the authority of our own lives while acknowledging the limits of those positions. Our work was about the "intimacy of solidarity that emerges from our mutual emancipatory labor" (Darder, 2011, p. 88). This work requires relationships of courage and honesty.

This collaboration is particularly important because of what Mayer (1997) names as barriers to white people working together toward antiracism, such as attempts to distance oneself from other white people (and align solely with people of color) or to position some white people as good and others as bad. As the majority of U.S. teachers and administrators (and university faculty) are white, this is crucial. We cannot do this work without collaborating with (which means both teaching and learning from) other white people.

What We Learned Together

This book is about what happened when eight white teachers collaborated with two white facilitator-teacher educators to get smarter about white supremacy and to enact concrete antiracist change in lives and schools. This work is critical to overcoming centuries of white domination, but it is never straightforward and rarely easy. These introductory chapters have introduced what RaceWork was and who was involved, as well as what we read and what we did together.

What follows in Chapters 3 through 8 presents learnings from this process, centering stories and examples of the eight RaceWork teachers and the ways in which we (Zac and Shannon) have theorized them, building on our collective work on those Saturday mornings. While the centering of the teachers' antiracist praxis has a different feel than the first section of the book, the organization of these chapters maps on to the tripartite model explained in Chapter 1. The personal, Chapters 3 and 4, explores fears and experiences of personal change. The local, Chapters 5 and 6, explores relationships and relational tensions within the contexts of schools and families. The structural, Chapters 7 and 8, focuses first on white privilege and then on accounts of seeing and getting "it"—of naming ways that white supremacy is reproduced.

These chapters take their names and foci from Shannon and Zac's work to understand the sophisticated ways these eight white teachers made meaning from their experiences in RaceWork and lived out their commitments to antiracism. (For further information on our research methodology, see Appendix B.) We examine the lived experiences, struggles, and sense-making of RaceWork teachers and their colleagues and students, with deep respect for the ways in which they worked to challenge the status quo of an educational system that devalues and deintellectualizes both students and teachers. In these chapters of *Building Pedagogues*, we center the teachers' voices and theory building so that readers can hear these teachers in intimate contexts and in conversation with the theoretical and practical tools of previous chapters. We present their and our learning in ways that we hope provide insights for others to learn from. The compromise is that these narratives and theories are not in chronological order; nor will chapters focus on any one particular teacher.

We have used this structure for two additional reasons. First, as authors of this text, we want to honor the group and the collaborative ethos RaceWork established on all of those Saturdays, as well as the years since spent reading and rereading what we produced together as a group. We want this book to echo the relational accountability we write about in

Chapter 5, for these words and contributions to hang together, to be together, because they were produced together. That togetherness feels important to honor and to share with those who continue this work through reading about it. Second, we believe these ideas can aid other antiracist educators in naming particular challenges and possibilities practicing teachers face; in naming them, we extend the invitation in our initial email to teachers to readers of this book, for us all to collectively continue building antiracist pedagogies in our own buildings, contexts, and lives.

PART 1

THE PERSONAL

CHAPTER 3

Fears

Working toward antiracism in schools means confronting the monstrous, seemingly insurmountable system of exploitation and oppression known as white supremacy. Once we understand the insidious and structural nature of white supremacy, it can feel overwhelming to imagine responses that we, ourselves, might take. As white people, we tend to fear such work.

This fear resides at the level of the personal, the first of our three levels for antiracist praxis. The personal comprises the space of our own mental terrain. The personal level of antiracist praxis necessitates close and careful introspection into our own identities: who we are, why we are who we are, and how we *could be* in our orientation toward racial justice. Within the personal domain, we ask teachers to place their own lives and work in contexts, based on their reflection on the purposes of their work in schools and classrooms. Importantly, we place the personal within interlocking frames; one cannot attend only to the personal and not to the local and structural and hope to accomplish any material transformations. Work at the level of the personal, then, is always fraught. It is always caught up in the internal struggles of our own minds, our own ways of thinking, and the ways we understand our own social experiences.

As they engage in antiracist praxis, white educators will most certainly be challenged by fears. While these fears can feel isolating and their circumstances might be unique, our experience as facilitators and practitioners as well as our time in RaceWork leads us to assert that these fears are quite common—and that addressing them can be mobilizing. Fear can be both pedagogical and productive in the context of its exploration and expression in community. Thus in this chapter we explore ways that fear—in particular, fears of getting it wrong, of not doing enough, of harming existing relationships, and of being called racist—animated the thoughts and actions of RaceWork teachers. As stories were such a central part of RaceWork, we examine these fears through examples from these teachers' personal and professional lives, intertwined with research literature and our own theorizing. While these circumstances may be uniquely personal to these teachers, we conclude this chapter by arguing that these fears, expressed in differing ways across contexts, can be figured as a productive part of antiracist praxis. As white people, we can acknowledge and then resist these fears in our own lives and as a collective practice; in other words, while fear exists at the personal level, sharing these fears in a hope-filled community (in a space such as RaceWork) can propel us through them.

Fear of Getting It Wrong

RaceWork teachers worried they might not know what to do to begin or were anxious about their abilities to enact their antiracist commitments. That is, they wondered if what they were planning to do to combat white supremacy would actually *be* antiracist, or if their actions to combat white supremacy might exacerbate oppressions. We call this the fear of getting antiracism wrong.

These fears connect to one of the central components of anti-oppressive education: that no practice is *always* anti-oppressive (Kumashiro, 2009; see also Kumashiro, 2000). For Kumashiro, schools are always already engaging issues of oppression. Many are doing so through negation; that is, in not acting to resist oppression, they are, by default, perpetuating oppression. He also cautioned that any focused attention on a particular form or enactment of oppression, such as white supremacy, is simultaneously a lack of attention to other forms of oppression. This is an inevitability, but it does create a need for reflexive engagement with anti-oppressive actions. For the teachers in RaceWork, these arguments resonated powerfully, even as they highlighted fears about their own abilities to act in antiracist ways.

An example comes from Amelia, who was working on her school's equity team the year after RaceWork concluded. The equity team was responsible for guiding the school's equity work, including antiracism. But this was not easy. Of her equity team colleagues, Amelia said:

> I don't like when people start going into [an] action strategy phase right away. I'm like: "whoa, slow down, that has to be right." We can't just get up there and throw stuff at them [other teachers]. Because then that reflects on us [the equity team],

and we're throwing stuff at them that doesn't work . . . I want to make sure that whatever we are going to tell them is good and true and backed by research; that's the credibility piece of what I want to see. To show that it's not just us, it actually is real; we're not making it up.

For Amelia, jumping straight into an "action strategy phase" is problematic and risky; she worried that a lack of grounding would reflect negatively on the equity team. In other words, she worried that what she and the equity team were going to facilitate with the rest of their staff would be wrong, and that in being wrong, the teachers in the school would miss out on the potentially powerful interventions the equity team was advocating. For instance, Amelia wanted to ensure that teachers in her building understood that she and the equity team were not "making up" the school's discipline gap statistics, with students of color, especially Black male students, disproportionately referred and suspended at higher rates than white and Asian American students. She linked this to "credibility": being "good and true" in fidelity to research findings. And the need to do this connecting, to ensure that teachers understood the research literature on the discipline gap, was anchored in Amelia's sense that not to do so is to make a mistake in antiracist work. She worried that too many teachers would desire to skip all those pieces that come before a "strategy phase" (though, as we argue, there can be no hard and fast steps for antiracist praxis), pieces required to ensure educators aren't undermining their own aims: that they aren't actually perpetuating oppressions as they seek to work against them.

Other teachers shared this fear of "getting it wrong" in enacting antiracism. Sarah, for example, felt that RaceWork gave her ways to act on her feelings of empathy with students of color. She told us, in characterizing herself before RaceWork, "I may care, but I don't know how to do it. I don't have any idea what I'm doing, I just, I care." Not knowing what to do is different from not having any idea what to do in terms of antiracist action, but both function as a fear: fear of being insufficient and doing the wrong kinds of things. Knowing more about what to do, this logic assumes, will help prevent missteps and mistakes, or more sophisticatedly, will help stave off the constant threat of perpetuating oppressions even as we seek to work against them. Knowing what to do is imagined as ensuring that nothing goes wrong, because, as Sarah acknowledged, caring, on its own, is not enough in antiracist work. Certainly, caring that is solely cognitive—without any materiality—is incapable of transforming oppressive conditions for students and teachers, but the actions that could follow from this care came with risks for Sarah: risks of getting those actions wrong.

Another example of the fear of getting it wrong came from Veronica. While her school had over 95% white students, when students of color were in her social studies classrooms studying histories of peoples of color, Veronica felt a special responsibility to make sure those lessons functioned as antiracist, both supporting students of color in white hegemonic social spaces and being taken seriously by white students. For instance, she had created a lesson on Ghana and the trade routes of West African peoples, which were vastly more complicated than those of their contemporaries in medieval Europe. For Veronica, including this unit and others like it was a major victory in her struggle to create more space for world history curriculum that did not center European and settler-colonial histories. She connected the inclusion of precolonial African histories to ensuring that students of color—in this case, Black students—were able to "see themselves" in the curriculum. Yet she was frustrated because she felt her students (worrying particularly about students of African descent) were not taking the lesson as seriously as they did those focused on ancient Greece and Rome. She also worried that her students (mostly white) would not engage as deeply with what they saw as less important or as less likely to be critical to their eventual score on an AP test.

In the interview in which she told the story about her fear, Veronica asked us what to do "in practice." She was uncertain how to address what she saw happening in her class in ways that would not alienate Black students or create the appearance that learning about the Ghana Empire was important solely because there were Black students in the course. Making such an explicit connection ran the risk of being racially tokenizing. This example became a powerful lesson for Veronica in the ways that curricular changes do not automatically produce more socially just outcomes for students. While of course a critical intervention, and a major success in terms of her self-designed antiracist praxis in her school, the inclusion of more African peoples' histories did not have an automatic impact on the hegemonically white character of Veronica's classroom and school. Veronica was unsure how her pedagogy needed to shift to help her students appreciate the importance of the content—that this material was indeed "a big deal," and worthy of their attention and interest. She feared getting these connections wrong, and what the results would be for the two students of color in that particular course.

For the teachers in RaceWork, the fear of getting it wrong was almost always connected to desires to know "what to do" in different pedagogical contexts. Yet their fears about getting it wrong speak to a sincere desire to do *something*—mediated by worries that the "something" might actually work against their antiracist aims. This is connected to a second fear: a fear that whatever they were doing would not be enough.

Fear of Not Doing Enough

A common concern RaceWork teachers shared was the fear of not doing enough: fearing that their antiracist interventions would not be sufficiently impactful to actually combat white supremacy. These fears ranged from falling back into old habits or practices to not doing enough for students in ways that could contest structural oppression as enacted in schools.

As we discussed earlier, white supremacy is deeply ingrained in our society, in our schools, and in ourselves; as Delpit (2012) has said, we have all "breathed the racism smog" for our entire lives. Deeply considering this can make us afraid. For instance, Charlie had much experience with the antiracism PD program based on *Courageous Conversations* (2006). These workshops had been really important to Charlie, and she encouraged others in her building to attend the optional sessions. But as she went back again and again, she began to feel stifled, and a particular fear manifested. She told us:

> I'm thinking back to my whole mentality after attending Courageous Conversations PDs [professional development sessions] and then coming here [to RaceWork] and realizing, like, "whoa, I need to go on a different track here." And that's what I'm nervous about is getting back onto that professional development track of very surface level and not going deeper and not having someone hold me accountable.

Going deeper during her first year in RaceWork made Charlie afraid that she would, in a way, regress to her previous comfort zone: the "surface level" engagement she experienced in Courageous Conversations. In particular, she feared not being able to engage on a "deeper" level and not following up. Charlie felt that the PD experiences most commonly available to her and other staff would not significantly combat white supremacy in her school because they didn't push analysis far enough and because they stayed isolated in the PD; that is, the mechanisms for continuing the work after leaving the PD space were not strong enough. Much of Charlie's past antiracism PD remained at an abstract level that left teachers without the responsibility to bring their learning into their own classrooms—as though going through the antiracism training itself *was* the antiracist intervention. Without a structure for accountability to act on the oppressions under consideration, Charlie feared she wasn't going to continue doing impactful work, as she had done in RaceWork. She was afraid these other forms of PD wouldn't do enough.

Veronica also shared a fear related to old habits or practices that were surface level or disregarded antiracism: She feared what would happen to the new social studies curriculum she had worked to bring to her school, a curriculum that was less whitewashed and more globally representative. In addition to her work in her classroom, Veronica made her department's curricular revisioning a major part of her engagement with RaceWork. Making more space for the histories of peoples of color before colonization and genocide was part of her antiracist commitments; she hoped that such inclusion would help rupture the "bubble" she described her school community as existing in. Yet, as other teachers felt pressed for time in the world history curriculum, she feared they would exclude sections focused on precolonial Africa, Oceania, and South America, resulting in a world history course that once again centered European and settler-colonial histories. Veronica "worried that in the end, when we get short on time, the units that are going to get cut are the ones that always get cut, anything that's not Europe." Even if she used her antiracist knowledges to push for curricular changes, with a shared curriculum in her school, if other teachers did not share her commitments, the curriculum would likely revert to its Eurocentric model.

In a different way, Sarah feared not "doing enough" in her role as Dean; her fears were related to not being able to change beliefs, practices, and policies that negatively impacted students of color. She shared her frustrations about feeling stuck with the discipline policies in her building, as they were established not by her but by her principals. As Dean, her job was to execute the policies, not to amend or augment them. When it came to student discipline, she often felt as though her position necessitated racial violence: It was her job to punish the (disproportionately people of color) students who got sent to the office for behavior issues. She told us:

> Racism is just perpetual. It's systemic and it's perpetual, and I'm doing it every day. I keep doing it, I'm a part of it, and it's awful. It's awful to like, to get to a point where you see it, and then you're still in the role [of disciplinarian and now have to say], "OK, now you're suspended," and you're like "Ahhhh!"

Sarah wrestled with her positionality, with her "role" as the school disciplinarian, and the dissonance she experienced between recognizing the reasons that students of color were disproportionately sent to the office for behavior infractions and her job as the Dean to determine their sanctions. She recognized the structural reality of white supremacy in her school, calling it "perpetual." She saw that the ways that students of color were read in the social and academic space of her school were different from the ways that white students were read, that teachers saw things like "disrespect" from students of color more frequently or failed to connect or make curriculum relevant, and also that the disciplinary policies themselves were biased (Delpit, 2012; Heitzeg, 2009). But this recognition conflicted with what she saw as her purpose and job in the school: to apply predetermined consequences for particular behavior infractions.

In the above quote, Sarah also recognized her own complicity in the overrepresentation of students of color for behavior referrals. She stated plainly: "I keep doing it" and "I'm a part of it." "It's awful," she concluded. Yet recognizing that she was part of structural oppression at her school was not enough for Sarah; it was not enough to understand how her role as Dean meant that she herself was part of the racist practices that produced this overrepresentation. As in her rhetorical example—"OK, now you're suspended"—Sarah knew that recognizing her complicity was not doing enough to actually change practices and their consequences: Students of color were still being disproportionately suspended, even as she named the ways that she herself was part of the "perpetual" system that targeted students of color for discipline.

This same fear of not doing enough and its negative consequences for students of color was shared by Charlie. Before our last interview, we (Zac and Shannon) had spent the day in her classroom, and we'd seen a surprising amount of fighting, name calling, and tears from the 3rd-graders she was working with. Charlie had been engaging more with school-to-prison-pipeline literatures and feared that if her students didn't have positive experiences in 3rd and 4th grade, they'd end up incarcerated. She told us:

> I don't know if they're going to prison, but unfortunately the system is set up for them to probably end up there, and if things aren't going well in 4th grade . . . 3rd and 4th grade [are] such a good predictor of how the rest of school is going to go, so it makes me nervous.

Charlie feared for her students, that because they were working-class people of color, "the system is set up for them to probably end up" in prison. Seeing 3rd and 4th grade as "good predictors" of future academic success, Charlie worried that the system was setting her students on a course for prison and that she wasn't doing enough to shift that course and prevent this "probable" outcome. She wasn't doing enough, as a teacher, to combat structural racism experienced by her students. Yet, as we will see later, her attempts to mitigate this were met by resistance from other teachers. This relates to a third fear: of damage to relationships with colleagues.

Fear of Harming Existing Relationships

"I just want to be well respected and well liked in my building. I think everybody does," began Amelia in a story about the work of her building's equity team. But the story was ultimately about an opposite outcome: losing relationships with co-workers because of her antiracist commitments and activities. She was not the only one with this fear. As Angela told us multiple times, in her building the attitude among the teaching staff was to "shoot the messenger" on issues of racial equity; other teachers would undermine and critique Angela, arguing that she was unfairly prioritizing the needs of English learners. Yet Angela saw her comments as reminding her colleagues that their school *had* English learners and that their needs were often not being considered. Relationships with other teachers can have serious impacts on what happens in classrooms. At times, the ramifications—perceived and actual—of engaging in antiracist work can mark teachers as "broken records" or "the person that talks about race and makes them feel uncomfortable" (quoting Angela). Fears of harming relationships with co-workers can block antiracist interventions before they happen. The teachers in RaceWork were deeply aware of this often unexpected outcome.

For Sarah, the risks of harming relationships with co-workers were hyperpresent because of the antiracist approach she took to reducing the number of referrals, particularly for Black male students, at her middle school, building on her recognitions shared above. Unhappy with the policies, she decided to take action. Her restorative justice-inspired approach involved recording the exact times that students were sent to the office for disciplinary reasons. After a student had been removed from the same teacher's classroom more than once, she set up a meeting with the student and the teacher to discuss the behaviors and make a plan together on how to resolve the conflict. In describing this practice, Sarah said:

> At first, I wouldn't really pull the teacher in on it because . . . that was scary to me, because I felt like they were gonna get defensive, which a lot of them do. So I wasn't sure how to do it. I wasn't sure how to do it without making them feel, you know, like I was saying they were doing something wrong, even though I kind of thought that they were.

Sarah recognized that many teachers would (and did) get defensive when called to meet with her and a student they'd referred. Often, there is a kind of automaticity regarding administrators' responsibilities to back up teachers who have sent students to the office. The administrator's job is to be on the side of the teacher and to help the student come up with a way to change their behavior. Taking seriously the notion that teachers themselves might have behaviors that need changing breaks the (unwritten) rule of teacher–administrator solidarity. This solidarity has to be broken, according to Sarah, when the teacher is not shifting their approach to particular students—meaning there have been moments for Sarah when her commitments to antiracism had to supersede her desires to be on the same side as her colleagues.

Sarah remained fearful about these moments when her antiracist beliefs and practices necessitated intervening in conversations and meetings with other teachers in her school. When asked if she was growing in her confidence and comfort in having these restorative justice conversations with teachers, she shared the following:

> I am comfortable to a certain extent, but that's still hard for me too. The hardest thing for me is to confront racial bullshit that comes out of those people's mouths that I care about, because I feel like my choices are to cut that person off, because they believe that way, or to ignore it, or to try to attempt, right, some kind of conversation. And I sort of bumble around with, I kind of do all three, you know? I won't talk to someone for a while and bitch about them to someone else, or I'll confront them, but not in a way that's helpful. It just ends up being combative . . . I think that's still the area that's scariest for me.

Sarah's approach to mediating teacher–student and, later, student–student conflicts had dramatic results, lowering the number of referrals and suspensions by half in a 2-year period. But she was doing this work conscious of her own fears about how her relationships with others would suffer because of it. She was still fearful: Confronting racist discourse, whether explicit or implicit, was profoundly complicated for Sarah when the speaker was someone about whom she cared. Further, she understood she was not responding in only one way to such moments, voicing three different tactics and stating that in practice she "bumbles" her way through versions of cutting someone off, ignoring them, or attempting a more substantive dialogue. Even when the outcomes were overwhelmingly positive for the purposes of racial justice, we see in Sarah an example of a teacher remaining fearful of how relationships with other teachers will be affected because of antiracist interventions. This was coupled with Sarah's desire for collegiality, as "I don't want to come off as having the answers, but rather, [asking my colleagues] will you try it with me?"

To complicate these fears even further, we have to remember that faculty dynamics are not solely conjured in relation to antiracist or racist beliefs and priorities. Relationships with colleagues are multifaceted and often impacted by structural elements of the schools, districts, and communities we work and live in. Morgan's experience offered a keen insight into just how difficult antiracist work can be when the culture of a building is already strained and a feeling of fearfulness permeates. In her 1st year at her elementary school, Morgan experienced a principal she described as "very old school." He had been, in fact, the principal at the school when Morgan herself attended. Morgan described the culture he fostered:

> He really played favorites a lot. And people were terrified to make the wrong move because if you were on his bad side, you were really on his bad side. He would transfer people without a request to other schools, to other grade levels, just to kind of force them out . . . So people were in a community based on fear really, and you just always had to watch your back . . . Everyone would always tell me, "Oh, always watch what you say."

But this did not change much when a new principal started during Morgan's 2nd year at the school, as staff reacted this way:

> People were really nervous about having someone new come in . . . [The new principal] would just kind of come to the classroom for 5 minutes, just to see what was going on, and people were really bothered by it. They thought she was coming to say, "Well, you're doing this wrong and that wrong. I'm going to write you up for this," and so that's kind of the fear that was in our building. And it's because of the old principal. We were just terrified.

The "culture of fear" that the first principal had created and maintained persisted after he left and functioned to block antiracist efforts. Let's slow this down and consider it in detail for a moment.

The teachers in the building were meant to be fearful of running afoul of their principal. They were on guard, encouraged to "watch what [they] say"; they taught in a building where the primary source of accountability was fear of termination or removal to another school. In such a context, we would expect teachers to develop ways to cope with these realities, practices that would ensure, to the best of their ability, that they would not be singled out for punishment. When a new principal came to the building, these same fear-based tactics and practices remained part of the staff's sense of how they did their jobs. The previous principal rarely visited classrooms, which created the sense among staff that anyone being observed was likely in some kind of trouble. To have the new principal visiting many classrooms amplified fears that already existed around observations and the role of the principal.

Further, if teachers were already in a school community "based on fear," we might expect resistance to work that seemed even potentially controversial. Take, for instance, Morgan's intervention to facilitate a critical reading group with the school's faculty. She chose Delpit's book *Other People's Children* (2006) to anchor their conversations, and hoped she would get the support of her new principal in purchasing copies for the entire staff. She also requested that at least partial participation in the reading group be mandatory. Yet, although she was excited about Morgan's work to bring more attention to antiracism in the building, the new principal worried there would be too much resistance among staff to actually make the meetings mandatory. A generous reading of Morgan's new principal balking at making *Other People's Children* required is that she didn't have a choice, given the context of the building and the ways that top-down mandates had been such a cancer in the previous principal's tenure. The climate of the building also made it difficult for Morgan to effectively advocate for students of color who were singled out for punishment by other teachers in her building. This relates to another fear: being called out as racist.

Fear of Being Called Racist

One of the first things Lisa said on our 1st day was that it really "ticks me off when kids call me racist." Many readers might have been expecting this fear—of being called racist—to dominate this chapter. It is, for the vast majority of white people we have known, talked with, and interviewed, something that must be negotiated. In other work we have suggested that to engage in antiracism as a white person is to bring oneself into social spaces that are likely to be read, at least by some, *as racist* (McManimon, Casey, & Berchini, 2018). That is, a white social actor is always negotiating their relative privilege and social capital as they take on antiracist stances and act on their antiracist convictions. Being involved in these conversations and practices is itself sometimes read as racist—not to mention that we might make mistakes as we do so.

In the 2nd year of RaceWork, teachers were making more antiracist interventions in their schools; they needed a space to dialogue with one another about these new roles and possibilities. In these moments, teachers struggled with questions of whether being on a school- or district-level equity team would actually open them up to ridicule from their colleagues—or if their work in these groups would come to be seen as racist.

Amelia was a compelling example of the ways that greater institutional power to shape antiracist initiatives can lead to fears about the possibilities of coming across as racist. She expressed it this way: "The fact that our principal even asks our E[quity] Team to do stuff is like what? You want *me* to do that? Because then you're vulnerable. You're putting yourself out there and waiting to be criticized." Amelia emphasized her own positionality regarding risks she felt in taking on equity leadership roles in her school. There's a certain degree of disbelief in her comments, as if she almost couldn't believe that she was even asked to lead her colleagues in serious work regarding the overrepresentation of students of color being suspended and referred and their underrepresentation in honors and AP courses. After questioning the equity team's roles, she then personalized it, voicing fears of the ways such work made her feel "vulnerable" and "waiting to be criticized." These fears are similar to the larger ethos of her school and district at the time, but with important differences.

The previous year, Amelia's district had engaged in a large-scale effort to reduce discipline gaps at every grade level. The resulting trainings and initiatives left many teachers "feeling like if they kick a kid out or send them to the office or anything, then that means they're racist." In other words, as the district made an effort to recognize the ways that students of color were disproportionally referred for behavior issues, many teachers came to see themselves as under attack, an attack in the form of an accusation of racism. The teachers in this district are racist, so this logic went, and that racism results in more students of color being unfairly punished. Thus, the response must be to *not* send students of color to the office for behavior issues. While Amelia did not view these questions in such either-or binaries, her efforts both independently and as a member of her school's equity team were mediated by these larger district-wide dynamics. Part of the vulnerability she experienced came not only from the threats to self that she herself was being racist, but that her work to help teachers understand the ways race and structural racism were playing out in their building would further the resistance teachers were already feeling in response to *their* fears of being called racist. Fear of being called racist can complicate white antiracist interventions in many ways: It is not only a risk to be a white person facilitating efforts aimed at combatting white supremacy, but it also produces multiple risks for other white social actors on guard for accusations of their own complicity.

These fears of being called racist can be further elucidated through the lens of Steele's (2010) work on stereotype threat. Stereotype threats occur in situations wherein we experience the potential to confirm a negative stereotype tied to one or more of our identities, particularly an identity about which we feel strongly. When we are concerned with not confirming a negative stereotype, we have very little other cognitive energy to expend on the actual task at hand. A person then actually underperforms. Steele's work, and a host of others, contains numerous empirical examples over decades, including stereotype threats for people of color around intelligence tests, women on math tests, and white men on athletic ability (see Steele, 2010). The fear (whether acknowledged or not) of underperforming and living down to a stereotype happens precisely when we care about the task at hand. Stereotype threats for white people include the threat of confirming white racism—as Nicole said, "what we do is so personal." If we apply the logic from these psychological studies, when white people are afraid of living out the stereotype that they are complicit in white supremacy (i.e., that they are, in fact, racist), there is likely very little other room for whatever else we might be asking them to engage in. We can thus imagine that many white teachers in Amelia's district were so concerned about being perceived as racist—living down to this stereotype—that they were not able to fully hear or engage with what Amelia was presenting nor engage in the work needed to ensure that building policies were actually advancing antiracism (not simply ignoring behavior issues from students of color so as to appear less/not racist).

This fear was linked to actual examples. Sarah, for instance, mentioned that her work as Dean of students—and the restorative justice practices she started—led to both students and parents calling her racist. This was hard: "I would get upset—I started sobbing after one phone call and couldn't compose myself." Her fear of being called racist came true. And it did so over and over. Another time, when a student called her racist in front of his entire class, "I was really upset and . . . pissed for a while." Later, she called the student in and told him: "The reason I got so mad when you said that is because it's something I really, really care about." As she talked about how much she cared about antiracism, the student made eye contact with her for the first time. Despite her fears and being very publicly called racist, Sarah used this occasion as an opportunity to talk with a student about her own work as well as the student's behavior.

At other times, our fears of being called racist stem from topics we might well be ignorant of. While many teachers are comfortable answering student questions about, for instance, a scientific inquiry, with "I don't know," moments that feel like they might confirm white racism take on a higher-stakes status. Veronica voiced this feeling this way:

> I still struggle with how do you deal with including groups, and then there's one Asian kid. What do you do with that? Right now we're talking about world religions, and one kid goes, "I'm a Hindu," and I'm like, "Awesome. I hope I don't screw anything up."

Veronica's discoursal move here—worrying about "how to deal with" including students of color—might well fall into the very traps she was seeking to avoid. Certainly, students of color should not be imagined as so "other" that we, as white teachers, must seek to "deal" with those differences. But what Veronica seemed to be aiming for here was actually the opposite of this connotation: She was worried about the possibilities that she would alienate a student who already experienced a host of moments in school that confirmed the ways in which the student did not fit the hegemonic ideal of the nearly all-white, affluent school. She didn't want to further reinforce these feelings: She *did not* want to "screw anything up." The risks, of course, were not only for this particular Hindu student, but also for Veronica to not come across to her students as racist-by-way-of-ignorance.

While these teachers did not overcome fears of being called racist, they did come to see such feelings as part of the work of antiracism in schools. That is, they saw negotiating the different moments when they might be accused of racism as evidence of the impacts of their work. To be engaged in antiracism as a white social actor is to invite accusations of racism; it is the negotiation of these feelings, not working to eliminate them, that can make this fear into a productive component of white antiracist praxis.

Resisting Fear: Not Feeling Alone

During our collective time in RaceWork, these fears did not feel pervasive. Only when we (Shannon and Zac) went back to read interviews, evaluations, and field notes did it become apparent how much time we (both as facilitators and as a collective) spent addressing these white teachers' fears. What was apparent throughout, though, was the importance of community. When we asked what RaceWork teachers found valuable about our time together, the most repeated piece of feedback was the sense of being in community with other teachers. Meeting together helped them feel they were not alone in this work; this feeling was often critical to sustaining their efforts to combat white supremacy in their classrooms and schools. As described earlier, as each teacher came from a different school and even district, the teachers felt free to speak their minds and take risks that would not be possible in building-wide PD settings. Having teachers from different contexts to brainstorm and reflect with was critical to RaceWork's success, but more important, it kept teachers from doubting their commitments when they felt like they were the only ones in their building who recognized possible interventions on the side of antiracism.

In her final interview, Lisa told us that while she often felt isolated in her school, knowing that the other RaceWork teachers had similar experiences helped her feel she was part of a larger community. She said:

> I'm used to having groups of people where I'm the only language teacher or I'm the only one that's [teaching] French. I'm used to kind of being the odd ball out, so it was kind of nice that we were all odd balls because no one really taught the same thing. That actually helped.

Lisa gave us a way of thinking about the group that we hadn't considered: Because no two teachers taught the same content or were in the same district, because each was unique and different from one another, we were all "odd balls." These differences, as Lisa signaled, were read and viewed positively by the teachers in RaceWork, who often compared our group and other PD. All of their other opportunities were either specific to their content area or to their building. RaceWork was the first and only chance these teachers had to dialog with others who taught much older or younger students in totally different schools in different communities.

For Lisa, the fact that no one taught the same content made it easier for us to focus more on the "why" of antiracist approaches to teaching, rather than getting stuck at the "what" that she described as the focus of content-area PD. Charlie shared a similar sentiment in a written reflection after our 1st year together. She wrote:

> The collaboration of this community/group has been amazing! I've stretched my thinking in different ways and brought attention to areas of injustice I never thought about. For example, I never thought that grading could be racially unjust until we started breaking it down and talking about it. It has been nice to work with a group of people that I'm not attached to through work or elsewhere. It has helped create a more honest space to talk, vent, and think.

For Charlie, the group offered new terrains upon which she could live out her commitments to antiracism. As she wrote, she had not before considered the ways that grading might reflect structural oppression and valued the ways that she wasn't "attached" to the others in the group through work. This lack of attachment made it possible to explore new and different questions about her own antiracist praxis. She credited the group for helping to "stretch" her thinking, a metaphorical description of the kind of scaffolding that was possible because of the different ways teachers brought in their own experiences, learning with others without fearing how what they shared might affect their professional and interpersonal standing in their own buildings.

Amelia shared a similar sentiment and tied her experiences in the group to helping sustain her own sense of hope:

> I absolutely wouldn't be able to do this work on my own, so having facilitators and a framework around which this work is centered has helped me tremendously. What I keep coming back to is hope—there always has to be hope. Hope for individual teachers, hope for our students, hope for a systemic change. In our own buildings, it can be so easy to lose hope, but when you come together with people you don't see all the time, it brightens and lightens the load a little bit—that the things we are doing DO matter, and that we can all help support each other.

Here Amelia calls particular attention to the space between sessions. Not seeing the other group members all the time helped her stay hopeful for the potential changes she was working toward in her own school. We also here see the sophisticated and multilayered ways that Amelia conceptualized different kinds of hope as essential for antiracist work in schools. This point on hope is worth exploring more, as it resonates with Freirean critical pedagogy in powerful ways.

For Freire, hope is a requirement for those seeking to transform our dehumanizing status quo. This hope is not naïve, nor is it utopian. Hope for humanization, for growing justice as central to the work of teaching and learning in classrooms and schools, cannot accomplish everything we need to transform our present social reality on its own. To think that schools can do this would lead us to see teaching on the side of justice as an end in itself, rather than as a political act in solidarity with other instances of praxis. Amelia was conscious of these frames in describing the kinds of hope she saw as imperative for her work. She even named layers of this hope—for teachers, more broadly for students, and then for a wider "systemic change." Breaking these groups up thoughtfully signals her recognition of the relationships between multiple layers of oppressions and opportunities to struggle for justice. In some ways, we might read Amelia's written reaction as her reworking and rewording of the tripartite approach to antiracism that anchored RaceWork. Hope became part of what helped Amelia resist feeling alienated and discouraged.

One final example of resisting fear and not feeling alone comes from Morgan, who wrote at the end of our 1st year together:

> A lot of my learning has taken place by listening to other people's stories, struggles, personal development, and successes. It is nice to know that there are other people in education that are working on the same types of goals that you are, that are struggling with the same things, and are wanting to learn about similar issues. I have definitely been more aware of what is going on in my classroom and school in order to be able to share and contribute on Saturdays.

The last move Morgan made in this reflection focused on her desire to contribute to the group, though earlier she shared that listening had been one of the most impactful elements of her learning. Morgan was soft-spoken in peer-group contexts, often opting to listen first before contributing. The result was that, when she did contribute, others took special note of what she said. This was certainly the case when she shared examples of the ways that different teachers in her building resisted the interventions she was suggesting. Still, the focus of her reflection centered on the feeling of being in solidarity with other teachers who were focused on bringing equity into their teaching and into their schools more broadly. Morgan was thus theorizing a balance between being aided by hearing from others facing similar challenges and taking on the responsibility to contribute in return. For Morgan, it was not enough to simply attend, listen, and feel part of a collective. Rather, she needed to act on her convictions and what she was learning with the group so that she could bring her own stories and examples for the group's benefit. This way, they could learn from her challenges and successes as she learned from theirs.

The most important lesson for us in our analysis of how teachers resisted and pushed past their different fears centered on their experiences of the group itself. The group was both the challenge and the comfort for these teachers. RaceWork provided a group of peers to share and think and grow with, outside of the complex set of relationships they each had with colleagues in their buildings. The group was their reason, when they needed a reason, to persevere and continue in the face of difficulty.

Fear as Reflexive: The Place of Fear in Praxis

As we analyzed interviews, written reflections, and field notes from the 2 years of RaceWork, we identified fear almost immediately as one of the most salient themes that cut across all eight teachers' projects and experiences. But as we dug deeper, we came to view these fears as having a pedagogical quality that made them important sources for learning in the context of white antiracism. Fear, in the case of RaceWork, was productive. It produced spaces for reflection and created new questions for these teachers that, had they been more *fearless*, perhaps would not have had the transformative impact so many teachers reported. "I see race everywhere now" became a consistent refrain, but this "sight" came with repercussions and consequences. Those consequences produced the fears we've detailed in this chapter.

Still, the process of addressing and living with these fears feels intimately connected to the personal work needed for white antiracist praxis in schools. If part of our responsibility as white antiracist social actors is to understand the ways that we ourselves are implicated in oppressive white supremacist systems of social reproduction, fear is a predictable response, considering how daunting the task of social transformation truly is. Fear thus becomes not something to get past or move beyond, but rather something to be *worked through*. This working through is the focus of the next chapter on the personal level of antiracist praxis.

CHAPTER 4

Personal Change

Perhaps one of the easiest ways to know if we have learned something is to ask ourselves if we have changed because of that learning. Rogers (1989) argued that learning is most significant when it influences behavior—when it conditions and shifts our practices. For the teachers in RaceWork, learning in our shared space felt immediately connected to their practices in their buildings, and to how they understood themselves, not only as teachers, but more broadly as white social actors in our oppressive social reality. Every teacher in RaceWork reported that their work with us had changed them in significant ways. Thus, we came to view personal change as an important complement to dealing with the fears detailed in the last chapter. This personal change relies on reflection; as Sarah put it: "Any time you can reflect back on how you're doing, it's going to be helpful, for the most part, if you're open to ideas or open to what you can change about how you're doing it."

In this chapter we unpack ways in which these teachers experienced personal change over their time in RaceWork, specifically in terms of their growing sociopolitical consciousness and racial fluency and the ways in which these were supported through various (re)sources. The stories of RaceWork teachers in this chapter share ways of thinking and acting, of "reading racially" across settings and applying locally, specifically in their schools. These examples are context specific, but we argue that enactments of sociopolitical consciousness can be supported elsewhere through readings and discussions in which white teachers engage in an ongoing process of antiracist praxis. This growth—as RaceWork teachers said, as well as lived—is a process, an ongoing becoming, not something to be finished with. In other words, we cannot measure personal change in the ways that we frequently measure in schools.

Growth as Metaphor and as Assessment

With important exceptions (see note 1 from Chapter 2), professional development (PD) for practicing P–12 teachers in the United States today, and the desired outcomes from long-term engagements such as RaceWork, tends to focus on "results." These results, for much PD, typically focus on high-stakes tests: Did student scores go up? Are they making progress? Is the PD "effective"? Such questions speak to the ways in which increasingly all forms of school activity, including PD, are measured and given value in our present neoliberal reality. These measures are, of course, limited; they conceptualize growth in a way that can be captured through multiple-choice questions.

RaceWork did not set out with a goal to increase standardized test scores for students who worked with the eight teachers in our group. To be clear, it isn't that we don't want scores to go up—it would be lovely if they did. But such means of reducing teaching and learning to narrowly defined, culturally exclusive, "mastery" of preestablished standardized measures stand in stark contrast to the aims of our work.

In RaceWork, we centered racial justice as both the prerequisite and objective: as both the point of origin and the destination. In contrast, much PD that aims for solidarity with oppressed peoples falls into the traps of traditional PD more broadly: overly instrumentalized into something that has meaning or value solely in relation to outcomes on standardized tests. Even when such programs strive to go beyond student achievement metrics, the ways in which we are hailed to understand them collapses onto "common-sense" notions of what PD should do and what the results of "good" PD should be (Kumashiro, 2012): If student scores don't go up, it isn't good PD. But a deeper and more insidious element to these logics can further undermine justice-centered PD: the notion of finality.

By finality, we mean completeness, an endpoint. While many critical race theorists insist on the "permanence of racism" (Bell, 1980; see also Delgado & Stefancic, 2014)—that is, the idea that in the United States no pre- or postracial historical moment is possible because we are always already in racialized space predicated on the oppressions and hierarchies of white supremacy—much PD appears to operate as if white supremacy can actually have an endpoint, at least in terms of the ways structural racism negatively impacts the "achievement" of students of color. Such PD programs often have certificates of completion or similar artifacts of finality: They signal that the work is over, when in actuality the PD is meant to scaffold and accelerate material practices that aim to transform the realities of oppression present in school spaces.

With this framing in mind, we return to RaceWork goals. We resisted easy ways of thinking about the impacts of our work because we knew that no matter how successful teachers' interventions were, we were not going to reach the "endpoint" of eliminating white supremacy. We have made this point with teachers and administrators in other settings as well. Even if we could eradicate every racist element of our particular school, this would not be enough: As soon as students walked across the street, they'd be walking back into the white supremacist reality we all experience daily in the United States. Thus, unlike many other kinds of PD, we anticipated that we would not—could not—actually "finish" the work we set out to do. Because of this unfinished quality, we see teachers' growth and personal change as a form of assessment of our work together. This chapter is about the ways in which teachers articulated their experiences of changing and growing at the level of the personal through their engagement with RaceWork.

What It Means to "Change": White Teachers Voicing Sociopolitical Consciousness

Among the most frequent comments teachers expressed in interviews were thoughts about personal changes they recognized in their work and thoughts before and after/during their engagement with RaceWork. In fact, every teacher in RaceWork shared that they felt they had changed significantly as a result of their work with us. Feeling that one has changed, in the abstract, does not actually give a sense of where one was to begin with and where one has moved to, however, and so the examples in this section are contextualized to help readers gain a sense of the range of experiences these teachers had with antiracism before their time in RaceWork.

Following are examples of what Ladson-Billings (1995, 2006b) has theorized as sociopolitical consciousness, one of her three tenants of culturally relevant pedagogy. She (2006b) wrote:

> The first thing teachers must do is educate themselves about both the local socio-political issues of their school community (e.g., school board policy, community events) and the larger socio-political issues (e.g., unemployment, healthcare, housing) that impinge upon their students' lives. (p. 37)

Sociopolitical consciousness on the part of culturally relevant or sustaining teachers is the ability to understand local phenomenon as part and constituent of larger social systems of oppression. Understanding schools and classrooms in context, as always already politically charged spaces, means understanding the work of teachers and students as constantly involving issues of oppression. As mentioned earlier, Kumashiro (2009) has explained that often the way schools address oppression is through absence: through *not* engaging the ways that they are and can be complicit in oppression. For Ladson-Billings, teachers must be sociopolitically conscious in order to support their students in developing students' own sociopolitical consciousness so as to connect their academic content with engagements in the world on the side of equity and transformation. RaceWork teachers frequently voiced changed sociopolitical understandings of their families, communities, and the world.

We begin with Lisa, who taught French in an immediate suburban secondary school with more than 90% of students identifying as people of color and qualifying for free and reduced-price lunch, as she seemed to have the least experience with antiracist approaches and perspectives. She attended the first session but missed the next two. While excited that she opted to remain with the group (missing only one other meeting over the remaining 2 years), we also felt that in missing some of the earliest activities and discussions she started off on a different note than the rest of the group. In her 1st-year interview with us, when describing ways she was thinking about students and parents differently because of her work with us, Lisa said:

> I guess I didn't really realize that just because the kid seems like they don't care in class doesn't mean that the parents don't care, and I kind of equated the kid attitude with, well, the parent is gonna feel the same way.

Before RaceWork, Lisa tended to think of her students as just that: students. Their lives outside of school, for her, mirrored their lives at school. So the students who were attentive and engaged were great kids, and those who weren't reflected the values of their parents and caretakers who, in Lisa's estimation, clearly were not modeling the kinds of behaviors needed to be successful in school. In RaceWork, Lisa realized that she didn't actually know much about how her students' families thought about school. She sought to learn more. Unfortunately, some of her attempts were blocked almost immediately when she couldn't reach the parents by phone. She reported calling numbers that were local restaurants and businesses, or leaving messages and never hearing back. After reading more about the ways that deficit frames often dominate white conceptions of families of color, she decided to challenge herself to connect with parents despite the obstacles:

> I mean, sometimes you have to go outside the box, but I wouldn't have done that earlier in the school year. I would have just been like, "well, phone doesn't work; oh well." But learning more about the attitudes of the parents being different from what I expected—just because they don't speak English doesn't mean they don't need to know about their kids. That was kind of a shock, kind of a slap in the face that I really needed.

Lisa's "slap in the face" came especially when she was able to work with interpreters who helped her connect directly with East African and Latinx families. While her school population did not have many French speakers, she was able to return the favor and translate a few times for other teachers as well. These experiences helped Lisa shift from a deficit perspective (i.e., seeing the parents of students who were not engaged as deficient) to a problem-posing stance: How did her expectations differ from those of her students and their families, and how could she communicate more explicitly? This orientation helped Lisa feel much more connected to her students and their families by the end of the 2nd year of RaceWork.

Lisa emphasized relationships as her primary goal for her work in RaceWork, and over the course of the 2 years she came to develop meaningful connections with most of her students and their families. In our last interview with Lisa, however, she discussed how these relationships were leading her to think more about what *else* she wanted to work on to be an even more antiracist educator:

> I feel like I need to do more to help them connect with, now that they connect with me, and they respect me, and we respect each other, I need to show the ultimate kind of respect by allowing them to see themselves in a curriculum that could definitely go white. It's French, for Christ's sake, you know; it could definitely go white Christian, Catholic, whatever, and so I really need to infuse more Africa, more Asia, more you know, Haiti—something to make it more culturally relevant to more of our students.

Lisa extended her work to build stronger relationships with students and their families into recognizing that these relationships must be coupled with curricular interventions. She explicitly wanted her curriculum to be more culturally relevant for her students. While other teachers in RaceWork focused on curricular interventions almost from the very beginning of their time with us, Lisa came to curriculum later. This does not mean Lisa was somehow deficient or behind others; rather, it signals that she needed first to understand who her students were and what expectations their families had for them before she began to worry about the ways her curriculum might be functioning to exclude different students. In other words, she needed to develop a greater understanding of the sociopolitical conditions affecting her students, her school, and her work. Lisa felt she grew in each area over the course of RaceWork.

As mentioned in Chapter 3, Sarah, the Dean of students at her middle school, described her approach to antiracism before RaceWork as worrying and caring about students (particularly of color), but not having any idea what to do with that caring. She knew her school was reproducing white supremacist outcomes, but she didn't know how to respond. In her final interview, Sarah reflected on how she was thinking about her work several years after beginning RaceWork:

> I'm not saying I know what to do, but I feel like I actually have some footing now [whereas before I thought] "that's too big . . . I can't think about that on a daily basis . . ." I'm really different, I feel like I'm really different, and I feel a lot more confident and other things have happened in conjunction to make me feel more confident. I feel like the role: not being liked was the scariest thing for me. Before I hated it, and it made me feel like I was going to throw up. And now I've just had to kind of deal with it.

For Sarah, "not being liked" referred to her shifting role within her building: Her 1st year in RaceWork was her 1st year as Dean of students, a position that meant she was in charge of both student discipline and annual high-stakes testing. Transitioning from being a well-liked and well-respected science teacher to being the person in charge of testing and discipline was difficult for her. While she knew the role was important and was excited for the challenge, she was not prepared for the shift in relationships with her co-workers. Sarah found in RaceWork a source of support during this transition. She also recognized ways that her role as Dean offered new spaces for antiracist interventions; she came to see the shift in her relationships not as losing popularity, but as part of the counter-hegemonic work she was doing.

Sarah challenged taken-for-granted assumptions in her building, questioned existing discipline policies, and took the critical step of conferencing with teachers and students after the second time a teacher referred the same student. Being liked felt important to Sarah, but became less so once she realized that it was more important to be fighting for more inclusive discipline practices. This is why she told us she felt "really different" but also more "confident." As she grew in her confidence as an antiracist white educator, she also realized that we ought to expect push-back when we transition to centering equity in our work in schools. Following from her growing sociopolitical consciousness, she aimed to support others in better connecting what they were seeing in their schools to the structural conditions and realities of their community.

Morgan shared that it also took her a while to understand the importance of taking a pedagogical orientation to work with others in her building around issues of whiteness and white supremacy. Reflecting on both years in RaceWork, she shared that in her school she had to remind herself that teachers had not had the same experiences that she had and needed time to work through ideas, without her jumping in to problem-solve. Over the course of RaceWork, she came to see a need to be generous with her colleagues, connecting elements of her own previously held ideas in what she heard from them. While frustrated at times with her colleagues' desire for quick solutions or for best practices, she explained to them why she did not have them, rather than offering an easy or quick way out.

Morgan's approach to leading her district equity team echoed Ladson-Billings (2006b). She did not want to solve other peoples' problems for them, but envisioned the equity team as a source of help in working through particular contexts and questions for themselves. This is a pedagogical orientation that follows from the years spent together in RaceWork: not learning about the best possible actions to do and then reporting on them, but rather taking time to learn together and struggle based on the actual contexts in which teachers worked. RaceWork teachers came to internalize the ethos of our approach to PD as building leaders on antiracist questions: The aim of our work cannot be to sound right, correct, or most critical. Instead, our work must respond to the material conditions and the actual communities we are working with. We can't tell others what to do, but we can support them in their/our work to respond in the most antiracist ways possible.

In trying to support others, the biggest issue Angela experienced in her building was the "broken record" effect she described early in our work together. Angela advocated for English learners in her school at virtually every faculty meeting and often via email between the monthly meetings. The result was that she felt most of her colleagues had stopped paying attention to what she was saying. As she repeated herself, she became more and more frustrated with how few of the other teachers in her building really heard her. Angela told us at our second session in the 1st year, when we each explained why we'd come back for a second session, that she'd come back because she thought RaceWork was talking about race and white supremacy in ways that might actually help her be heard by more people in her school; she came back because she "*had* to—well, not had to, but need to" as she needed a place "to feel vulnerable but also to feel strong."

A few months later, she announced to the group that she had made an important discovery in her own thinking about antiracism and conscientizing white teachers: "Everybody is on their own journey, and the point is to *be on* the journey, not where you are on it." In her attempts to advocate for students, she recognized that she came on very strong and "thus maybe burned some bridges with colleagues" unnecessarily. She described this more after our 1st year together:

> Everybody's on their own journey; everybody's experiences are different. I don't have to judge them because they don't get it. My position should be to help them understand it, and that's not a process that takes place over night . . . You don't just say to somebody, "well, you know blah blah blah" and they get it.

Angela had approached advocacy for English learners in her elementary school as akin to explaining why these students needed different kinds of supports than the mostly white and middle-class students the school had traditionally served. Because she explained this regularly, many in her building dismissed her, until she shifted her approach to one that was more *pedagogical* in orientation.

This pedagogical shift for Angela began by honoring the others she was working with in her school as *learners*: as folks who bring with them the host of their past experiences and knowledges that they can scaffold to greater understanding of race and white supremacy in their building. Angela shifted from thinking that her task was to say the right thing, in the right way, to show that she was antiracist, to thinking about how she might be a support for others to appropriate for themselves the ways in which their work was complicit in maintaining white supremacist realities for students and how they might work to challenge this. This critical shift led to her feeling much more "heard" in her building the following year. She explained that, for the first time in over 20 years in the classroom, she finally felt like she had others on her staff to whom she could really talk and get/give support in antiracist work. For Angela, growing her own sociopolitical consciousness enabled her to work with others in her building in reciprocal and collaborative ways to better understand their sociopolitical contexts and to respond in culturally relevant ways with and for their students.

Racial Fluency or "I See Race Everywhere!"

During our final interview, Morgan told us:

> I just want both of you to know how impactful this has been in my life. I mean, my classroom would be completely different had I never gone to those Saturday mornings, and I feel like I would really be doing an injustice to my kids if I wasn't conscious of the things that I am now aware of. So thank you to both of you for doing this.

While we include this quote with some trepidation, as it is as much a glowing endorsement of our work as a piece of "evidence" for the claims we are making about RaceWork, Morgan centered the experiences of her students as central to the shifts she perceived in herself. While she began with the impact to her own life, the details of this claim were classroom based. She drew a direct connection between her experiences in RaceWork and the lived realities of her students. This speaks to the initial framing of this chapter, in thinking about PD as deriving its value from impacts on student performance. While she didn't mention test scores, she did center her students and their needs. Antiracism for white teachers does not mean that white teachers reach a certain level of understanding of themselves as white social actors *for their own sake*. Rather, antiracism necessitates an ongoing praxis with and for students, in order to realize antiracist outcomes. Morgan's antiracist stance began to influence everything she did—in her classroom, in her school, and in her district. Morgan grew in her racial fluency; she became confident in speaking about race and white supremacy, and she used that confidence to push for more antiracist PD in her district and to lead the effort to create her district's first equity team.

Further, RaceWork seemingly seeped into all areas of Morgan's life. During the same interview, she related an experience she'd had the day before:

> This is really random, but I picked up teeth whitening yesterday at the dentist. And the back of the box said on it, "white has never been so right." And I was like, "Oh my god! I know this is a totally different context, but oh my god!"

Morgan was recognizing the way that racially coded language and framing permeates our everyday environments—and what her responsibilities were because of this:

> I think my goal is always to just talk about real life with my kids. So that's always a continuing goal, 'cause it's always a new group of kids. So I think through me being aware, the people around me are also being aware, and now we're all having a conversation together. I guess since it's been a focus in my classroom, it's just kinda spread into all areas of my life.

Morgan expressed an assumption that we have had about critical teachers for a long time: Critical teachers are critical not only in their classrooms, but in their lives outside of school as well. They *are* critical; they don't *do* critical things at certain moments and then turn it off. Our pedagogical commitments bleed into our interpersonal commitments, our social and familial relationships, our civic relationships, and so on. Morgan saw her abilities to recognize and understand evidence of white supremacy as supporting others in her life in also being more aware. But importantly, she did not assert that she was "teaching" the adults in her life about race and white supremacy. This is again a sophisticated pedagogical gesture, one that sees others not as fixed and static characters but rather as fluid and dynamic: as learners.

Morgan was definitely not alone in the ways RaceWork enabled her to read race and racialized oppression in a variety of spaces. Charlie, for instance, said that RaceWork facilitated

> such a shift in my thought process and even just the way I talk about it now with friends or with my husband. I just feel like I can be a little more upfront about what's really going on, like the system and why it's inequitable.

As she said in our final session at the end of year 2, RaceWork had helped her to start "to understand structural and historical events" and to develop the "vocabulary" to talk about it. RaceWork teachers broadened their racial literacy and fluency, by which we mean being able to "read" racially: connecting multiple pieces of information to past knowledges, placing this information in context through the lens of white supremacy, and then applying these knowledges. Such "readings" offer white teachers ways of understanding their work in local contexts, enabling them to respond in generative ways and to resist moments when the white supremacist character of our society becomes explicit in school settings. For the teachers in RaceWork, working monthly to name and read race in explicit ways together resulted in a shared phenomenon among the group: They came to see race everywhere.

Lisa had perhaps the biggest shift in racial literacy, explaining that she came to "understand other perspectives, more about the inequities that I didn't know existed before I started RaceWork. And now I see them everywhere." For her, because of RaceWork, "it's like I have a decoder ring" through which to analyze differently and to recognize the racialized space of school and the relationships therein. Prior to RaceWork, Lisa thought that students who were being systematically excluded were *choosing* not to engage in their schoolwork the way they were supposed to. She connected this to home environment, thinking that students who were successful in school had strong home environments where schoolwork was important and celebrated. When students struggled, for Lisa this had signaled a home environment that did not value and respect school enough. Students were thus mirrors of their home lives, with no need for a racially explicit lens or understanding. But she pushed herself to connect with families. For instance, one Saturday she shared a story about reaching out to a Black mom, only to find out that while her son was getting Ds and Fs in all his classes, Lisa was the only teacher to reach out to his mother. Their conversation inspired Lisa to connect even more. By the end of our first year, when Lisa shared her response quoted above, she was deeply self-critical of her initial approach to understanding students and saw RaceWork as part of her growing racial consciousness. She came to recognize how structural white supremacy played out in everything from racialized microaggressive comments among students to how families felt ostracized from the structures of schooling.

For Veronica, racial fluency meant recognizing that she was now different from people with whom she'd grown up and even some of the environment in which she was now teaching:

> It's a gradual thing. And then you don't keep up with everybody and then you realize they're still right there and didn't have any kind of journey . . . My high school group: the comments that they make, they don't realize that what they say really hurts other people. Or . . . they'll make some sort of comment offhand about race or something but then it seems okay for them, because they look around, and there's no one of color in the room. It's a safe space for them, and I don't always want it to be a safe space.

Importantly, Veronica recognized that she had grown, but also that this growth contained both pain and potential. She couldn't go back to the safe white space she grew up in, went to college in, or even was currently teaching in. She recognized that being antiracist was *not* just about when people of color are present, but all the time. Race could never be "off the radar" for her. Likewise, in the spring of our 1st year, she recounted talking with a student teacher about his Eurocentric approach to history: "In talking with him, I realized, 'Oh, I was there. I can see growth and change in myself.'"

Amelia also expressed a similar sense, stating after the 1st year of RaceWork, "I see race in *evvvveryyyythiiiiiing*!" For her, understanding race and racism in "everything" included recognizing all white spaces with friends and family as racialized—particularly as white spaces. Still, her growing ability to read race left Amelia uncertain. When asked to elaborate on this statement, she shared the following:

> I'm starting to see it everywhere, so I'm starting to think I'm really smart, like "look at me go, right?" But I know that's not safe, that's not good either, so I don't want to get to that point. There always has to be something to learn, to grow, to challenge, I guess. I don't know what my antiracist classroom would look like or my antiracist justice would look like. I don't know.

To borrow Angela's metaphor, at this point in Amelia's "journey," she acknowledged both that she was recognizing race more and more and simultaneously that she had much more to learn, particularly regarding how she might apply these knowledges in her classroom. She was laughing to herself a bit as she said "look at me go, right?" Yet her self-mocking tone was coupled with deep introspection. For Amelia, coming to understand white supremacy included a series of challenges that she had not fully anticipated. She did not know what her "antiracist classroom would look like" nor what antiracist justice would entail. She also recognized that RaceWork was not going to mean that she came away "with a toolbox," as was the usual expectation of professional development.

She carried these questions into the following year of RaceWork as her role shifted dramatically within her school. Amelia became a leader on her school equity team, facilitating multiple PD days for the entire staff and becoming one of the go-to people in her building on questions of racial equity. Yet her self-questioning remained. In our last interview, she shared the following about her process of asking these kinds of questions:

> I do feel like it's paralyzing a little bit, and then I feel like I'm just being jaded or just overly critical now, overly sensitive. 'Cause that's always been a question about it too: is it always

about race? Is it always there, is it never, aren't there sometimes like really does it? . . . Am I always thinking about it? I don't know.

Amelia's uncertainty is clearly present. While she experienced a huge transformation in confidence as an antiracist educator over the years of RaceWork, she never lost her deep-seated questions.

Inside the Course: (Re)Sources for Change

As with how they addressed fears, the role of the group itself came up often in formal evaluations, interviews, and teachers' writing with regard to how they were understanding their own personal change. Our monthly gatherings provided sources and inspiration that continued to push these teachers. They credited the group for the ways that they experienced personal change, sharing examples of how the group helped or sustained them. This happened through readings and subsequent discussions in which teachers learned from and with each other. This dialogical learning inspired confidence in their ability to both do this work and to *be/become* antiracist.

Nicole, an English teacher, was concerned about how the small but growing Latinx population in her exurban school was made invisible by the traditions and norms of a "college town" whose P–12 population was disproportionately middle class, white, and from homes with families who had had significant success in the U.S. educational system. She came to RaceWork seeking ways to help other teachers in her building understand that just because their classes did not have a significant number of working-class students of color did not mean that race and white supremacy were not constantly present in their school. Nicole was especially disturbed by the literal train tracks running through the town that separated the middle-class single-family homes from the trailer parks and working-class homes in which almost all of her students of color lived. She wanted help theorizing and then talking about this with other staff.

For Nicole, RaceWork readings seemed different from other kinds of past learning experiences:

> It was all things I hadn't read before so it all felt new. And because I was choosing to come . . . sometimes my readings for class [e.g., for an MEd program] feel like something I have to do, but because [RaceWork] was something I was choosing, to come to this space, I had the attitude that I'm going to put all my thought into reading this; I'm not just going to read it

to get it done. And I'm going to read it and then think about, connect it as I read. So I always try to make notes in comparison to my classroom or my school which is probably, unfortunately, something I hadn't done before, but because I felt like if I'm going to come here, if I'm going to this, I might as well.

Nicole viewed RaceWork as both a "class" and as markedly unlike her other course experiences. She found herself engaging in a different reading practice than she usually did, focusing on connections and comparisons in ways that she hadn't before her engagement in RaceWork. The newness of the readings felt important too; she was engaging with literatures that she did not typically take up, ones she felt she had little other access to. She then brought these readings and ideas to her building, helping other teachers understand more about the ways that, often unintentionally, their school functioned to privilege middle-class white students and further marginalize working class students of color. Nicole saw these connections as stemming from the different type of reading she did with us; drawing on elements of her disciplinary pedagogical content knowledge as an English teacher, she used reading as a way of connecting more with other teachers—and students—in her building on questions of access and equity.

For Angela, it was not the readings we explored together but the conversations in which we explored them that were the source of a shift in her thinking, a shift from thinking of herself as information sharer to pedagogue. That is, over the course of her time in RaceWork, Angela repositioned herself as someone who recognized other white teachers as *learners*. Before, she saw most of her colleagues as willfully ignoring the realities of oppression faced by students in their school. Drawing on experiences with the younger teachers in RaceWork, she came to think of these differences with colleagues as akin to being on different parts of the same "journey." While there is no way to know how far others are or were willing to go on said journey, the notion of the journey speaks to a pedagogical quality that Angela did not articulate in our initial meetings. Importantly, this does not mean that Angela came to excuse the relative racism of her colleagues in relation to English learners. In fact, during our final interview Angela indicated that fighting for the inclusion of her students in the school remained her biggest struggle. But what RaceWork teachers offered Angela was a way of recalibrating her understanding of other white teachers as learners about race and racism. Recognizing that the teachers in RaceWork brought different kinds of commitments and had very different experiences from one another, she transferred this approach to her own building as well, finding ways to better scaffold for those teachers rather than responding solely to their dismissal or defensiveness.

Along with Angela, other RaceWork teachers believed that the long-term engagement of RaceWork and the relationships built within the group encouraged them to go beyond what they had experienced in other racial equity PD, which felt like a kind of Racism 101 wherein white teachers learned about their relative privilege and the ways that whiteness norms are ubiquitous in schools. For the most part, RaceWork teachers came to our group firmly aware of these ideas. They wanted to know more and hadn't found spaces to do that. For Charlie, the question was

> How do I keep pushing myself? Because I wouldn't have known half of these things to read. I wouldn't have known any of them, or any of the authors that you guys have suggested that weren't in session, like I'd [still be only] reading Glenn Singleton.

These new resources and approaches were important to Charlie because she felt she had plateaued in her learning about race and white supremacy. She shared the experience we've written about with others (see Lensmire et al., 2013), wherein learning about white privilege comes to stand in for all antiracist work. Charlie felt stuck in a kind of whiteness PD loop: She would once again confront her relative privilege, feel like this was in itself a kind of action, and then be disappointed at the lack of momentum for antiracist transformation in her building.

In our last interview, Charlie told us her confidence "has been boosted from RaceWork" and that this confidence was assisting her in her role as equity leader for her building—and also an equity leader for her district. While she was already seen as a leader on questions of equity in her school before her time in RaceWork, Charlie connected her growing responsibilities to confidence stemming from her time in RaceWork. This confidence was common across the group: Every teacher reported growing in confidence around engaging questions of race and white supremacy. As Morgan described it, writing after the 1st year of RaceWork:

> I am much more comfortable talking about race with any particular group of people. I feel much more confident in my understanding of race related topics than I did back in September. I think a lot of that confidence came from being able to "practice" talking about race in a safe environment on the Saturdays that we met. I feel that I am able to be a leader for my school in starting a discussion about race and that I am no longer concerned that I will upset or ruffle feathers. I think because of all the talk focused on race I have been a part of I am able to be much more honest with what I am observing in

my school, classroom, and in myself. Before I was hesitant to point out race related issues for fear of what that could mean for me or my school. Or even how others would interpret my viewpoint. Now that fear is gone and in its place is a need to confront what I am seeing and start to discuss ways to change it and myself. I am okay with admitting that I have work that I need to do.

While there was another year of RaceWork yet to come, Morgan was already articulating a significant shift in her thinking about race and racism in relation to her school. Being fearful of what addressing race would mean for her and her school was no longer a possibility: Such fears had to be abandoned in favor of the "work" that Morgan knew she had to do, including confronting her internal struggles in coming to a more robust and materialist conception of white supremacy. Morgan recognized that focusing on maintaining positive relationships with others in her school could potentially work in opposition to her desires for equity and instead felt the need to "confront" white supremacy in her school and in herself. This attention offers a way of placing the tripartite approach to antiracism in context: Morgan was grappling with the intersections of the personal (focusing on herself) and the local (focusing on her school).

Change as Ongoing: White Antiracism as Becoming

Morgan's admission of all the work we have yet to do and Amelia's self-questioning provide a reminder that white teachers do not have to wait until reaching some kind of firm and confident stance on their own abilities as antiracist educators before acting on antiracist commitments. Waiting until they are certain that no move they make will cause concern among teachers or administrators or harm students is likely to result in complete stasis—and worse, continue the racially oppressive status quo. Amelia did not wait for this certainty, and her example can serve as a model for others who have worried that they do not possess enough experience or have a clear enough vision of antiracism to work toward their aims. Amelia's experience shows that someone can enact concrete antiracist changes—in her case, creating more opportunities for students of color to access Advanced Placement courses and ensuring that every staff-wide PD contained a racial equity component—while still questioning their own credentials and skills as an antiracist educator.

In fact, we must think of change as ongoing, as becoming. In Sarah's final interview, she said that RaceWork teachers see antiracist work as

integral to what we're doing with our jobs and our lives. . . .
You've moved things forward for so many of us. . . . It has
changed the way that I'm always going to be in education, and
I know that that's true for the others in our group as well.

Sarah's description of RaceWork's impact described a shift from a focus on "doing" to a focus on "being." She asserted that her experience with the group in RaceWork changed how she was "always going to be" in her work in classrooms and schools. This challenges more instrumentalized conceptions of PD that are concerned with questions of "doing": "What am I going to do on Monday?" "What should I do if this happens?" These questions are not unimportant, but from the perspective of culturally relevant and sustaining pedagogies, they ought to be secondary to issues of ontology: who we are being with and for students. Ladson-Billings (2006b) situated cultural relevancy not as something someone *does*; rather, we *are* culturally relevant with and for our students. For Ladson-Billings, being culturally relevant will take care of the question of what to do. Sarah had internalized that antiracism is not merely a series of steps that, if performed correctly, will always yield a particular outcome. Rather, she demonstrated that she had come to understand her work in schools as a question of who she was being with and for students, not merely what she was doing to them.

We thus conclude our discussion of the personal changes experienced by RaceWork teachers with the notion of change as ongoing. This pedagogical commitment follows from Freire's (2000) conception of human beings as never finished, as always in the process of becoming. From a Freirean perspective, much PD is a form of banking, even as the content often advocates for more student-centered and multicultural approaches. RaceWork's approach to antiracism with white teachers follows Freire's notion that we are always reinventing and rebeginning as critical educators: We are never finished in our development as white antiracist educators. To feel finished is to signal an inability to evolve our pedagogy, to stop emphasizing who we are being with and for students, and to regress into the instrumental obsession with technique and best practice.

For the teachers in RaceWork, our years together did not have a clear and neat beginning and end. As discussed earlier, we continued as a group together in our 2nd year not because it was part of the plan, but because the teachers did not want the group to end. At the end of the 2nd year of working together, we concluded our time together primarily for pragmatic reasons. As academics who had completed PhDs, we (Zac and Shannon) had found jobs away from Minnesota that would make it impossible for us to continue meeting monthly.

In our final interviews with each teacher, completed a year after our last session together, we heard more about the ways that RaceWork had never actually ended for these teachers: They were still in the very same processes of becoming. Again, Amelia's case makes for an excellent example. In her interview after our 1st year, she told us:

> It's still just me in my classroom, I'm not, I'm just focusing on how can I be a better teacher, how can I help my students better, how can I, I mean even in terms of school I'm not, I'm still struggling with my identity at school.

Amelia's deep uncertainties, as discussed above, were ever-present in her 1st year in RaceWork. Yet these uncertainties did not lead to her leaving the group, nor to deciding not to actually try antiracist interventions in her classroom and school. By the time of our last interview with Amelia 2 years later, after spending the day observing in her classroom, she told us:

> I know that I have some skills that other teachers don't have, and I know that other teachers have skills that I don't have, but I know that I am unique in some ways. And it's taken me a long time to say that, you know that. I want to be around to see it through. I want to be able to say I helped things change in our school, and I never thought in a million years that I would do that.

Over the span of a few short years, Amelia went from being a teacher who did not know who she was, who did not feel that she had an antiracist identity or desire to act as a change agent in her school, to being the co-chair of her building equity team, responsible for the official communications between the equity team and the rest of the faculty in her high school. One of her ongoing goals was to be "bold and brave." This change was not a result of pre-programmed curricular choices on our part as facilitators, as if we knew ahead of time what Amelia's needs were and could successfully anticipate where we wanted her to go. If such a series of steps were part of RaceWork, we doubt seriously that Amelia would have remained in the group. But without requiring a series of affirmations or feelings of finished antiracist consciousness, we were able to support Amelia in her own self-appropriation, in her own learning.

While we certainly believe that our efforts in RaceWork had direct impacts on the teachers who worked with us, we do not believe that we, as facilitators, are responsible for the growth of these teachers. The changes they reported were, indeed, *personal* changes—evidence of their sincerity in thinking seriously about what they took up with us and putting it in contexts of their own realities, conflicts, and desires. As Veronica said: "I feel like it took me a long time to get to where I am now." Too often, antiracist work with white teachers assumes white teachers to be, in Lowenstein's words, "deficient learners about diversity" (2009, p. 164). Antiracist work with white teachers is then imagined as responding to these deficiencies, correcting them. Our approach stands in stark contrast to this deficit-orientation, understanding white teachers to be complex social actors who bring resources and strengths with them to their work in antiracism. Yet we must also be attentive to the uncertainties, fears, and worries of white teachers. We must do both, simultaneously, which calls on us to be humble, in the Freirean (2006) sense, to not believe that as PD facilitators we can fully know either where learners are coming from nor where they are going, in any kind of complete way. Instead, we can make space for their self-appropriation of meaning, for them to chart the course of their own personal change, with scaffolds and support along the way, on the side of antiracism. These scaffolds can then become sources of engagement in the immediate contexts in which teachers find themselves, in their classrooms, schools, and communities: the space of the local.

PART 2
THE LOCAL

CHAPTER 5

Relationships

This chapter starts the section concerned with the level of the local in our tripartite framing of antiracist praxis. The local is sometimes left out in our antiracist imaginations. Often, when white social actors conjure the ways they ought to orient their antiracism, they think of two possibilities: the work they need to do for themselves, in their own mind and consciousness (the personal), and the immensity of structural racism that requires long-term, coordinated efforts across society (the structural). In other words, change yourself and/or change the world. Space is created, however, between the personal and the structural any time we find ourselves in positions of systemic authority. For instance, a white woman in her late 20s in the United States is far from the most hegemonically powerful social position in our society. (Think, for instance, of the makeup of the U.S. Congress.) Yet, when she is transformed into Ms. Martin, 4th-grade teacher in room 223 in Huntington Elementary School, she occupies a position of structural advantage over every one of her students. The local is the space between the personal and the structural wherein we have a form of institutionally sanctioned power over others. Thus, one of the most potentially transformative sites for enacting white antiracism is the classroom.

The local is not *only* in the classroom. We are positioned hierarchically in relation to others around us at different times in our lives, even at different times in our day. The bus driver might not make as much money or have as much social capital as the law professor, but when the professor is on the bus, who is in charge? Who would authorities and the public trust in a dispute about the professor/rider not paying the fare? Other examples include service-oriented relations, patrons asking to speak to managers, rigid hierarchies among cooks in a professional kitchen, and so on. The local gives us access to instances of the structural, localized by our encountering them in our own personal way. In this way, the local becomes perhaps the best practical location for white antiracism. It is a way of actually living out the notion of doing something *productive* with one's own relative white privilege. Or, more pedagogically, it is the immediate context for the problem one is working to critique, get smarter about, and transform.

This pedagogical focus on the local brings us to Freire's centering of love in his conception of critical pedagogy. Freire (2000) saw love as essential to revolutionary struggle and thus to any pedagogy that aims to be in solidarity with those who are oppressed. Freire (2000) argued that we need "*courage to love* (which, far from being accommodation to an unjust world, is rather the transformation of that world in behalf of the increasing liberation of humankind)" (p. 176). Love connects pedagogical concerns with antiracism in the abstract to the embodied enactments central to this chapter: relationships.

All teaching and learning is relational, concerned with the social exchange among people engaged in the praxis of education. The teachers in RaceWork were, of course, in relation with one another, and with us as facilitators, but also with the many people they work with in their schools and classrooms. Parsing through RaceWork teachers' conversations about relationships, we (Shannon and Zac) identified several characteristics of relationships that enabled teachers to pursue their antiracist aims: They worked toward humanizing outcomes based on shared purposes, they took time and trust-building, they were based in understanding the complexities of a racialized world, and they occurred across settings and roles—meaning with other adults, including colleagues and students' families, and with students. With students, these relationships were based on honesty and high expectations. Further, relationships built on these values and listening to each other's stories fostered relational accountability to each other as humans and to antiracist praxis.

For RaceWork teachers, relationships figured centrally in their antiracist praxis. Yet these relationships are not automatically pedagogical and supportive. Following this chapter on positive relationships that nurture relational accountability for antiracist aims, the next chapter focuses on relationships with colleagues that produce tensions and marginalizations. While these tension-filled socializations are relationships, they are not pedagogical in character and orientation; in these cases, relationships with other adults in their buildings functioned in opposition to RaceWork teachers' antiracist desires and activities. First, though, this chapter offers examples of different approaches to and understandings of relationships that (can) function on the side of antiracism: relationships among RaceWork teachers, with students, with students' parents, and with like-minded others.

Relationships within RaceWork: Rethinking "Accountability"

"If I can be frank," Amelia said, I have "a sense of obligation . . . I didn't want to be a flake . . . I didn't want to let you down . . . but [also] I just wanted to keep learning. I wanted to keep hearing other people's stories, to hear that my story was somehow validated and that it's okay to struggle with these things." Again and again, both during the Saturday mornings we spent together and in our conversations with RaceWork teachers, we heard that RaceWork enabled these teachers to not feel alone in doing the hard work of countering white supremacy in their classrooms and schools. They felt, as Amelia said, obligated to do this work, or as Nicole said, "You said we're gonna do stuff. And I was like, 'okaaayyyy.' We're going to try stuff . . . instead of just wishfully think about stuff." This obligation, "trying stuff," felt and sounded very different from how it is often characterized.

In the context of U.S. schools in the 21st century, accountability is broadly part of the neoliberal regime of treating any and all elements of P–12 education like a business or corporation (Casey, 2017). Rhetoric and policy form a chain of accountability linking student performance on high-stakes tests, to teacher quality, to the ability of principals as school leaders, to state departments of education. The overriding logic is that in the recent past, these social actors were not being held accountable, and greater and greater accountability has been the stated remedy in most educational policy. Accountability in this lexicon stands in for a host of complex educational laws, policies, and procedures. It is the official narrative for why students must take so many tests, why teachers can't be trusted, why teacher education standards have been remade, why there are more tests than ever before in order to become a teacher, why so many schools are being shuttered or charterized, and so on. Given this framing, accountability—because of the links between neoliberalism and white supremacy (see Casey, 2016)—was the last thing we expected teachers to talk about regarding their experiences of RaceWork; for us, as educational scholars, accountability is a catchall term for the dehumanizing realities teachers faced in their schools, not the humanizing work we took up together on Saturday mornings.

And yet, despite the nearly constant refrain of accountability discourses in education, teachers in RaceWork said they felt accountable for the work they took up with us. In this way, perhaps the ancient French roots of the term are partially visible: The Middle French *acompter*, the source of the English word *account*, meant to count or enumerate, but also to relate or to tell. Thus, accountability is perhaps a useful way of framing the relationships the teachers in RaceWork established with one another and with the group.

When we asked Nicole after our 1st year what kept her coming back month after month, she had just been telling us how inspiring she found Angela's passion and advocacy for her students. She continued:

> But she wasn't the one I was going to be accountable to; it is to [the] group as a whole for sure. If I had come back and hadn't done anything, you know? So I guess there's this real investment and care on the part of the group that they remembered what was going on with each other . . . I can't even remember what I had for lunch the other [day] and I could remember what Angela was worried about with her student.

Nicole juxtaposed being accountable to the group "as a whole" to being accountable to us (Zac and Shannon) as facilitators or to a particular person, here, Angela, whose concerns about supporting EL students she shared. Being accountable to the entire group meant, in part, that she had to do something between sessions to respond to the "investment and care" she felt from the other teachers.

Lisa shared this sentiment. In response to the same question, she said, "I kept coming back because I still wanted to hear how the other teachers in the group were coming along with their goals." She also connected this to a felt sense of accountability:

> I really enjoyed setting a goal and having that forum to be able to share what your goal is because it helps you be more accountable, and then coming back and talking about your progress toward your goal and maybe how you want to shift your focus or change it or improve.

Sharing a goal and progress on it was a significant motivating factor in why she persisted in RaceWork. But again, like Nicole, she connected this to accountability, saying that the format of each teacher working toward their own antiracist projects in their distinct school and classroom contexts helped her feel "more accountable." But what does Lisa mean by *more*? More than what?

We pushed Lisa to theorize further, to describe what she meant by accountable in this sense. She said,

> It's a good accountable. I mean it's an intrinsic accountability. I mean you feel accountable for yourself, but the group helps to make you, 'cause everybody's accountable. Then everybody's got their own thing that they're accountable for, but you know

you're not the only one that's responsible for the project. It was also motivating, you know, 'cause every little step that I took toward my goal, I was seeing progress and then . . . it didn't feel like an accountability of, "oh man, I've got this big project!" It was: we'll see how it goes and if it's not working, I can try something different, but I still want to give it a shot.

Lisa sees accountability as a universalizing outcome of the format of RaceWork. If everyone is accountable for their own work between sessions, they're *de facto* accountable not only for the work, but *to* one another. Lisa then connected this to motivation. Her felt sense of being accountable to the group produced the motivation she needed to continue to push herself in her own antiracist work in her building. But she also voiced a critique of a different kind of accountability, which she described as "this big project," distinct from a more open-ended sense of "see[ing] how it goes." This comparison functions as a partial critique of the hegemonic character of accountability described at the beginning of this chapter. Lisa critiqued a more common negative sense of accountability to explain why she felt the constructive sense of accountability in the group that propelled her forward. Policymakers could take a lesson from Lisa—namely, that accountability is desirable only if it produces continued efforts at working for more humanizing outcomes. If accountability fails to propel social actors to improve on their practice in ways that offer agency and support, it is hampering rather than accelerating progress.

Angela shared a similar sentiment in our final interview. Asked how she was thinking about the group today, she responded:

I miss the collegiality; I miss being able to once a month sit down with people who are all there for the same reason. No matter where they were, they wanted to know more; they wanted to talk. They wanted to think; they wanted to share.

As mentioned earlier, Angela consistently called out how RaceWork teachers were on "different paths" or at different places "on their own journey" of antiracist consciousness. What Angela learned most from her time in RaceWork was that a group of people can share aims without all sharing the same reasons for *why* they want to work toward realizing those aims, if, as she said, everyone is "there for the same reason." A shared purpose created a space for a group of people with varied experiences, and at times radically different settings for their work, to support one another.

For Sarah, accountability also functioned as a positive and motivating force. She stated that the format and structure of RaceWork was helpful to keep feeling like there was some kind of progress. It kept you thinking about the things that made it feel worthwhile, or the hard things kept coming up . . . Totally there's an accountability piece that makes you feel like, "okay, I'm going to keep working on this and focused on this," without it feeling like homework.

Sarah described RaceWork as a class, but then nuanced this description by saying that what she was doing between sessions never felt "like homework." She felt a forward momentum, "some kind of progress," from session to session, and connected this to a feeling of accountability. But like Lisa, Sarah's feelings of being held accountable were motivating for her, creating an experience of being in a "class" that asked her to complete work but not burdensome "homework." Morgan shared this feeling, stating that she felt responsible for reading and thoughtfully reflecting because "it kinda was a big deal because there wasn't a ton of people so I had accountability . . . I need to make sure I have things to contribute and it even caused me to think deeper about the readings." Like Sarah, Morgan felt responsible for coming to sessions prepared, but she also felt accountable because of the structure of RaceWork and the ways we made time for each teacher to share what they were experiencing in their antiracist work.

Charlie's sense of accountability also kept her thinking about the group between sessions:

> Just thinking about it so I have something to share, something to contribute for the next sessions. So, I guess that's how I felt accountable, and I knew that you guys [Shannon and Zac] and the people in the group would push me so I could challenge myself in those ways.

Like Morgan, Charlie brought up accountability in the context of wanting to be sure she had "something to share, something to contribute" when the group next met. This accountability motivated and challenged her to continue antiracist interventions in her school. Veronica told the group that our built community was important in ensuring that her antiracist work did not become a "lost priority" amid all her other work; the "sounding board" of RaceWork and teachers from different schools and subjects helped her to place her work in her classroom into larger contexts.

Importantly, as Veronica noted, this accountability was to people *outside* of each RaceWork teacher's particular building and district. Morgan, for instance, said that she thought "a lot of it has to do with that we're all from different schools so you can be open and honest." Often, antiracist professional development involves an entire building's faculty in the same session. When prompted to think and talk about ways that the systems of the school might be working on the side of white supremacy, many teachers feel they can't voice what they've experienced for fear of professional consequences. It is difficult to critique, for instance, the hiring practices or discipline policies of one's school if the department chair and principal are at the very next—or the same—table. RaceWork teachers nearly all expressed that RaceWork was different for this reason, allowing them to be open and honest.

To our surprise, RaceWork teachers independently used the discourse of accountability to describe what kept them coming back month after month. They related *to* each other through this accountability, mediated by both the work (readings and discussions) we took up together on Saturday mornings and by sharing stories and getting advice on the work they were doing in their own buildings between our meetings. This positive sense of accountability is relational, functioning outside of neoliberal models of education, nurtured instead by the type of "armed love" Freire (2006) wrote about.

Relationships with Students

While relationships among group members and the accountability to the group these relationships produced were significant, relationships with students figured heavily in the daily work of RaceWork teachers. For many, these relationships were central to their antiracist interventions. After the 1st year of RaceWork, Sarah stated: "Once you have a relationship with that kid, it's a different—it's not a faceless idea." The local rejects any sort of "faceless" approach to antiracism, and relationships are a way of making certain that the faces—and minds and bodies—of our students are centered in any and all antiracist interventions we may take up.

For Amelia, building relationships centered on creating a classroom where everyone worked toward supporting one another as learners. While we hear such discourses often in elementary school settings, applying this to high school chemistry can present challenges. To overcome these, Amelia characterized her approach as working to be more "honest" with her students and saw this approach as critical to her success in creating more opportunities for students of color to access AP courses. For example, she told us about her work in a particularly challenging science classroom:

> Just being more honest with them, I think, has also helped our cause, because I do feel like I have their support and they're rallying—if nothing else, at least to just get the class quiet because they know what I'm trying to do.

Amelia's discourse, with its Freirean overtones, is striking. Many teachers talk about "my class," not "our cause." Amelia, emphasizing "our cause," voiced her own positionality as a co-learner *with* her students. Her students, she asserted, recognized this; because of her "honesty" with them, they would help her to get their peers to pay attention when Amelia was addressing the entire class. Working together to support one another has antiracist implications, especially when the students are people of color, as was most often the case in Amelia's school. Further, Amelia's "honesty" meant being explicit and open with her students about racialized patterns in discipline and access to AP courses. Part of her students' response to these explicit conversations were efforts to support Amelia in multiple ways, including helping to quiet the room down when they needed to hear instructions.

Building honest relationships through time in such ways is not a surface-level or "touchy feely" approach, nor does it happen overnight. Two years before her statements about how honesty in the classroom affected students, Amelia had said:

> Part of what I've been thinking about this year is relationships: how am I strengthening that piece of it while also, you know, walking the line, not trying to be too buddy-buddy, but also hold these expectations too.

The caveat she offered, the worry to not be "too buddy-buddy" with students, is important: She was not advocating for relationships that settled for low expectations or diminishing the role of academics. Amelia carefully rejected these notions; building relationships could not come at the expense of lower expectations for students' academic efforts or behavior. Rather, "walking the line" was required: Teachers need to build capacity with and for their students, which includes knowing them as whole and complex people.

Building relationships with students, knowing who they are as people, was also central to Sarah's work to address the disproportionality of students of color referred to her for disciplinary reasons. She recognized that her role as Dean meant that she needed to foster relationships between students and their classroom teachers. After the 1st year of RaceWork (also her 1st year as Dean), Sarah wrote:

> In our work, I have learned that building relationships with students and their families is one way to close the discipline gap in my middle school. I wonder/worry about how to convince other teachers and staff about this method—it seems that some teachers decide that they are done with a student once the student has shown disrespect or poor behavior in their class.

This leads to the breakdown that must be addressed. I wonder about the best way to approach the situation with the adult, especially when the adult is frustrated and does not appear to be interested in repairing the relationship.

Sarah had noticed "the breakdown in relationships between the teachers and the kids and how that was perpetuating referrals and discipline stuff." A relationship "breaking down" necessitates repair, and so she began reading more about restorative justice practices and the ways in which they could foster connections between students and teachers and restore the pedagogical possibilities of those relationships. This was particularly important, she noted, because students themselves might not identify that the problem was with the teacher, instead saying things like, "I hate science," when what they truly didn't like was what was happening in the classroom. She thus began a practice of meeting with students and teachers after a second behavior-related issue, mediating a conversation between the teacher and the student to repair the broken relationship, even as she acknowledged that bringing in teachers along with students was "scary."

Sarah brought a generous posture to her role, taking an explicitly pedagogical orientation to working with students *and teachers*—particularly as the teachers in the district were "really, really white." Early in her work, she was struck by so many teachers seemingly taking on an attitude of being hurt by a student whom they had referred. This got in the way of the teachers seeing themselves in a pedagogical role in their relationships with students. Instead, some teachers in her building seemed to "decide that they [were] done" with particular students. Rather than working with students, they kicked them out, creating a discipline gap that also kept students from "learning and achieving academically."

Through such work on repairing relationships, Sarah came to understand that her building needed to frame behavioral referrals differently as well: not as personal insults or an inability to "behave," but as a skill, analogous to an academic skill such as multiplication. After several years of doing this work, Sarah described her approach this way:

> We decided together this year that we wanted to do something with teachers that had to do with relationships with and engaging Black and Brown boys. That was our thing 'cause we were . . . looking at the data and you're looking at who you're dealing with all the time, who we're dealing with every day, all the time. If they [teachers] can start to see the behavior as a lack of skill instead of [as] a character trait, I feel like the relationships won't fall apart as easily and maybe they'll feel more invested.

Sarah consistently used a discourse of "skills" to describe student behavior. After working with us to name the ways that many white fears of people of color become pathologies of people of color, she started making a point to explain the racist essentialism teachers were calling upon when they described student behavior as caused by their race (e.g., "character traits"). In Sarah's school (and across the United States), students of color are vastly overrepresented in behavioral referrals. Instead of turning this into an attribute or characteristic of students, Sarah took a pedagogical orientation: Student behavior can be learned. Thus, teachers can teach desired behavior—"skills"—so long as they maintain relationships with students. Sarah worked with teachers to repair bruised and broken relationships with students so they could teach the "skills" that students needed to remain in the classroom and learn productively.

Relationships with students and their families were the primary focus for Lisa's antiracist work in her school over the 2 years of RaceWork. In our final interview, she said:

> I recycle. I keep my kids for years so if I bust a relationship my first year, it's gonna take a while for [them to] trust me and feel like I am back on their side, and I may never get some of those relationships back.

As one of a small number of French teachers, Lisa might have the same student for as many as five courses during their secondary school experience. In addition to the pragmatic concern of a "busted" relationship resulting in a student dropping French, Lisa demonstrated her concern for students, who were nearly all people of color: She wanted them to know she was "on their side."

For Lisa, this was related to knowing who her students were and, in particular, the effects of white supremacy on their lives and bodies. Clarifying what it meant to be on the side of a student, she said:

> You need to be aware of where the hurt comes from, and you need to be aware of why it comes from there or why it exists. Because you can't become responsive to that, you can't fix it, you can't try to build those relationships with those kids if you don't know where that comes from. You can't fix what's going on in your classroom if you don't know why it's happening in the first place. And that's what RaceWork really did help me understand: why or where it came from. I might not be able to make it all better, but at least I can be aware of where it is and help to, you know, navigate around and through it.

Prior to RaceWork, Lisa did not know how to name "where the hurt comes from"; she did not have contexts or nuances to understand the racialized patterns in her school and community that then played out in her classroom and in relationships between herself (a white teacher) and students of color. Without these knowledges, Lisa later asserted, she would not know how to respond in the classroom and to build strong, rather than "busted," relationships. She gave an example of a student of color who "fought me tooth and nail." Lisa worked hard to understand where this student was coming from and to recognize that the ways she was engaging—or failing to engage in class—were due to circumstances of the student's life, not willful misbehavior. Lisa, in fact, built such a strong relationship with this student that another teacher commented, "Wow, that girl really attaches herself to you, doesn't she?"

But this was not just about being friendly with or supporting students. Returning to Lisa's last point in her above statement is particularly important, as she sophisticatedly contextualized her students' experiences with oppression. She carefully centered the experiences of her students, positioning them as agentic in their learning and in their efforts at humanization. She wanted to "help" students "navigate around and through it." While the sentiment began with a desire to understand "where the hurt comes from" in a linear way so as to "fix" whatever issues may be present, by the end she focused on her role as a supporter of her students in *their* navigating of white supremacy. The concept of working with and through, rather than getting over or pushing past, was central to Lisa's conception of her role as an antiracist educator with and for her students.

For Lisa, this meant she needed "to build and maintain those relationships and make sure that I don't do anything either inadvertently or on purpose to break those relationships with my kids." Through RaceWork, Lisa came to understand the ways that white teachers can undermine relationships with students of color by focusing only on their own *intentions* rather than on the *impacts* of their actions on students. She moved from a stance that often centered her own conceptions and experiences to thinking about students' multiple interpretations of the same phenomenon. Being able to take on these different perspectives, to recognize that it is not only what we do "on purpose" but also what we do "inadvertently," is a critical skill that white teachers can cultivate through greater engagement with pedagogical approaches to white racial identity and white supremacy. In other words, working to theorize not only the formal curriculum of our classrooms, but also the hidden curriculum, can offer new possibilities for forming more robust pedagogical relationships with students.

While it can seem as though all teachers are always engaged in relationship building with students, these relationships can be scaffolded through the lens of antiracism into functioning in opposition to white supremacy. Teachers asserting a need to center relationships with students is rich with possible meanings that need further exploration. In other words, it is important to know what the aims and pedagogical contexts are for such a focus, as it is sometimes at a surface level: Focusing on relationships can be an escape from engaging the actual lived realities of young people if those relationships are concerned only with their identity and role as *students*. Pedagogical relationships with students then necessarily require attention to students as complex social actors who are not *only* students. To be in genuine relationship with them, teachers must also be in relationship with their homes and communities.

Relationships with Students' Parents and Caregivers

Nicole articulated the relationship in this way:

> I think really passionate teachers aren't going to fix what's wrong with schools until families and students can really actively, vocally, clearly communicate what they want and need, in a positive sense, but also what's wrong and what's not okay . . . being their own advocate.

While the teachers in RaceWork spoke much more about their relationships with students than teacher–parent relationships, they also came, like Nicole, to see these relational spheres as intersecting. Relationships with students as whole and complex beings require relationships with the people who love and care for them when students aren't in school. In some ways, these relationships are instrumental in character, because they are supporting the more central and critical relationship between teachers and students. They take on a pedagogical orientation when read through a funds of knowledge lens (González, Moll, & Amanti, 2005): when students are viewed as experts of their own lives and experiences and when teachers see home contexts as assets that support student learning at school. Thus, teachers' relationships with caregivers and parents are primarily about teachers' relationships with students.

An example of a pedagogical approach to working with parents on the side of students comes from Sarah:

> I would call them [parents/caregivers] this year when their child was doing well, which I know is kind of an idea that you know

you would do. It's not some great idea, just I had never done that. And they really, really, really loved it, and it made them kind of trust me more.

Sarah said "really" with increasing volume, sounding more like parents "really, Really, REALLY loved it." The notion of calling caregivers to report on the good things their students were doing in school *does* feel like an old and almost cheesy idea, like "caught being good slips" and winning the chance for pizza with the principal—things many of us felt we were too mature to take seriously by the end of elementary school. We might also tell ourselves that most caregivers are busy with jobs and other responsibilities; if their child isn't in danger and isn't putting anyone else in danger, there's no need to alert them to what is happening in school. But this changes if we think of understanding the pedagogical necessity of parent–teacher relationships as important to and for student learning; then, phone calls home regarding successes help to cement the positive relationships teachers and administrators have with students. These calls build trust, according to Sarah, and this trust is especially important when the repeated pattern is a white teacher or administrator calling a parent of color about the misbehavior of their student of color. To interrupt the citational violence of the discipline gap, calling home to let caregivers know about successes can help make the times when the call is about mistakes function on the side of working to teach "skills" needed to stay on task and not land in the Dean's office.

Similarly, Morgan spoke of a student with whom she had a challenging relationship, going so far as to say that "there was a month period in the winter that was really, really hard." But she worked to build a relationship with the student, learning to read his body language and to adjust to what worked for him. As she did so, Morgan said that "he had to warm up and figure out who I was. And I had to figure out who he was, and that just took some time." Supporting this was her relationship with the student's mom: "Mom's wonderful. Having that parent relationship probably helped, too, because if there is the bad day, I can call her. And she will process with him too at home. And then he usually comes back the next day, and he's totally ready to go." In other words, Morgan developing a relationship with a parent helped to support a student, allowing him to continue his learning and processing outside of the walls of the school so that he came to school again ready to learn.

Charlie took this relationship building with families even further. In our 1st year together, she led an effort to create more welcoming spaces for African American and East African parents and families in her school. She helped start a parent-advisory group made up of Black parents and started a now-yearly fall carnival to celebrate Black families with East African storytelling, crafting, and food. Through her work with Black families in the community around her school, she made connections to readings we took up in RaceWork about home visits (e.g., Pollock, 2008). By our final interview, Charlie had become a certified home visit trainer, working with teachers across the metro area to make more powerful connections with students' families so as to support classroom learning. Charlie explained:

> So the model is you visit them in the fall. You're not bringing any paper work or anything with you; you're just getting to know like, what are your hopes and dreams for your kid? What do your kids like to do? Tell me about your family. Things like that.

Understanding historical distances between white people and people of color or between people from different economic backgrounds as well as disconnects between home and school, Charlie respected families' privacy; if they didn't want her in their home for these visits, she did not try to talk them into it. Instead, she told us, "I'll suggest somewhere close by that they'll feel comfortable, like a Starbucks, or McDonalds, or a park bench. It just needs to be close; it has to be in the actual community they live in." For Charlie, the point of these home visits was not to see a family's home, but to understand more about her students and to build relationships.

Charlie had a number of difficult years in the classroom, with a lot of tension among students. In addressing these challenges, she could rely on the relationships that she had started with the home/community visits and the ways she and the families could be people together. So, following up later with families by phone, Charlie remarked that parents

> hear my son crying in the background or something, and they know I'm a normal person. I feel like it becomes about our relationship. So even though it's been a hard year, I have really good relationships with most of their [students'] parents.

These relationships then helped Charlie to address what was happening in her classroom. As with many highly engaging teachers, especially those seen as equity leaders in their buildings, Charlie's classroom that year had far more students with IEPs and histories of struggling with behavior. These students were placed in Charlie's class because administrators saw her as a strong teacher. The last time we visited her classroom, she made clear to us that knowing she had many of the "toughest" students in her school didn't change her commitment to connecting with their families so as to support their children's learning. As Charlie noted, relationships with parents are especially important when our relationships as teachers with students are challenged. If we can work in solidarity with caregivers, we have a better chance of restoring the fractured relationship with students.

Finding Comrades: Building Relationships Outside of RaceWork

A final way RaceWork teachers worked to build relationships was with other adults in their own schools or districts. Although most RaceWork teachers felt alienated at times in their buildings, they did not find themselves only in solidarity with other RaceWork teachers (as detailed in Chapter 4). Every teacher described ways they worked with other teachers in their buildings or their districts toward more just and antiracist outcomes for students. As Amelia said: "I've found allies in my building that I've been able to connect with and share and ask really tough questions and I know will give me really honest answers."

Morgan, for instance, returned to the student she had been building a relationship with all year. She worried about what would happen once he moved to middle school and didn't have the stability of one primary teacher. She talked with him about who his "person" would be at the middle school: "We even approached a teacher and talked to her. She's actually come down and met with him a couple of times, so he actually knows that there's somebody there for him." After building a relationship with this teacher through their work on the district equity team, they together developed a plan to support the student's transition to middle school. Morgan thought of this strategy after taking "a little bit of other people's ideas [from RaceWork] and try[ing] to find a way of how they could work here for our kids and our setting."

However, relationships such as this one with Morgan's colleague were rare. More often, relationships, even around antiracism, were inequitable, often positioning RaceWork teachers as resources who could provide simple solutions. For instance, Morgan shared after the 1st year:

> I think part of it is [that] they have to figure it out for themselves, so they have some sort of investment in it and want to continue to learn about this instead of just being like, "alright, I'm gonna read this book, and I know I'll have this information. But if anything actually happens, I'm just gonna go to [Morgan]; she'll tell me what to do." I want them to hold themselves accountable too.

While accountability reappears here, we also see the pedagogical approach to colleagues that produced the title of this book. Morgan experienced this regularly, as teachers looked for quick fixes to issues that were far more complex than most of these teachers were making them out to be. She also focused on what Rogers (1989) called "self-appropriation" of knowledge: The things we know best are things that we have worked, ourselves, to learn. Morgan critiqued the notion that simply reading a book or having more information would somehow transform practices that function on the side of white supremacy in the school. Instead, teachers need to want to learn for themselves, not go to someone they see as more knowledgeable for *that person* to explain "what to do."

Morgan found a colleague willing to help build the district's equity team who didn't take the stance of having Morgan simply tell her what to do. In our final interview, Morgan said:

> I've been more vocal with what my feelings are about equity and things like that. I definitely see that a little bit more. There's a coworker that had kind of come along with me on that journey with equity, so I do think that we have certain students placed with us that just might do better because they know we'll take the time to listen and hear them out.

Morgan alluded to the practice mentioned earlier in Charlie's school, where many of the "toughest" students are placed with a particular teacher who is seen as especially strong working with a "type" of student. Morgan's discourse about this was far less veiled than typical euphemisms for working-class students of color. She named what distinguished her and her colleague from other teachers in their school as "tak[ing] more time to listen and hear [students] out." To listen and to hear students of color, we have to first understand the ways that white supremacy is reproduced in schools and articulate, for ourselves, the ways that we seek to work in opposition. Teachers have to want to do this; otherwise, they fall into the practice Morgan critiqued of going to whomever they see as best at equity-related work and asking them "what to do."

Sarah's work with restorative justice practices provided both an example of "what to do" and also moved beyond a reliance on her. Instead, teachers were "excited about doing that [repairing relationships] all year . . . so now it wasn't just coming from me [but from] this group of teachers." Further, RaceWork, she said, encouraged her to link up with someone in her building. Her "next step," then, was to find

> someone else in my building that I'm aligned with that I can go to and be like, "Look what's happening over and over and

over and over! Look at this!" And he's like, "yeah, I know, so how can we now start to do something?"

With this colleague, she began to devise a plan—one that unfortunately was blocked, as described in Chapter 6.

Building Pedagogical Relationships

Finding comrades in antiracist work can be especially difficult, but working to center pedagogical relationships with students means cultivating relationships with other adults, including parents/caregivers, teachers, and administrators. Angela felt particularly strongly about connecting these relationships and helping her colleagues understand that "you don't need to be afraid to talk with parents who aren't white—while also not saying that directly." One Saturday morning, she told a story about talking with one of her students, during math time, about an upcoming music concert. She discovered that the student had a contentious relationship with her classroom teacher, who had been making disparaging comments about never being able to reach the student's mom and thus the teacher's disappointment that the student never went to music concerts. Angela called home herself. The student's brother told her to call back at 10:15 that night when their mom got home from work. She did. Not only did Angela speak with the mother, but she helped make arrangements for the student to attend the school's music concert despite her mom having to work. Angela said, "I just needed permission. What did I do differently?" In this brief example, she demonstrated the need to build relationships among all the partners invested in a student's learning, rather than dismissing them, as the student's other teacher had done.

To work in isolation, only in one's classroom, is not to recognize the full complexity of the antiracist frame of the local. White teachers on the side of antiracism need to work toward building pedagogical relationships with folks in their buildings, even when this means they often find themselves figured as "experts" in ways that can undermine antiracism. The teachers in RaceWork came to understand that their role(s) needed to be pedagogical the whole way through: not only with their students, but with families, teachers, and administrators as well.

The aims of antiracism, especially for white teachers, can never be simply to be "right," to say the "right thing," to use the "right terms," and to scold anyone who isn't "right" on their wrongness. No. We have to use our skills as *pedagogues* to follow Morgan's directions to create opportunities for others to desire *for themselves* a deeper understanding of white supremacy and antiracist praxis. Of course, this does not mean that we cannot support others in this work—we must—but we cannot take shortcuts or compromise authentic learning for the sake of expediency. This is precisely what Freire (2000) warned readers of in *Pedagogy of the Oppressed*: We cannot utilize banking methods to speed through explanations of "what to do" in terms of antiracist praxis, or any other humanizing aim. Even if this means we are working with learners who have more experience than we do, we can and must adopt a pedagogical orientation that sees all social actors as capable of learning and growth and support them (and ourselves, as always unfinished) to the best of our abilities. And we should expect significant resistances to such efforts, as discussed in the next chapter.

CHAPTER 6

Tensions

Conflicts with Colleagues in Three Movements

For a decade, we have talked about how little has been said in research on white teachers, and white social actors more broadly, about the costs of engaging in counter-hegemonic work. By "costs," we mean that too often white people (and both of us have also fallen into this trap) believe there will be no negative consequences to actions that work toward antiracism. After all, doing the right thing should not have negative repercussions, right? But common conceptions of racism (especially among white people) fail to explain the pervasiveness of the system of white supremacy, how deeply engrained it is. Challenging the system carries visceral and emotional risks and costs.

For most white people in the United States, "liberal individualist" conceptions of racism dominate (Lipsitz, 1995, 2006). A liberal individualist conception understands racism as discreet acts by particular persons who support white supremacy. Rather than recognizing white supremacy as a system of meanings, practices, and values, liberal individualism sees any and every racist incident as isolated and discreet, the result of a particular person's choices and agency. Liberal individualists thus are critical of explicit racism but ignore instances that are not tied to malicious intent. In this framing, racism can be corrected with a narrow form of education: Racist individuals need to learn not to be racist.

So, what happens if a white teacher does not subscribe to a liberal individualist conception of racism, but rather understands white supremacy as the intentional outcome of centuries of colonialism, exploitation, and plunder reproduced ideologically and materially through social systems and structures? We can expect that person to become the target of liberal individualist resistances to structural conceptions of white supremacy. This chapter is about the tensions teachers in RaceWork felt with other teachers in their buildings as they sought to create more antiracist classrooms and schools. It is an account of the costs of doing antiracist work in schools as white teachers and the ways that liberal individualist resistance functions on the side of white supremacy.[1] We begin by returning to fear, sharing examples of fears teachers had, before naming three specific ways Race-Work teachers' fears were realized in conflicts with their colleagues: as they were blamed for calling attention to white supremacy ("shooting the messenger"), as they stuck up for students, and as institutions reproduced white supremacy. Teachers can address these fears through a pedagogical orientation to the educators in their local sites.

Returning to Fear

In Chapter 3 we focused on fear at the personal level. Here, we return to the topic of fear in theorizing how white fears have implications at the local level as well. The teachers in RaceWork feared the very outcomes this chapter describes: They worried their relationships with their colleagues would suffer as a result of their antiracist praxis. They were also fearful of their own failings and missing pieces: of not doing enough, or of engaging in work that actually reinforced, rather than challenged, white supremacy.

One example comes from Morgan, who wrote this reflection during our 1st year together:

> A big concern of mine all along has been the continuous [number of] students of color that are sent out into hallways, partner classrooms, or to the office that I see throughout the day. I am concerned that I am not doing enough myself to combat this issue and that I need to be learning and thinking as much as possible to learn more about cultures and customs. It has also become evident that this is not an issue that is seen by

---

1. We would of course be remiss here if we did not note that while white supremacy harms white people and people of color and Indigenous peoples, these harms are both qualitatively and quantitatively different. In acknowledging the costs and risks to white people, we are not either making comparisons or equalizations. As Rankine (2016) wrote, "Though the white liberal imagination likes to feel temporarily bad about black suffering, there really is no mode of empathy that can replicate the daily strain of knowing that as a black person you can be killed for simply being black" (pp. 145–146). Yet we also do an injustice to the hard labor of antiracism if we do not acknowledge that it can cost white people, too.

the staff at my school. Other teachers and staff members seem to be unaware that this is occurring or even defensive when it is brought up.

This writing evidences Morgan's deeply generous approach and outlook to work with others. Her first inclination was to give other (white) teachers in her building the benefit of the doubt that they might not have noticed what she had: that virtually every student who was kicked out of a class was a student of color. When she brought this up with others, they sometimes got defensive. A defensive position in this context requires unpacking. *What* is being defended?

On first examination, the answer appears obvious: A white teacher is defensive about why so many students of color are perpetually being kicked out of class for behavior reasons because the teacher does not want to be seen as racist. This defensiveness is an enactment of a liberal individualist conception of racism, but it is also a defense of white supremacy. This is a glimpse of what is meant by *structural* racism: teachers following procedures in place in their schools, not individual acts of meanness on the part of teachers (although these might also occur), produce an overrepresentation of students of color being referred and suspended. Teachers are doing "what they are supposed to be doing," and the result punishes people of color through one of the most powerful Ideological State Apparatuses (Althusser, 2008).[2] White teachers who take a defensive position on questions of why so many students of color find themselves in trouble are defending white supremacy, but they are often doing so because they see *themselves* as in need of defending. This is how liberal individualism distorts structural realities.

When schools and districts seek to center the work of racial justice, these liberal individualist positions can become shared across entire staffs. Amelia, for instance, told us during her final interview:

> We know that there's more staff willing to talk about it [the racialized discipline gap] but feel that there's an environment of fear in our building that they can't talk about it because there's another majority of teachers trying to keep it from everybody else. And it's really hard to speak up against that, especially when they're super involved and are older and they're just everything I'm not.

---

2. Althusser argued at the time he was writing, in the 1960s, that schools were *the* most powerful Ideological State Apparatus, replacing the church as most effective in protecting hegemony.

Because she was relatively new to her school, she felt especially deferential to more senior teachers with longer institutional memories and experiences at the school—those who were "super involved" and "older" and "everything I'm not." Amelia interpreted some teachers' resistance to the antiracist work she was championing as part of the equity team as a critique of her relative inexperience and lack of time teaching in that particular school. Amelia cited one teacher in particular as an example of what she meant: her building's union representative. Since he was a vocal advocate for teachers' time and work, Amelia was dismayed when her union rep was one of the loudest voices opposing her building equity team. Through mechanisms such as citing experience or calling on union policy, teachers hid behind liberal individualist notions to deny their own complicity in white supremacist practices.

These two examples constitute a miniscule fraction of RaceWork teachers' many accounts regarding conflicts with colleagues that emerged because of their work on the side of antiracism. When first analyzing interviews, written notes, and our own field notes, we treated these conflicts as falling into the same category: They were stories of liberal individualist resistance to structural critiques and localized responses to white supremacy. As our work to (re)read our data continued, however, we became persuaded that we needed to further delineate these different moments of conflict, because these resistances are expressed and experienced in multiple ways. We have thus divided the following section into three "movements," or subgenres, of the overarching phenomenon of liberal individualist resistance to antiracist praxis on the part of white teachers. These movements are (1) "shooting" (i.e., blaming) the messenger;[3] (2) sticking up for students; and (3) acting institutionally in reproducing white supremacy. We treat each in turn, with examples from teachers in RaceWork.

Movement Conflict One: Blaming ("Shooting") the Messenger

Describing how she was positioned in her own building whenever she voiced the issue of English Learner (EL) students being made invisible, Angela cited

---

3. As explained in the section below, while we are deeply troubled with the violence of the metaphor "shooting the messenger," we use it here because it was a quote from Angela and became a shared way of naming the moments when someone is attacked or belittled because they called attention to something that made others uncomfortable. With the preponderance of school shootings and active shooter drills, we want to clarify that we use this metaphor only because it was used by the teachers in RaceWork.

the common tactic of "shooting the messenger": others blamed Angela for raising issues, thus avoiding any substantive discussion of the *content* of what she was saying. "Shooting the messenger" is a violent metaphor, one that carries particular resonances in the contexts of ongoing mass violence in schools (and other settings). Yet this metaphor also captures the psychic assault that RaceWork teachers sometimes felt; we use the phrase here because it was Angela's exact wording. "Shooting the messenger" became, for the group, a way to reference those times when other teachers would blame the teacher voicing a criticism of a practice or policy for whatever violation that teacher was calling attention to. This is akin to the earlier discussion of the white supremacist logic that argues that to bring up race, as a white person, is racist. Talking about the ways students of color are overrepresented in behavioral referrals, when read solely in a liberal individualist frame, becomes a critique of individual teachers who maliciously and unfairly target students of color for punishment. Yet, for the teachers in RaceWork, this was rarely what they wanted their colleagues to take from their comments.

For instance, Nicole's colleagues viewed their majority white exurban high school as not needing to discuss race. Because of the relatively small (but growing) population of Latinx students and the school's history and record of high achievement, racial equity was not on the minds of virtually any of the teachers Nicole worked with. When we asked during her last interview with us how her work to make race more central to PD and staff meetings in her school was going, she answered:

> It got brought up a couple times in different meetings, you know like, "how do we talk about race? And how are we bringing it?" And it's always—it's never actually taken too seriously. Like, "Oh, well, that's not really an issue here." That's usually the response with them: "we don't really have any issues here with that."

In a school context where teachers see no racialized patterns, attempts to discuss race and racism feel uncalled for, and perhaps even racist. Why would someone (i.e., Nicole) insist on bringing up race at every staff meeting? And when they do, how can a white teacher not take it *personally* that one of their colleagues is in effect calling them out as racist in front of their co-workers? Nicole theorized this in the same interview, speaking of a particular incident where a teacher could not *hear* Nicole's point. Nicole argued that the school functioned primarily for white students, pointing out as evidence that EL students (who were Latinx) had classes in a building removed from the main sections of the school, with almost no interactions with students who weren't also ELs. Nicole wanted her colleagues to discuss why this was the case. Instead, a colleague challenged her, accusing Nicole of calling the entire staff racist. They blamed her for creating tension. Nicole put it this way:

> Teachers are sensitive folks, right? It's so personal. What we do, teaching, is so personal, and I was just being honest. Like, "I don't see that," so it's hard, you know? I wasn't saying you were a bad teacher.

Nicole heard from other teachers in her building that they "didn't see that," referring to evidence that racism was alive and well in their school. Multiple times, Nicole shared with RaceWork that she continually found that other teachers were seemingly incapable of thinking about race at all, let alone thinking about ways to make their school more antiracist.

Nicole was not alone in feeling attacked for encouraging her colleagues to discuss race and white supremacy more explicitly. As Amelia put it frankly (while laughing) during our 2nd year together, "I have full confidence people are saying things behind my back, just not to my face." Amelia was responsible for all of the communications from the equity team to the whole staff. Thus, while she was a member of a *group* that organized the equity-related aspects of PD days and staff meetings, emails came from her, and thus she became the de facto leader and voice of the school equity team. As a result, Amelia learned that one of the things we can expect as white teachers engaging in antiracism is that others in our building may change their thoughts about us.

Sarah also experienced this, saying, "People used to like me a lot more before I got in this position. Honestly, they just get pissed about things. They get pissed about decisions I make about consequences, and they get pissed about testing." As Dean, Sarah did have an official leadership position, unlike Amelia, but like Amelia, she came to stand in for a number of other decision makers in her building. While not a principal, because of her role in organizing all of the high-stakes testing and discipline in her building, she was regularly positioned as speaking for the entire administration. And when the voice of the administration openly discussed the ways that young men of color were five times more likely to be sent to her office, most of the teachers in her building took this fact as a personal attack.

One last example of shooting the messenger comes from Morgan. After successfully starting her district's first equity team, she experienced colleagues reacting to her in new and unsettling ways. In our last interview with her, she told us that

> a lot of people are really, really resistant to it and I know or experience it. At our last PD on equity stuff, I was about to sit at the table and so was someone else, and they saw that I sat down there. So then they went to a different table because they don't want to be around me because I have so much passion about it.

Knowing that the topic was one that Morgan had been a leader on in the building, her colleague opted to sit somewhere else. Morgan theorized this as a reaction to her "passion" for antiracism, but also coded this as evidence that some of the staff were "really, really resistant" to discussions of racial justice. There were consequences to Morgan's passion and willingness to talk about race.

Shooting the messenger is a defense tactic that protects the interests of white supremacy, mainly because it misplaces the causes of structural racism found in so many schools. The old adage "out of sight, out of mind" explains the stance of many teachers when it comes to questions of racial equity in their schools. And if they can't see racial injustice, when someone insists that their school isn't doing enough on the side of antiracism, the suggestion triggers a reactionary questioning of the motives of the person who first brought up the issue. Often, the result is blaming racist outcomes on the very teachers who are the most vocal advocates for students and families of color. This solidarity with students and families of color produces a second "movement" regarding ways in which white teachers in RaceWork came into conflict with colleagues as a result of their antiracist praxis.

Movement Conflict Two: Sticking Up for Students

Whenever RaceWork teachers advocated for students of color and their families, they risked conflicts with co-workers. Of the three movements discussed here, we heard most often about sticking up for students, and thus also of times when aligning with students or students' families put teachers at odds with colleagues. Every teacher in RaceWork shared stories; the examples that follow are just a few of the many we could have included. Sticking up for students is another instance of how doing the right thing can lead to tensions with colleagues.

Lisa's school served a number of diasporic communities, with about a third of the students speaking a language other than English at home. In Lisa's quote below, the reference is to Latinx families, the second largest group of students in her school. (Black students made up around 40% of the student body and were the largest racial group in the school.) Lisa, by the time of her last interview, had come to be deeply critical of teachers making sweeping generalizations about entire student populations in her school. She challenged other teachers when she heard these kinds of remarks.

> I heard from them: "these kinds of parents don't care." 'Cause I hear that from staff sometimes, and I have to be like, "that's not true." They say that notoriously these parents don't care about their kids' education. I'm like, "that's absolutely not true; you just maybe need to get a translator."

Recalling Lisa's initial comments in RaceWork—that she used to give up on trying to contact parents if they were at all difficult to reach—makes her transformation into a fierce advocate for Latinx students and their families' investments in education all the more remarkable. As she shifted her understanding and her advocacy, Lisa often found her colleagues becoming defensive when she addressed their white supremacist bias against parents; further, they were often surprised when she called attention to their essentialism. Note that here she also offered a solution: Communication would be more successful if there were a translator. Yet she didn't feel that her remarks were heard.

Amelia shared a similar example, this time about student behavior. She was struck that teachers were so personally offended at what students sometimes said to them, telling us, "Teachers take it personally and they say, 'this child verbally accosted me; they swore at me; they said the F word at me.' Like, yeah, they did. Yep." For Amelia, it was difficult to understand why teachers would not see these student behaviors as evidence of other kinds of difficulties and discriminations students were experiencing, rather than seeing them only as personal attacks. Because they were teachers, Amelia reasoned, they should be able to rise above the immediate conflict and respond pedagogically to a student. Like Lisa, Amelia found that her attempts to call attention to larger questions were met with silence.

Sarah witnessed the same dynamic when listening to staff dialogue about the upcoming school year:

> We have a huge group of kids [of color] this year and the teachers are like "oh my gosh. I think they're . . . I think it's going to be hard." And I'm like, "what's gonna be hard? What part is

going to be hard?" And I can't get them to answer really, but I think that's what it is. I think they're worried because there's so many kids of color.

When Sarah heard (other white) teachers in her building talking about how "hard" the year would be because of the growing number of students of color, she challenged them to confirm the white supremacist but unspoken element of their dialogue. Challenging them with this question, she could not "get them to answer really." Sarah had seen this tactic of questioning and problem-posing in practice multiple times in RaceWork, and she did the same: asking her colleagues questions, rather than openly condemning their (liberal individualist) racist comments. Still, she was troubled by the essentialist character of so many staff in her building: Hearing there would be more students of color automatically meant the year would be "harder" for them—and constructing such a stance would make it all the "harder" for students to form meaningful connections with teachers.

Morgan also wanted to become a stronger advocate for students of color, particularly regarding the discipline gap in her school and the lack of connection that this demonstrated. After the first year of RaceWork, she stated:

> I need to get more comfortable. As comfortable as I am, I need to be much more comfortable talking about race or talking about immediate discrepancies that I see happening in my building. I need to have the courage to go and talk to those teachers about not only what I'm noticing, but what my kids are saying to me. And right now I'm just not there yet. I know I need to get there, not for myself, but for my kids that are having those struggles, [to] have that hard conversation, not necessarily calling [other teachers] out, but just having a conversation like, "my kids are feeling this way when they're in this space. What's your perspective on it? Or what can we do so that they're not feeling this way?"

Morgan had recognized the overrepresentation of students of color kicked out of classrooms and sent to the hall in her school. While growing in her abilities to name and connect where these practices came from, she still felt that she needed to be bolder in having "the courage" to talk with other teachers in her building about what she was seeing. By the end of her statement, Morgan is rehearsing what kind of approach she would take; once again, the pedagogical character of her (hypothetical) intervention is telling. She offered two questions for a colleague that centered students' experiences and feelings of being marginalized because of their race in their school. Similar to Sarah, this is not an example of a "call out" moment—Morgan here was not interested in being right or "correct," nor was she most concerned with identifying and pointing out racialized patterns in student discipline. Instead, she centered the feelings and experiences of students and worked to make a connection for her teacher-listener to the students' experiences. This centers the immediate context in ways that can help scaffold for those who might resist thinking about their work as complicit in oppressive systems. Instead of blaming a particular teacher's discipline policies for the whole of white supremacy, Morgan's questioning offered ways to focus the discussion on the materiality of the experience of students of color.

One final example of sticking up for students came from Charlie. She shared a story in our first interview about a student named Marcus to whom she had given permission to go to the bathroom. Another white teacher (whom Charlie had talked about on numerous occasions, "the one that can be a bit of a jerk, who is on my team") knocked on her door, saying that Marcus shouldn't be allowed in the hallway by himself. When Charlie said that Marcus was just going to the bathroom, the other teacher, Mr. Clarke, replied, "Well, I saw him in the lockers; he was touching lockers," insinuating, with Marcus standing there, that Marcus was stealing. Charlie asked Mr. Clarke if he had actually seen Marcus take anything out of the lockers. He had not. He had just been walking down the hallway back from the bathroom, close to the lockers. Mr. Clarke insisted that Marcus be punished; Charlie did not. She concluded her story:

> And I felt kind of bad, and I remember shaking and I cried afterward. I was just so nervous to have this interaction with a senior teacher. And this is the situation that always pops in my mind when I think about how important this is. And the kid, you know, eventually we came back in [to our classroom], and I talked to him one on one. I said, "you know, I believe that you didn't take anything, and let's just move on with our day." Because he was obviously upset about being accused of stealing. And then throughout the rest of the year I had a great relationship with this kid.

Charlie shared this story in the context of talking about the receptivity of teachers in her building to discussions of racial equity work. Earlier, she had said that Mr. Clarke was especially resistant to anything that specifically focused on race, and that because he was a veteran teacher in the building, many other teachers followed his lead. Her own experience with him and Marcus left her "shaking" and later made her cry. She felt pressured to implement some kind of punishment, when Marcus had simply been dragging his hand along the lockers in the hallway as he walked back from the bathroom. The fact that Marcus was Black made this story especially relevant for Charlie in the context of her work with us.

As described earlier, Charlie came to RaceWork with a number of experiences in other antiracist PD settings. She had learned a lot about her relative privilege, and her initial theorization of the Marcus story centered on Mr. Clarke's white privilege. Because he had privilege, so this theorization went, he saw Marcus as deviant and sought to make sure his deviance was punished with the support of another white (privileged) teacher. But this theorization was missing a critical component: How was it that Mr. Clarke's relative racial privilege could *cause* him to racially profile a 3rd-grade Black male student? Charlie saw RaceWork as providing the missing link for her in this theorization. Mr. Clarke certainly experienced privilege in the context of the school he worked in, and more broadly as a white cis-male social actor, but that privilege was/is the outcome of white supremacy. Charlie knew Mr. Clarke was acting in ways complicit with maintaining white supremacy, but she had only one code available to her: white privilege. She came to recognize that the ways teachers act locally are enmeshed in the structural realities that function to determine our lives. It was not Mr. Clarke's white privilege that *caused* him to profile Marcus, but his enmeshment within the codes and practices of a white supremacist system. This relates to the third type of conflict with colleagues.

Movement Conflict Three: Acting Institutionally— Reproducing White Supremacy

Over the course of our work together we recognized a pattern that connected the disparate contexts that each RaceWork teacher worked in. While the particularities of resistances to equity work markedly varied, many stories had a consistent refrain: white teachers acting institutionally. Acting institutionally means placing an organization's procedures and policies beyond critique and upholding said procedures and policies even when they conflict with humanizing pedagogies. Sometimes this can appear as an absence: the lack of challenge to institutional logics that harm students and communities of color. Other times it is an instrumentalized response: responding to long-term issues with short-term strategies that don't connect to a shared aim of racial justice. And, predictably, at times other teachers and administrators are outright obstructionists, actively blocking efforts at antiracism.

In Nicole's district, other white teachers seemingly refused to acknowledge any kind of racial injustice in their schools and community. Nicole told us:

> Honestly, they think there aren't any problems. It will be a while before anyone starts to think we should do something about race. I think the [local paper] had an article about East Park [being] one of the most segregated communities in the state.

How can a school in "one of the most segregated communities in the state" not think they needed to engage in careful study of how that segregation was affecting their classrooms? This was Nicole's central question for both years of RaceWork, one she struggled to bring to the attention of more of her colleagues. In not acknowledging the ways that a segregated community produced segregated and inequitable school experiences and outcomes, Nicole's school was culpable in reproducing white supremacy through inaction.

Another way white supremacy is reproduced in schools can spring from efforts that actually began as antiracist. In Veronica's school, teachers had formed a SEED group years earlier that served as a space for reflections, readings, and activities centered on equity and justice. Veronica described it this way:

> Because the group, it was sort of an intro to a lot of topics we talk about [in RaceWork]. And well, some people who had been there again and again and again were now leading it. But there was a lot of new faces that were like having moments all the time, and I wanted something a little more deeper than that and not just another group.

Veronica's critique of the SEED group at her school was that it never went further than an introductory level. It centered on "having moments," which for Veronica meant white people coming to a recognition of relative racial privilege. Many of her accounts of these "moments" sounded like confession narratives, described earlier, wherein white people are hailed to confess their relative racial privilege as though such a confession can actually alter white supremacy. The SEED group thus created a cycle for itself: Create opportunities for people who have not engaged deeply with anti-oppressive work to "have moments" wherein they recognize their complicity; have those same people become facilitators of future groups; engage in the exact same "moment-inducing" introductory materials that were initially presented. While SEED's aims are absolutely antiracist, the enactment that Veronica experienced served to function on the side of white supremacy because there was no space to excavate what local interventions were possible. Focusing only on the personal and the structural is a recipe for stasis: The only work to do is on one's self, because no one person could ever hope to transform the systems of oppression we live under. And, thus, if the only group dedicated to supporting antiracist efforts in a school or district becomes stuck on an endlessly repeating loop of introductory materials and "moments," existing inequities are not being transformed.

Amelia's school was also trying to be antiracist, with a district focus on reducing the number of suspensions and referrals for students of color. Yet this open goal was not having the intended effect. Instead, teachers in Amelia's building were, in her opinion, unable to think differently about student behaviors and were instead afraid simultaneously of violating the mandate to lower the suspension rate and of their students themselves. She characterized these white teachers' perspectives in the following way:

> Because we had such a vibrant class come in that also lent itself to a lot of discipline issues, [teachers think] what our schools needs is discipline. The kids need to know how to behave, and we need to make sure the teachers are feeling safe in their classrooms because teachers are being verbally, if not physically, accosted a lot. It's all like—it's all the kids' fault. Like the kids don't know how to do these things, so we need to make them fit into our school.

In this quote, Amelia voiced the perspective of other white teachers in her building, saying that students must learn to behave, to have discipline, because teachers were not feeling safe. Amelia saw this as a way of removing teachers from the responsibilities of adapting their practice to respond to the contexts they were working in; in other words, Amelia's notion of students needing to "fit into our school" avoided the responsibility of teachers to make accommodations in their practice to respond to the actual needs of the students they worked with. If all behavior issues are always already the students' fault, a teacher need do nothing but simply enforce the discipline policy as such, and continue teaching as they always have. Such a stance of inaction, or demanding that the only change or shift come from students themselves, reinforces existing inequities in schools and furthers deficit-laden notions of working-class students of color and their families.

Amelia took a pedagogical role in response to her colleagues' critiques of their students and of the attempted shifts in district discipline policy. This was challenging in a school in which "a large number of teachers will say, 'we don't need to talk about white privilege; institutional racism isn't real.'" As an equity team leader, Amelia worked in PD settings to respond to teachers' critiques of student discipline. But often in those spaces, institutional norms and logics blocked the critical work Amelia and her colleagues sought to engage staff with, as she described:

> Equity was pushed around on our April PD day. We requested certain things at certain times for certain reasons to try to maximize attendance and participation, and we got the exact opposite of what we wanted. And I sent a scathing email to the PD committee and admin saying, "we wanted these things for this reason and those were not met and we feel like that's because you guys don't value . . ." I mean to summarize that; I said it much nicer than that. Oh, they were pissed. So that, I think, kinda sealed the deal for me setting fires around school.

Amelia's administration did not follow up with the equity team's requests for activities to engage the staff in actually addressing discipline in their building in real ways, rather than through lip service. Instead, they scheduled competing initiatives and committees at the same time as the equity session, creating opportunities for many of the teachers who stood to benefit most from more time engaging questions of racial equity in their classrooms to opt out. Amelia saw this as a reflection of the values of her administration: Because her principal did not value equity work, the equity team and their initiatives were treated on the same level as other kinds of teacher committee work. This is not to say that such committee work was not important, but rather to argue that an *equality* approach to PD and committee work can often thwart *equity*. If a sense of equality results in the equity team not getting what they need in terms of scheduling and resources, administrators are placing equality before equity—sameness before fairness. This institutional logic maintains the status quo: No social actors are working consciously against antiracism, while producing outcomes that stifle racial equity.

Likewise, in Sarah's school, existing school disciplinary policies served to further reinforce white supremacy. Sarah put it this way:

> I would say if I didn't think something seemed right, there was no addressing, you know, structural inequalities. It was just like, "if this kid did this, then this is the consequence." There was no kind of mediation or any kind of teaching; it's just action-consequence-action-consequence. This is a suspension; oh, he's already been suspended? Now it's a 2-day suspension.

Sarah's role as Dean of students positioned her as the person primarily responsible for student discipline, but policies themselves were set by her principal and the district. Sarah shared multiple instances in which her principal felt forced into a particular response to student behavior. There was no space for context or specificity; whatever violation of student conduct had been committed, a policy was already in place that determined the punishment for that violation. Her principal did not feel he had the ability to make exceptions or accommodations, so Sarah was forced into the same logic.

These types of institutional logic also played out in nonofficial ways. Another example was Angela's frustrations with other teachers in her building not understanding how demands on working-class families of color created difficulties in attending afterschool events. One teacher in particular regularly scheduled evening programming that Angela's students, English learners, could rarely attend. Angela told us:

> She always questioned why the parents would not be able to get their kids to the events. Like, "well why not? . . . This is a parental responsibility." And I would say, "the parents often don't have more than one vehicle, and they work different shifts and sometimes it's just not possible." We have 44, and I believe this year it's higher, percent free and reduced [price lunch] in our school, and I know that is just forgotten at every faculty meeting. That is a fact that is just not even acknowledged.

After-hours programming for recitals and performances, as well as community engagement events such as conferences and back-to-school night, were common in Angela's suburban school district. Many of her co-workers took the attitude that all of their students' families had the means and ability to attend these afterschool programs, but Angela recognized the exclusions that such policies produce. Only those students whose families had the means to get them to and from the afterschool programs could attend; many of Angela's students were excluded by default from being able to fully participate in their school. Angela's recurring frustration with her co-workers was that they ignored the realities of their students and that the regular activities of the school reproduced exclusions unintentionally. This functions as institutional complicity in white supremacy: Without adapting to the shifting needs of its student population and merely continuing what it had always done, the school was choosing to exclude many working-class students of color from attending afterschool programs.

One final example of how acting institutionally reproduces white supremacy came from Charlie. Policies intended to respond to demands of school safety were a major impediment to her efforts to connect with families in her school community. She explained:

> We want parents to come and volunteer, but oh! They need a background check, and they have to pay for their background check. And [other teachers] are like, "why is it so hard for them to go on a field trip with their child or come in and read with a kid?"

In the name of protecting students, parents weren't allowed into the school building without paying for their own criminal background check—in a school context where the vast majority of students qualified for free and reduced-price lunch. Further, in the context of a class-based and racially unjust criminal justice system, parents might have had arrests that would bar them from the school, yet which presented absolutely no threat to the children or school. In this instance, structural problems, like school safety, produced local responses that functioned to reinforce other structural problems, like white supremacy. Further, without an understanding of the structural nature of both poverty and the criminal justice system, it was impossible to even have these conversations and to consider what other possibilities could exist. This was especially true when there was already a deficit-based, essentialist perspective of students' families, exemplified by a teacher-written song about their school that was, as Charlie described, "really cute until the chorus, when one of the lines was 'our parents take drugs.'" Despite all of this, teachers blamed students' families for not being more involved in the school or for feeling unwelcome there.

In the buildings of many RaceWork teachers, school policies and practices functioned to harm students of color. These teachers named instances where white supremacy was being reproduced without anyone in the building seemingly acting with intention to do so. But this is yet another powerful reminder of the foundational antiracist logic that argues that intention is irrelevant in the context of citational oppressions. That is, if it *feels* or is perceived to cite past oppressions centered on race and racial violence, then whatever was *intended* does not override such feelings and perceptions. In Charlie's case, parents of color were being systematically denied access to fully participating in their children's school. While not the aim or intent of the background check policy (indeed, we could argue that protecting children is a positive aim), that was the impact. Working through examples of ways that acting institutionally reproduced white supremacy helped the teachers in RaceWork further hone their critical awareness of the relationship between the structural and the local. But naming powerful structural mechanisms alone is incapable of working against oppression, unless it is coupled with local responses. That's why the teachers also shared examples of how they were working to respond to the resistances they encountered.

For a Pedagogical Orientation to Work with Colleagues

As much as this chapter has focused on very real obstacles to engaging in antiracist work and the potential costs to relationships with colleagues, RaceWork teachers also made clear that their ability to name these constraining tensions—the ways in which they experienced pressure from multiple directions—did not prevent them from continuing both to work toward more antiracist outcomes for their students and to remain hopeful in the capacity-building character of their work and possibilities for greater transformation in their schools and classrooms. For instance, while Veronica was critical of the stasis of her school's SEED group, she maintained an asset-based approach to her colleagues in the group:

> I think they wanted to get to changing things, but there are so many people that don't know that things have to change because it's such a mixed group as far as where people are at that you can't ever, always get to change, even though some people are getting there.

While the group centered on introductory materials meant to elicit "moments," Veronica found herself wanting to address institutional racisms—to act on her growing consciousness—but didn't find the space to do so in SEED. Yet she saw potential: "some people are getting there." Veronica did not adopt an overly deterministic perspective on SEED's *potential* as a transformative space, as something that could *never* focus on "changing things" rather than people not knowing "that things have to change." While she named a present constraint of the group, she saw her colleagues as working toward greater consciousness of injustice and was hopeful this would connect them to material actions on the side of antiracism.

Amelia's reality was that teachers in her building reacted to equity-centered work in personalized ways. She noted that teachers commonly complained that "the Eteam makes us feel like shit." While she continued to experience colleagues who were dismissive and resistant, she remained committed, in nuanced ways, to growing the capacity of her building's faculty to work for greater antiracist outcomes:

> I know people . . . are recognizing the work that our equity team are doing. And they know that it's a tough building; they know that it's a tough crowd. So in terms of what it's going to take in terms of change, I want to see it happen. I'm not really confident, though, that it will happen, and I hate not feeling that comfort about my building and the teachers that I work with, but something's gotta give either way, right?

While Amelia was not fully confident that change was possible in her school, she also "hated" this lack of confidence. This example reinforces earlier instances wherein Amelia engaged in antiracist work in spite of not feeling fully confident in her identity as a teacher. By the time of our last interview, she had shifted from lacking confidence in her own identity and abilities to act to counter white supremacy in her building to someone who lacked confidence that her *co-workers* would support antiracist changes in their school. But this later lack of confidence was mediated by her clarifying that she was *working* on this feeling, in ways that reflect her earlier struggles. Amelia was now engaging her co-workers in ways that echo the pedagogical stance she took to her classroom-centered antiracist work (explained more in Chapter 9) in her 1st year in RaceWork.

While this pedagogical stance to teacher colleagues was repeated in different ways at different times by the teachers in RaceWork, they also shared ways that were challenged by their colleagues' positioning of them as experts on race and white supremacy. Angela put it this way:

> I think sometimes people view me as, I'm the race expert. But I voice things that make them feel uncomfortable, and so am I really the expert? No, I'm just the person that talks about race and makes them feel uncomfortable.

Angela minimized her capacity and resisted an identification as an expert on race. But contained within this example is the important pedagogical concept of discomfort.

Kumashiro positioned discomfort as a powerful place of learning, asking us, "What would happen if we explored approaches to social justice that were premised on being uncomfortable?" (2009, p. 52) For Kumashiro, far too many people have experiences in schools that function in comforting ways, but further oppression. Feeling comfortable in spaces that discriminate against people requires questioning one's own culpability in maintaining that discrimination. Feeling comfortable in any and all classroom spaces or learning contexts might actually work to further oppression. Such recognitions often produce discomfort, which Kumashiro wanted us to explore as a powerful space for learning. When uncomfortable, we can search for meaning and can better "trouble" elements of our existing knowledge that our comfort has conditioned us not to question. Using this lens, we can understand Angela's example as wanting to distance herself from the mantel of "expert," yet still aiming to produce a pedagogical discomfort in her work with other teachers.

Morgan offered an example of how discomfort is often avoided in antiracist PD contexts:

> We did a couple PDs like that, always talking about those four agreements.[4] And as the year went on, our principal said, "we really got to get the discomfort in here—people are not uncomfortable enough with this; it's just an easy conversation; it's not any reflection." . . . So we're still kinda working on how do we bring that into it without pushing it too far [so] that people totally shut down.

Morgan pointed to the limits of discomfort, or what makes something pedagogically uncomfortable and not dehumanizing, while also critiquing the lack of depth with which her staff had been engaging questions of racial equity. While Morgan was successful in bringing more antiracist professional development into her building through her work in establishing the district's first equity team, her principal agreed with her that teachers were not engaging deeply enough. Pedagogically, Morgan acknowledged needing to approach her co-workers as learners, not aiming to create discomfort that made people shut down but rather engaging them more deeply. She elaborated:

> Having that lens that you view things through . . . can change how people treat you in your building. . . . That just helped me to realize people are at where they're at, and I can't force them, but I can certainly give them resources and let them decide where they want to go from there.

Morgan saw her co-workers as learners in ways that called on her to act on her pedagogical commitments. She didn't want to "force" her colleagues into anything, but did want to "give them resources" that supported their own decisions about "where they want to go." Again, this is an example

---

4. Morgan is referring to *Courageous Conversations*' "Four Agreements": Stay engaged, experience discomfort, speak your truth, and expect and accept nonclosure (Singleton & Linton, 2006, pp. 58–65).

of self-appropriated learning: For learning experiences to be lasting and meaningful, they must feel like our own; they need to be lessons we have actively worked to learn. Morgan saw a difference in her own "lens" on race and that of most of her co-workers, but she saw this lens as one she had built herself in her own conversations and learning, and in RaceWork. In response, she wanted to create opportunities for her co-workers to build their own approaches to antiracism, rather than attempting to somehow "force" them into a position or activity that did not feel like their own.

The local tensions that teachers experienced with their co-workers had material consequences for both themselves and their students. Yet while their relationships with other teachers changed over the course of their time in RaceWork, those shifts were not only negative. In response to the tensions they faced, teachers took on a more pedagogical attitude to their colleagues to encourage building capacity for antiracist work. As Charlie put it:

> I definitely have my moments, but I try really hard to stay calm and freak out in my head but not let it come out of my mouth . . . if I come at you calling you racist, that's not going to work, you know.

Instead, Charlie found different ways to talk about and to be confident in her assertions about white supremacy in schools. Charlie and others took an asset-based approach toward their colleagues, one we more often think of in relationship to students. When teachers adopt an asset-based approach to work with their students, they see potential and possibility connected to the skills and dispositions students bring with them as learners to the classroom. Similarly, a strengths-based and agentic approach can enable a pedagogical stance with co-workers, one that is not condescending but that creates a different and more humanizing approach than most white privilege–based approaches to antiracist PD with white practicing teachers. The teachers in RaceWork thus worked to respond to their co-workers as learners in ways that paralleled their criticality with their students. They worked in, on, and through the tensions they faced in their antiracism at the level of the local.

PART 3

THE STRUCTURAL

CHAPTER 7

White Privilege

We initially did not want to include this chapter. After all, in some ways RaceWork was conceived in response to desires *to go past* what white privilege frameworks have offered white social actors—and white teachers in particular. This of course does not mean that we do not recognize the existence and persistence of very real structural advantages white people possess based on race in a white supremacist social context like the United States. White privilege can be understood broadly on two planes: the presence of racial advantage, and the absence of racial disadvantage. Many times, white privilege is actually the absence of oppression, or the granting of what are broadly constructed as human rights, such as access to homes in areas one wishes to live in, quality schools, health care services, and so on.

Yet, importantly, white privilege does not mean that all white people's lives are blissful and burden free. Many white people live at or near the poverty line. According to the Henry Kaiser Foundation (2018), in the United States in 2017, twice as many white people were living in poverty as compared to Black people. However, 8% of all white people live in poverty, compared to 20% of all Black people—that's one Black person in five. Of course far more white people than Black people live in the United States, but if one is white, rather than Black, they are significantly less likely to live in poverty. White privilege is an explicitly *racial* privilege. It does not explain the entirety of anyone's life, but rather names a social effect of white supremacy.

White privilege is thus a way of orienting the third of our tripartite levels for antiracist work: the structural. White privilege is an example of a structural phenomenon that conditions and determines the personal and the local. The structural can be thought of as systems, webs of meanings, practices, values, discourses, and norms that are larger than any one social actor or any one particular social space or location. The public education system can be thought of as a structure, for instance. But so too can the English language, the news media, and white supremacy. They are structural because while they have a coherency in terms of hanging together and reproducing themselves, no one social actor could ever completely transform them through their own will power, actions, or aspirations. This does not mean that they cannot be acted upon, but such actions will be local and personal, mediated by the structural conditions of the particular local and personal contexts in question. In examining and acting against oppression on the level of the structural, we must consider both how it is produced and how it is reproduced; without an understanding of these mechanisms, interrupting them is impossible.

This is why it is important to note that white privilege is not a *cause* of racial injustice. Rather, it is an *effect*, an outcome of racial oppression. Oppression produces privileges and marginalizations, and to focus on only one without the other is to miss what is truly responsible for our present social reality. Yet white privilege has too often underemphasized the marginalizations and overemphasized the privileges in a white supremacist society (Leonardo, 2004; Lensmire et al., 2013). Leonardo, for instance, offered a companion list to McIntosh's immortal list of privileges that detailed historical acts, laws, and decisions of white supremacy and settler colonialism. Our work with the Midwest Critical Whiteness Collective (Lensmire et al., 2013; McManimon, Casey, & Berchini, 2018) has sought to understand both the explanatory power of white privilege and the ways that pedagogies that follow from it can function to stifle rather than to accelerate antiracist momentum.

In this chapter we discuss how teachers in RaceWork wrestled with white privilege as both a powerful way of naming their own racialized experiences as well as a barrier to engaging their colleagues more robustly in antiracist work. A primary focus is on the ways that the idea of white privilege, and the pedagogies that follow from it, influenced the work of RaceWork teachers, both with us and in their buildings.

(Re)Defining White Privilege

White privilege in many PD contexts is overcoded: It comes to stand in for all of the work we, as white people, need to do. White privilege is often positioned as *the* reason for the discipline gap, educational debt, and struggles to connect with families and communities of color. Because of this, white privilege can become fetishized in PD contexts. By fetishized, we mean that white privilege can be seen as possessing more features than it actually does; further, this fetishization can escape actually explaining the causal mechanisms that underpin the realities that "white privilege" seeks to name. As a result, while many buildings have PD experiences centered on white privilege, careful attention is not paid to *how* white teachers understand the role(s) of white privilege in their teaching.

Amelia explored this in the context of struggles over how to respond to uneven understandings of white privilege among her building's staff. She said, "but we've never really had the conversation: 'What do we mean when we say white privilege? What's the definition of racism?' " To Amelia, such questions felt foundational to the work of the equity team and became regular features of their time together. The equity team regularly talked about white privilege and included it when they facilitated schoolwide PD sessions; at the same time, these discussions were not without challenge. One member of the equity team, for instance, didn't "want to be on the Eteam right now because she thinks we don't need to be talking about white privilege." For Amelia, these conversations were important because

> not everybody maybe knows what white privilege is. We think we do, but we don't. So it's hard to come at it from like, "I'm going to educate you on white privilege, and we're going to have a history lesson on education." You're one of the people making them talk about white privilege every month.

What does it mean when someone on a school's equity team does not believe that a majority white teaching staff should learn about white privilege? Further, teachers who were *not* on the equity team, according to Amelia, lacked an in-depth understanding of white privilege and racism that most of the equity team shared. Their conversations were surface level; there was a right answer: A teacher understood white privilege in terms of factors such as those named above, or they did not. There was no room to discuss multiple understandings or nuance.

We have seen this over and over. Discussions of white privilege, on their own, in a vacuum, often lead to stasis. Ironically, this can happen in two ways: either by limiting meanings (e.g., white privilege is a list of "things") or by being so undertheorized that white privilege describes everything. If we cannot be specific about how and why we are naming practices and policies as functioning to further oppression in our buildings, reducing all of those meanings to a taken-for-granted, catch-all concept like "white privilege" can undermine and work against our aims. This is not to say that we should not welcome multiple meanings and understandings, but that we need space to engage that multiplicity: to put varied conceptions in context to work toward greater shared understandings. In RaceWork, we aimed to build such a multiplicious approach to the concept of white privilege. In what follows, we do so through examples of the understandings of white privilege that RaceWork teachers brought with them when we began.

Reflecting back on the beginning of our time together, Angela was especially struck by what she understood as the difference between how we conceptualized white racial identity, white supremacy, and white privilege compared to how authors she'd read in the past had. She told us in our 1st year of work together:

> I do remember the unpacking, 'cause I came from an "unpack your suitcase" and white privilege . . . I remember listening to you talk about and also reading about the whole Ruby Payne thing and kinda having this moment of well, you know, understanding that that's not the only way to think about it. It's just one step in the process.

For Angela, concepts from a McIntosh-style "unpack your suitcase" (knapsack) approach and Payne's (2005) notions of "cultural poverty" hung together, representing her primary orientation to understanding her relative privilege as a white teacher. This logic worked in the following way: Her students of color did not have as much privilege as she did, and part of that privilege produced the schisms in cultural norms that could explain different school outcomes for students based on race.

But Angela's connections between Payne and McIntosh need further consideration. The connection is produced largely through a lack of clear definitions and through PD experiences that collapse students of color and students living in poverty. This combination produced, for Angela, a connection between theorists who in many ways are diametrically opposed to one another. McIntosh wrote at length about the ways that structural forces limit the life chances of people of color, resulting in privileges—specifically, white privilege—for those who do not face the same sorts of limits. For Payne (2009), however, race was not a salient identifier—class was. Payne has characterized her work in the following way: "My work looks at poverty primarily through the lens of class, not race, ethnicity, gender, disability, age, or other criteria" (p. 372). Reading these two authors together feels almost impossible: One argued that structural determinants produce white supremacist outcomes, while the other argued that poverty should be studied and understood without regard to "race, ethnicity, gender, disability, age, or other criteria." What then does it mean that these concepts ran together for Angela?

Angela's experience links to Amelia's, in that far too many staff lack a shared and coherent understanding of concepts such as "racism" and "white privilege." But this also did not mean that there is *one* single conception; this idea opens space for both articulating a person's own understanding but also avenues to situate their colleagues. Angela came to see her earlier understanding as "just one step in the process," but she was thankful that RaceWork offered her a new and different perspective from that she had been working with for years. Frequent references to "process" signaled that, for Angela, engaging in anti-oppressive work and struggling to understand were more important than waiting for a complete understanding. She appreciated that not everyone in RaceWork shared (or was required to share) exactly the same approaches to antiracism in schools or the same antiracist identity. Angela saw this as a kind of rebuke of her prior combined McIntosh-Payne conception of cultural poverty and white racial privilege. In RaceWork, she experienced other possible explanations that acknowledged privilege or cyclical poverty but were critical of dominant conceptions of racial privilege and Payne's work. For Angela, this provided space to articulate her own approaches to antiracist work in ways that did not continually produce feelings of self-flagellation or require indicting others. Before RaceWork, she'd understood her colleagues' resistances to her advocating for EL students and working-class students of color as evidence of their unchecked white privilege. Learning more about how a "best practices" approach to this work can have unintended and oppressive outcomes and how there can never be one best or only way to engage in antiracist work in schools allowed Angela to read her co-workers in more complex and nuanced ways than the protocols she had previously learned had allowed.

Like Angela, Charlie found in RaceWork a broader understanding of white supremacy and a way of moving to action—in other words, praxis (action and reflection), rather than solely reflection. Based on her work in other PD, Charlie had "a clear understanding that I have white privilege," for instance, referencing the idea of the moving walkway, the idea that a white person who is unaware and not actively working against racial oppression is carried along with the white supremacist status quo, like being on a moving walkway. Charlie *knew* she had white privilege and, in some ways, enjoyed learning about it repeatedly. Part of why she sought out PD experiences centered on whiteness and white privilege was that the feelings they produced in her felt impactful: White privilege frameworks made her *feel* her relative privilege and reflect on her complicity in powerful ways. But, she shared, something was always missing from these experiences. While she learned a lot about identity, no immediate actions were produced from her reflections and growing understandings of privilege. What RaceWork provided for her that more stage theory or privilege-centered PD had not was a focus on the "why" of white privilege. While she experienced white privilege in the present and could articulate those experiences, they were in many ways decoupled from history. Focusing on "why" helped her understand privilege not as causal, but as an effect of white supremacist oppression. Charlie's extensive experiences in white privilege PD contexts had not led to discussions of the history of white supremacy and white racial identity in as much detail as she found in RaceWork. She connected this growing sense of the "why" to a "focus on what action we can take."

Despite the frequency of white privilege PD, RaceWork teachers reminded us that white privilege discourses produce a multiplicity of meanings that are often left unexamined and that leave participants unsure of "what's next." Assuming everyone to have the same conception of white privilege can often backfire; simultaneously, the need to ensure that everyone has a shared understanding produces the problem of always starting at the beginning, rendering all discussions of white privilege an introduction. In RaceWork, then, we instead started with situating the "why" in history: to explain where white privilege came from historically and institutionally.

Institutional Power: Hegemonically "White" Spaces and Practices

In RaceWork, (re)defining white privilege included expanding our understandings and connecting to the structural—not just white privilege, but the meanings of whiteness itself in a white supremacist society. For a white person to experience racial privilege, social spaces must have existing mechanisms to reward behaviors associated with hegemonic whiteness. By hegemonic, we mean the most dominant conception: Hegemonic whiteness is the range of experiences that center white subjectivities, white peoples as always good, whiteness as free of sin, white (cultural) norms of politeness, seriousness, respect, and so on. Of course, many authors have engaged the hegemonically white character of schools and the ways students of color regularly confront features of school that hail them to "act white" (e.g., Carter, 2006; Delpit, 2012; Pollock, 2004). We bring attention to hegemonically white spaces because they speak to the structural mechanisms present in schools. There is a great deal to understand about how privilege manifests in schools and how different social actors receive differential treatment based on the privileges they experience in the context of the social structure they are participating in.

Returning to Amelia's school, her Eteam colleagues thought they shared an understanding of whiteness, but their discourse and actions made clear that they did not, nor did some people want to engage more deeply. In hegemonically white spaces, calling attention to race is, as we have stated, at best impolite, and at worst a racist act in and of itself. White people may feel personally attacked when asked to think broadly about race and white supremacy, and many hegemonically white spaces can uncritically reinforce those discomforts and offer ways to avoid engaging altogether—as in Amelia's school, when teachers could choose which PD sessions to attend, thus creating the sense that each session was equally important. Such a practice is rooted in good intentions: Professionals should be allowed to select what they want to engage in. But treating antiracism in this way actually works in opposition to racial justice. When such options offer ways out of engaging in discussions of marginalizations and oppressions, they reinforce the oppressive status quo. Antiracism is not the same as, for instance, how to teach stoichiometry. Rather, antiracism must be infused throughout curriculum, throughout pedagogy, throughout behavior expectations.

A refusal to engage these ideas is in and of itself not, however, what was ultimately at stake here. For Amelia, more importantly, it produced a schism, stifling any kind of *action* on the side of antiracism. Antipathy toward white privilege and particularly what it can fail to explain when examined without contexts—that is, without consideration of whiteness as hegemonic—can function to thwart collective efforts at antiracism. Amelia, for instance, connected this refusal to the staff's stuckness with regard to disciplinary practices, stating, "It's the same thing with high expectations and classroom engagement. No one can agree with what they really mean, so we think they're subjective terms." Amelia wanted to explicitly connect whiteness to what it meant to have high expectations and what classroom engagement could or should look like. But without a shared understanding of how whiteness functioned within their school—an understanding that a primarily white staff was expecting all students (even in a school of nearly all students of color) to conform to white norms—this was not possible.

We can perhaps see the hegemonically white character of most school buildings most clearly with regard to student discipline. The teachers in RaceWork all worked in schools in which discipline was disproportionately racialized: Students of color were suspended and referred at higher rates than were white students. We collectively theorized this as an incongruence between white teachers' expectations and cultural norms and practices of their students of color. In other words, discipline was a white (supremacist) practice in schools.

Yet teachers in their buildings did not have the language to theorize this or contexts in which to situate it, which often made them reluctant to address what seemed blatantly obvious to RaceWork teachers. For example, Sarah told us:

> As far as the teachers, it's a really white district. Our school is becoming less and less white, and there's a lot of what we're talking about, kind of white guilt. I don't hear as much of this "I don't see color stuff" any more. That seems to be kind of moving on. But there's a lot of teachers who act or feel sort of guilty if they point out anything about race. So it's this weird kind of hiding all of it, even though I know that if we have more informal conversations, you'll hear things about their prejudice or their decisions.

Sarah read her colleagues as experiencing white guilt, but white shame might actually name her co-workers' feelings more accurately. For Thandeka (2006), white shame is an emotive response resulting from the "failure of the self to live up to its own ideals" (p. 108)—in other words, as white people, we may intuit that white supremacy makes unreasonable and unforgiveable demands on us, but we are participants in this system *because we are white*. As we cannot reconcile the demands of participating in this system, in a white supremacist society, "this [white] self, seeing its own brokenness, feels shame" (p. 108). This feeling of shame, Thandeka theorized, is part of what it means to be white in our society. We feel shame because we are white. In contrast, feelings of guilt result from feeling bad about something a person has *done*. If I understand that something I did was wrong, and I recognize it as wrong, I can feel guilt for my wrongness. But shame names something beyond my own individual purview. It names the feeling that something within my self is flawed and wrong; there is no immediate response available to shake such a feeling. White shame can name a salient aspect of the discipline gap and, more particularly, in the example from Sarah, can explain why simply pointing out race—which may or may not be related to anything a white person had actually *done*—evoked feelings of shame. This then led to avoidance.

Naming shame and other feelings associated with understanding what it means to be white in a white supremacist society was a central feature of our work together in RaceWork. Nicole shared early with the group that she felt "like even in high school and junior high I had this profound sense of guilt of being white and not even wanting to think about it sometimes." Nicole's statement showcases both relative privilege and white shame, placing them in causal relation. Feeling shame, though she called it guilt, resulted in Nicole "not even wanting to think about it sometimes"; this ability to choose when and if to think about race and racism is a white racial privilege. Feeling and naming shame is not somehow an "out" for white people looking to rid themselves of their relative privilege. Rather, it is a way of articulating feelings of brokenness over an inability to fully live out our deepest commitments to others. We feel shame for our complicity—not for intentional and malicious acts against people of color, but for our linkage to past and ongoing acts of white supremacy and structural violence.

If we conceptualize whiteness as hegemonic, we can understand these shared feelings; we can also acknowledge the ways in which white teachers' feelings—particularly that of shame—circumscribe our ability to even have conversations about race—what DiAngelo (2018) has named "white fragility." Hegemonic whiteness *affectively* conditions us. But we cannot stop there, as it also materially conditions us and our institutions, such as schools. Thus, we must also examine racialized discipline differences as a result of hegemonic whiteness: Most schools are white spaces, where white norms and practices are valued. Students who are white have likely learned these norms and practices at home, through the media, and other ways. This is quite evident when we consider a common reason that students of color—particularly Black male students—are referred for discipline: disrespect. What is "disrespect?" If we can move past the shame white teachers feel and get to actually interrogating this concept, eventually we will land on the reality that "disrespect" is culturally constructed. White teachers must *interpret* actions or languages of students of color as disrespect.

But this is also an opening. Over our years together, RaceWork teachers often talked about student behavior not as a fixed, immutable category, but rather as a set of skills that could be learned. Amelia, for instance, understood her students as arriving to school with different behavioral skills than those that were rewarded by the disciplinary policies and practices of her building. This then provided a pedagogical opening: A task for teachers can be to equip students with the skills needed for success in navigating their school. This necessitates two actions on the part of white teachers: both interrogating and challenging the hegemonic whiteness of school spaces and helping students build the skills to navigate school successfully.

Sociopolitical Consciousness of White Privilege: Pushing Past Confession

Often, white privilege frameworks don't provide spaces for white people to process feelings such as shame; instead, when a white person seemingly denies or misunderstands white privilege, they are shut down, furthering a sense of guilt that draws upon white shame. Further, in many spaces, white privilege discourses are themselves hegemonic: There is no space to question them. They thus remain unquestioned and unquestionable.

In RaceWork, a challenge on this basis came pretty early our first morning together. Zac emphasized that the point of antiracism work for white people is *not* to divest ourselves of privilege (as if this were even possible—as if that privilege is not deeply rooted in structures and thus much bigger than any individual's control) but to work against oppression. Pete countered: "I have learned that I have white privilege.[1] I can't go back. I'm working on it, but I will always be racist. Understanding white privilege is really important. You can't do this work without this idea." Pete was doing what we as white people have been taught to do: confess our privilege. Zac pushed back. Pete responded that as the only males in the room, he and Zac also had male privilege. Privilege became the central word, the only word that really mattered.

But we—Zac and Shannon—had deliberately set out to do something different from the vast majority of antiracism trainings we had been to. We wanted to create a space for white practicing teachers to analyze white supremacy and then to act on this analysis; we didn't know what would happen, but we knew we would start from a different premise. The pushback was nearly immediate: We weren't following the script.

But we also were nearly immediately affirmed in our sense that practicing teachers wanted and needed something different. Following some back and forth between Zac and Pete, Angela talked about how important historicizing race was and how a white privilege workshop she had facilitated for her colleagues had been a complete mess. Charlie was excited to dive deeper, saying that half of every workshop she had attended had been about white privilege, but she felt she ended up running into a wall: Privilege discourses couldn't tell her where to go next. And Sarah, who had taken a course with Zac, suggested trusting the process that we would go through.

Together, we faced our first crisis: a challenge to the very model that we were attempting to build as we went. Zac's skillful facilitation (according to Shannon) of this potentially shattering confrontation set the stage for our work together—almost as if we had planned this. Instead of pitting the "good" white people who get "it" (meaning understanding that we as white people have privilege—see Chapter 8) against the "bad," resistant, racist white people, we built solidarity. For instance, all of us raised our hands when asked if we had ever *not* confronted or corrected a family member who said or did something racist (intentional or not). At the end of the session, Angela said, "this is the first time I can wrap my head around *why*—I got goosebumps when you said how

---

1. Because of a family crisis, Pete was able to attend only the first session of Race-Work. A white man, Pete had taught for about 20 years in an affluent suburban elementary school with a growing population of middle-class students of color. He described himself to us as a "PD junky."

Germans, Swedish, [and others] became white. Now I understand *why* I have white privilege." From the beginning, we were acknowledging our deep embeddedness in racialized systems of oppression—and our desire to work against these structures.

The teachers frequently referenced this difference, juxtaposing RaceWork with other spaces they had experienced. For Veronica, her school's SEED group had a repetitive quality; as she explained, "we start with a lot of sort of confessions." Yet confessions are incapable of actually accomplishing anything on the side of antiracism because they do not have a material impact on the life chances of people of color. They exist solely at the personal level, decoupled from the local and structural because they center liberal individualist conceptions of racism. Veronica wanted something that could go deeper than her SEED group and relished the chance to share openly about her frustrations with others in her building in a space where no one else knew the people she was talking about. The confessionary approach of her school's SEED group was part of why Veronica theorized it as a space for "having moments" rather than working together to challenge white supremacy in their school and classrooms. The absence of such confessions was part of what made RaceWork a productive space for Veronica, a feeling she shared with Sarah, who summarized her understanding of RaceWork's approach to antiracism in this way:

> So it's not about, necessarily having some big, you know, "I'm white and I've had so many privileges." I feel like I went through that, but not anymore. It's like, "OK, yeah, yes, yes, yes, and also, you know, I was born here and other people aren't and I was taught this religion and other people aren't." If you stop there, then nothing can happen.

If we stop at the level of confession, Sarah argued, nothing can happen in the context of white antiracism. Sarah articulated her own experiences of learning about privilege, but being able to push beyond narrow confessions was critically important because of the problem of action: because we must *act* on felt commitments to antiracism for such commitments to be anything more than navel-gazing reflection for reflection's sake. Her examples of nationality and religious privileges are worth honing in on further, because she voiced them as examples of privilege discourses run amok. This is not to say that there aren't very real and material privileges connected to U.S. citizenship and Christianity in the United States, because there absolutely are. However, dwelling on such privileges on their own, absent engagement with the material oppressions that produce those privileges, can never function in solidarity with those who are oppressed in those systems.

Perhaps the trouble with white privilege discourses producing confessions was best articulated by Charlie:

> I just felt like I had a pretty good understanding of my privilege. What I didn't have a good understanding of was how do I use that? Or . . . how do I translate that into a way that you can teach kids about their identity?

Teaching white teachers about their privilege is often imagined as having direct causal impacts on their practice. But as Charlie often reminded us, "teachers want the checklist." Charlie resisted such approaches, rejecting the notion that concrete steps will work in any and all spaces for any teacher working with any group of students. Still, she wanted more explicit connections between her growing understanding of her own relative privilege and how that could support students of color learning more about their identities. She wanted to know how to "translate" her understanding of herself into practices that supported students of color in her classroom.

But we also need to emphasize that saying that a program such as RaceWork has raised sociopolitical consciousness is a rather empty statement when it's not coupled with actions that follow from that consciousness. This is what Freire (2000) called *praxis*: action and reflection in equal measure on the world in order to transform it. To return to Angela's metaphor of "process," we argue RaceWork was a site of consciousness raising, but only because of the concrete actions the teachers took up between our sessions. The space to reflect, to dig deeper, to connect contexts and histories is valuable only if it speaks to the present activity of those doing the reflecting. Reflection for its own sake is empty work. But so is action for the sake of action. We are thus not arguing here for an anti-intellectual stance that asserts there is nothing to be gained through careful study and dialogue with others. Rather, we learned through our experiences in RaceWork that reflection can take on special importance in sustaining antiracist efforts that go largely unheralded and often are resisted by others. A critical space with others, even if not everyone approaches their work from the exact same set of political and theoretical locales, can sustain and propel everyone involved. This is partly why teachers who had engaged this work for years, like Charlie and Angela, felt they took as much from their time in RaceWork as teachers like Lisa and Amelia, who were far less experienced with antiracist PD and activity in schools before RaceWork. Their experiences were assets, to be drawn on and scaffolded from so as to support the group in building greater and greater meaning together in service of sustaining material antiracist work in their buildings.

For the End of the "Beginning" of Antiracist Work with White Teachers

As a field, teacher education has been concerned about "low expectations" for a long time. Low expectations, of course, refer to teachers who approach students with a fixed mindset that results in giving some students less engaging work and holding them to lower standards than others. We argue that low expectations permeate most PD that targets white teachers in the context of antiracism and white privilege. These low expectations produce an overemphasis on the most resistant learners as stand-ins for all others: Antiracist PD with white teachers thus aims to reach those who are seen as being the most resistant and possessing the least amount of prior knowledge; anyone who might have more prior knowledge is blocked from deeper engagement because of the low expectations held for the entire group. This is why so many teachers in RaceWork felt they had learned about white privilege over and over again, in the same kinds of ways, and such learning didn't seem to lead anywhere. They named the problem of always starting with a deficit approach to white teachers.

The introductory quality of the white privilege workshops most teachers experience produces a secondary issue, described above as the "overcoded" quality of white privilege as a concept. Charlie shared a story of her own efforts to engage staff in PD that would do more than rearticulate white privilege, but ended up circling back to privilege because it was central to how teachers in her building had learned how to talk about racial equity.

> I was just nervous that there was going to be just one more of those meetings where you hear about your white privilege. So we tried to take that away, and white privilege did come up a lot because it's all they—it's every other training they've gone to. . . . So it definitely came up, but we kept trying to steer it away like, "how can you use this? You're understanding it now. Let's move forward." And that's something where I'm still struggling; how do I push people forward, aside from just recognizing their privilege?

What happens after the recognition of privilege? It's as if we have only ever attempted White Privilege 101. What about White Privilege 201? Or

501? Charlie's aims to do more than rearticulate white privilege were stifled by the past experiences of her building engaging in so many activities that focused on white privilege. White privilege became the name for all of the work to do; the task was/is for white teachers to learn about their privilege, and if we can accomplish that, we should then see shifts in oppressions like the discipline gap and educational debt. But do we?

To engage in antiracist work in P–12 school contexts in the United States today increasingly is to engage populations of white people who have learned something about white privilege. From Teach for America to university-based teacher education programs, one is hard pressed to find teacher certification programs that do not include the concept of white privilege at some point in the curriculum. Often, in fact, teacher candidates learn in multiple spaces about racial privilege. Perhaps because we've assumed a more direct and causal sequence of events that is supposed to follow greater awareness of privilege on the part of white teachers than is actually the case, it still feels to many that if we want to engage white folks in taking up more antiracist stances and practices, we must always first help them understand their relative privilege. But what if we started from a different set of assumptions? What if rather than seeing all white teachers as always already novices in the context of white supremacy and racial privilege, we saw them instead as capable and able learners who bring with them experiences that can be scaffolded to greater and greater critical engagement in antiracism?

Such an approach is actually what we should be called toward if we affirm culturally relevant and sustaining pedagogies as the aim of teacher education and PD (Ladson-Billings, 1995; Paris, 2012; Paris & Alim, 2014). We cannot treat our students as if they do not bring their own funds of knowledge to their work with us (González, Moll, & Amanti, 2005). And so it would seem that we then actually have many already available alternatives based on what we understand from critical multicultural education. We can do more to contextualize privilege and localize practices that challenge white supremacy. We can develop more explicit ways of talking about expectations and the reasons behind those expectations and their citational power. We can develop shared plans of action and the means to understand the impacts of those activities. Most important, we do not have to continue engaging in the exact same white privilege workshop Charlie dreaded recreating for her colleagues. The teachers in RaceWork demonstrated that we can make strides on the side of antiracism without waiting for complete or full understanding, especially as such completeness is anti-pedagogical. As Freire (2000) insisted, the world is never finished but rather always becoming. So too are teachers never finished. It is time for professional development for white teachers that goes beyond introducing privilege and instead approaches them as capable learners who are hungry for ways to act on their antiracist commitments. What is needed is space to try, to struggle, and to get feedback. RaceWork serves in this way as one possible model.

CHAPTER 8

Seeing and Getting "It"

During our Saturday mornings together and then again as we read transcripts and listened to audio recordings, we were struck by "it." Yes, "it": over and over. RaceWork teachers talked about who did and didn't "get it" or "see it"—including the ways in which RaceWork helped them to see "it." "It," we realized, was shorthand for the structures of white supremacy. Thus, in this chapter we parse out how RaceWork teachers connected the personal and local with the structural: how they came to "read racially" by naming "it" as well as what happens when other educators, particularly those in their buildings, are complicit in and by *not* getting "it." RaceWork teachers often named others as not getting it when they resisted the antiracist approaches RaceWork teachers were attempting to enact in their schools. Yet, as mentioned before, RaceWork teachers also recognized that "getting it" is a process, not an endpoint; we always have work to do to read the structural system of white supremacy and to recognize the ways it is enacted personally and locally. Further, getting it is not just about the way we talk, the politics of language, or knowing the "correct" words to use. Fundamentally, getting it is about materially enacting antiracism.

"Reading" Racially: Naming the "It"

It is not possible to live in the United States without absorbing white supremacy. We thus might expect that RaceWork teachers would have numerous stories of naming overt racism in their buildings, of describing explicit moments of white supremacy and its material impacts on students and families of color. Yet RaceWork teachers asserted some version of "they don't get it" much more frequently than they called other teachers or administrators in their buildings or districts "white supremacist" or "racist." This is not to say, of course, that they didn't sometimes do this as well. Morgan, for instance, named several teachers as some version of "old school racist," telling us about how they treated (particularly, punished) students of color or how she had to point out to her colleagues that every one of the students they named as "potential trouble" was a student of color. So this is not to say that RaceWork teachers were afraid to name what they experienced, particularly when students of color were adversely affected.

As discussed in previous chapters, white people in the United States have also developed and been socialized into sophisticated ways of avoiding talking or thinking about race and white supremacy. Thus, in examining instances of not getting or seeing "it," we realized that what teachers were pointing out was actually how others did not see the structures of white supremacy, thus missing how the level of the structural was playing out in their classrooms and schools. "Seeing it" or "getting it" was a vernacular for knowledge about how white supremacy, regardless of intention, shapes lives and interactions and what this meant in personal and local contexts. This is the excess that white privilege has trouble naming; the "it" here was most often *not* about the advantages or privileges that attend being white in a white supremacist society, but about the structures of that system. In other words, to "get it," a white person had to accomplish more than understanding their relative privilege; one needed to know what caused and what sustained that privilege: the ongoing practices and structures of white supremacy.

In RaceWork, teachers came to "see it" and name or get it in new ways—in other words, to read racially. "It" became more concrete, more apparent in words, deeds, and structures. Amelia, for instance, wrote after our 1st year:

> Every single thing I read, listen to, talk about, think about, is now through the lens of race. I feel like my observation skills have been sharpened because I'm so much more attuned to how race shapes our conversations that stem from our beliefs.

Amelia, as mentioned in Chapter 4, noticed how race influenced everything. Here she also described a sense of connections, of the ways that structural oppressions *actually structure* our social reality. Morgan also recognized that she might be reading the world differently, through racialized lenses. She stated in an interview that "we had some diversity when I grew up in [the suburb], but not nearly as much as I see now. But then I also think, well, maybe I just didn't notice it as much either." The question of racial diversity for Morgan was thus at least partially conditioned on the ability to recognize diversity, something she was now able to do differently than before her time in RaceWork. Nicole's written reflection took Amelia and Morgan's "it" further:

> As the RaceWork class progressed, I began thinking about racism in less abstract ways and more about the real manifestations—both small and large—of racism in my personal space each day, in places like my classroom, the staff lounge, meetings, watching the news, etc. I found myself "feeling" racism more and experiencing it as a tangible aspect to my life as a teacher, and less as an academic concept or abstract idea. The process of digging through the readings [that we did in RaceWork], but then discussing and applying what we were reading to our own spaces and helping each other discuss those spaces helped me see and interact with racism for the first time, rather than just knowing about it and knowing academic language and concepts.

Our work together, providing academic resources and examples as well as time to discuss and apply ideas, meant that these teachers were naming actual instances of white supremacy and racialized space in their own settings, recognizing how race "shapes" everything, as Amelia said.

Two years later, in her final interview, Amelia remembered that when we started, she didn't "know how my whiteness affected my classroom." The thinking that we'd done together enabled her to recognize it; she was reading racially, including understanding how both her own self (her whiteness) and the politics and structures of her classroom and school played out with students, curriculum, and more. At the same time, she acknowledged, "You're not going to be perfect all the time with it, but there are things you can mostly muddle through without giving away too much of yourself." The "you're" in Amelia's framing was meant to stand in for "white teachers," signaling in particular that white people are prone to mistakes and failures as they work ambivalently in antiracist contexts. Knowing that we, as white people, will fall into well-worn territories of re-centering whiteness can help us sustain ourselves and persist in this work; it can help us from giving "away too much" of our self-concept and drive as antiracist social actors.

RaceWork, these teachers asserted, helped them not only to recognize and name how "it" (white supremacy) was embedded in their schools and in their daily interactions, but also their own roles in maintaining "it," even as they desired and worked to challenge white supremacy. While we looked at the following quote from Sarah in Chapter 3, here we call attention to the role that "it" plays in her descriptions. Speaking of established student discipline procedures that reproduced a racialized discipline gap, Sarah said:

> Racism is just perpetual. It's systemic and it's perpetual and I'm doing it every day. I keep doing it, I'm a part of it, and it's awful. It's awful to like, to get to a point where you see it, and then you're still in the role and [have to respond to a student], "OK, now you're suspended" and you're like "Ahhhh!"

In this brief statement, Sarah calls out "it" seven times. In other words, explicitly seeing and getting "it," being able to name the structural nature of white supremacy and its impact on the lives of students of color, was not enough. She also had to grapple with her own complicity in it.

Not Getting "It" and/as Complicity

For RaceWork teachers, then, "it" named white supremacy, which meant coming to understand that "it" is much bigger than any of us, that our actions and best wishes alone cannot end white supremacy. Importantly, this understanding acknowledges that structures are much larger than any of us or our individual institutions and that these structures are firmly rooted historically, socially, politically, and economically. We may not (likely will not) be able to dismantle these structures completely, but we can't even begin if we don't "see it."

For RaceWork teachers, in reference to other people, "not getting it" appeared to be shorthand for unthinking complicity in maintaining structural oppression. When RaceWork teachers said that others—be they administrators, teachers, or their own families—didn't get it, they were actually saying that these were the people who refused to acknowledge the structural nature of white supremacy, making these adults reactionary. As researchers, we see how the vernacular and shorthanded nature of the term "they don't get it" accomplished much for RaceWork teachers. Yet we must also push past a narrow reading and imagine RaceWork as producing, in some ways, our own sorts of vernaculars: our own ways of speaking and listening that are ultimately *for* one another. While we could possibly read such frequent references on the part of white teachers to seeing and getting "it" as a tactic of racial avoidance, we understand RaceWork teachers' use of "it" to mean a tripartite conception of white supremacy and antiracism as at least partially constructed in and by our praxis in RaceWork. "It" can accomplish a great deal when interlocutors already share a robust sense of context for how "it" can be employed in a discoursal space. And when one is talking with the same group of others for the 15th time about white supremacy, sometimes the best use of time to describe reactionary responses to antiracist work on the part of teachers and administrators is to say, "they don't get it."

Not "getting it" carried a particularly heavy weight in contexts that were predominantly white, such as Nicole and Veronica's schools. This is not to say that Lisa and Amelia, for instance, in schools where most students were of color, did not also name this problem—but in their schools, race could not be outright ignored. In Veronica's disproportionately white building, "not getting it" played out in multiple ways, including among students and among staff. In her school, race itself often remained unnamed, as she said in her last interview:

> I think one of the big things is that most of our kids think that all of the kids that are not white *are* white. You know, it's that idea that, "oh, you're white. I don't think of you as Black; I don't think of you as Asian." You're basically white because you're here. I don't recognize your race, which they see as a positive, but it's not a positive thing.

In other words, the (racial) identity of students of color was erased, which, of course, means that "it" (racialized oppression in curriculum, pedagogy, or policy as well as in interactions between students and between students and teachers) could never be named. Veronica had pointed out this problem 2 years earlier, stating that in her school's SEED group, one of the few places where equity was discussed in her building, we "never really get into the problems within the school." The group instead kept things abstract. Refusing to name race happened both with individuals, students, and staff as well as at the school level; thus, staff and students in this building missed opportunities to connect what they saw around them with larger systems. Refusing to name "it" (race *or* racialized oppression) meant not addressing it, meaning that the staff and students remained unthinkingly complicit in white supremacist structures.

For many RaceWork teachers, frustration about their colleagues "not getting it" was greatest because of the damaging consequences for students in their schools. They recognized the violence of white supremacy in their schools, and knew that students did too. Nicole, for instance, spoke of how whiteness allowed white students to get away with a lot in school, particularly if the student was a "star," such as academically or athletically. In reference to a recent incident at her school, she said, "All the students have to see is him [the white student] not getting in trouble . . . So [for teachers] it doesn't have to be 'I do or don't write more referrals for students of color.' It just has to be they see this well-liked boy get away with it." Refusing to talk about race and in particular, about whiteness, meant that such experiences were not examinable. White teachers in Nicole's school were complicit with white supremacy in not acknowledging that whiteness, in instances such as this, provided white students with a free pass—and that students, both white and of color, understood this. Nicole was theorizing a hidden curriculum of white supremacy within the disciplinary regime of her school; students were learning from the *lack* of a white student being disciplined as much as from seeing students of color overrepresented in detention.

Morgan also was frustrated with her colleagues' refusal to acknowledge white supremacy as a structured system that affects everyone, even small children. Trying to talk about race in her elementary school, Morgan got push-back from a kindergarten teacher, who wanted to know at what point in life kids start noticing race because "this doesn't happen in my classroom." The kindergarten teacher asserted that "this" (i.e., white supremacy and differential treatment—another way of saying "it") wasn't happening in her classroom, so it must happen sometime between kindergarten and 5th grade, when students got to Morgan's classroom. In other words, because the kindergarten teacher worked with 5- and 6-year-olds, she was attempting to remove culpability from herself, asserting that kids that young don't "see race." If this were true, then the racialized patterns that Morgan was pointing out must be *someone else's* responsibility.

But this refusal to see "it" locally (e.g., in the kindergarten classroom) means unacknowledged complicity with racialized structures, as young children certainly *do* see race (see, e.g., Winkler, 2009). Thus, Morgan's rhetorical response to this teacher:

> Something happened also in kindergarten. Not directly by you—you didn't purposefully put these ideas, thoughts in their head, but something that we're doing is causing this, whether you see it right away in kindergarten or by the time they're in 5th grade. It goes all the way back to all of us.

In this interaction with a kindergarten teacher attempting to remove herself individually from complicity, Morgan asserted over and over that as white people, we are all complicit. This complicity is not necessarily malicious, intentional, or the result of us being "bad" people; rather, complicity is a consequence of living in a white supremacist society. She said, "you don't want to think that you're doing that [inequitable treatment]. But everybody is, whether they're trying to or not. That's why they can be aware of it and then try to do something about it." For Morgan, a refusal to "get it" in relationship to one's own classroom meant that teachers were complicit with racialized oppression.

Another way this came up was when other teachers or administrators denied their complicity by stating they already understood. They claimed they got it. Check: done. For Amelia, the response of many teachers in her building to equity team proposals or professional development sounded like, "We don't need equity; we're over that. We don't need that; we get that. What we need are strategies: we need ways to discipline our kids." Over and over, when Amelia pointed out racialized patterns in behavior referrals and academic standing, teachers in her building insisted they understood equity and now needed something concrete. But Amelia had come to understand that "strategies" were not outside the racialized systems of the school and society; responding to students exclusively as individuals was a way of refusing to acknowledge the system and teachers' complicity in racialized structures of oppression. Amelia insisted that strategies would not fix "it" if these larger patterns—based in the structural—were not addressed.

In contrast to these teachers at Amelia's school, Lisa, after participating in RaceWork, took an opposite position: "I'm still obviously learning and trying to figure it out, but that first day was almost like a, 'I need to figure this out' and almost a call to action at the same time. I have to do something, and I have to figure out how to make this not be my classroom." In contrast to teachers at Amelia's school, Lisa learned about the system of white supremacy and read herself into the structural, naming her own complicity and lack of understanding and using that as a push to action. Lisa, like other RaceWork teachers, recognized that "getting it" was a process with which a white person was never finished.

Getting "It" as a Process

In *Practice Makes Practice*, Britzman (2003) implicitly argued that we never finish learning how to teach and that our common-sense ways of understanding teaching (such as a cultural myth of teachers as self-made) do a disservice to both teachers and learners. She wrote: "The teacher as expert, then, is in actuality a normalizing fiction that serves to protect the status quo, heighten the power of knowledge to normalize, and deny the more significant problems of how we come to know, how we learn, and how we are taught" (p. 229). Instead, she argued, "practice makes practice," making teaching always a "complex dialogue between practice and theory, biography, and social structure, knowledge and experience, and difference and commonalities" (p. 238). The idea of teaching as a dialogic process of construction describes our collective experience of RaceWork: Just as we are never finished with learning how to teach, we are never finished with understanding and combatting white supremacy on the personal, local, and structural levels. This work cannot happen in isolation.

White people working against white supremacy need to consider who we are in solidarity with. RaceWork teachers kept coming back to our Saturday sessions because of their desire for colleagues with whom to struggle constructively—colleagues who were working *toward* "getting it" and acknowledging when they didn't. As Veronica wrote, "Because of this group, I am much more cognizant of race and racialized ideas. I teach in a predominantly white school, but once you start looking for it, you do see race everywhere." In other words, this was a process of learning. Importantly, though, RaceWork teachers came to recognize that "it" was never and could never be finished. This necessitated a change in their posture toward other white learners who were or weren't working on "getting it."

For Amelia, who did and didn't "get it" in her school was particularly salient. She spoke often in our years together about her school's hostile environment. This hostility was sometimes directed at members of the equity team, who, because they were openly addressing race, became the scapegoats for frustration that would have been more correctly targeted at the structural oppressions students and teachers faced and labored under. While she hadn't experienced this hostility directly, Amelia said that

> other teachers on our [equity team] have had more attacking conversations where they've been on the receiving end of teachers verbally putting down our work. Which makes it hard. So there's that atmosphere in our building. It's not a healthy place; it's hard to talk about the need for change when people don't see the need for change and when people don't think that they're a part of anything.

Amelia asserted that the majority of teachers in her building disregarded the work of the equity team, instead taking the stance of, as she put it, "I'm just going to do what I do without any acknowledgment of kids in my classroom." Despite the equity team's work to point out racialized patterns in their school and to connect these patterns to larger systems (the structural), Amelia and other teachers on the equity team were positioned as the problem: If only the equity team could provide some strategies for student behavior or if teachers just put their heads down and worked, without acknowledging the racialized identities of students in their classroom, problems wouldn't exist. This furthered the hostility in the school environment, creating an "us" versus "them" mentality, with "us" being those who were working to understand white supremacy and its impact in their immediate environment and "them" being those who were not.

Amelia looked to her equity team colleagues for support and solidarity. But a strict "us versus them" dichotomy, Amelia came to understand, could not fully explain what she experienced. This dichotomy (which can take the form of "good whites" vs. "bad whites") can actually function on the side of white supremacy, positioning some of us as finished with our learning and thus not making mistakes. Amelia stated that the equity team was

> trying to feel like we get it. And one of our members will say something totally off the rocker. And [my response was], "No, that's not it. No." I'll try to just not feel alone . . . and to feel validated in what I've learned but also to realize that I'm still learning too.

What Amelia found in RaceWork that often felt missing at her school was an understanding that learning is a process. As her equity team functioned in such a negative environment, a protective mechanism was to position the team as the ones who got it. But this meant that learning had stopped, that it became a space in which they couldn't help each other to learn more. Thus, Amelia ended up feeling very alone.

Morgan also recognized learning about white supremacy as a process, which helped her to be more pedagogical in how she approached friends and colleagues. Morgan shared a story in our last interview about a conversation with two friends, Laura, a white woman with whom she had long been friends, and Talia, her roommate, a woman of color with whom she had frequent conversations about race. She said:

> Laura made what would seem to anybody else a really racist comment about something along the lines of, "well, should I be expected to give up my privilege for other people? I don't understand; what am I supposed to do about this, be unhappy that I have it? . . . I don't get in other countries—how does this play out?" And Laura was really just trying to understand, but for Talia to hear that was like, "that was really a racist comment you just made and proof of your white privilege." But because [Laura] didn't understand white privilege, she didn't know that was her putting her privilege out there.

Morgan was able to mediate this conversation, she said, because of her time in RaceWork. She explained that what Laura was saying about privilege reinforced privilege itself but saw this also as an important pedagogical opportunity. She wanted to help Laura understand why Talia would hear what she was saying as evidence of her privilege. In other words, she used the conversation as an opportunity to raise consciousness. Morgan experienced herself stepping outside of this conversation and observing it as it happened:

> I could see that Laura didn't have enough background knowledge about what privilege actually is to be engaged in the discussion she was in. And Talia just naturally assumed that because [she] and I talk so freely about race and because Laura is my really good friend, that maybe she was on the same level that Talia and I were at. So Talia just had this natural assumption that Laura knew what privilege was.

In this moment, which almost devolved into an open and bitter conflict, Morgan recognized that Laura had not learned what Morgan had learned over the past several years. She was able to see both herself and Laura as in the process of learning. She positioned both as learners, but at different places in their learning and application. She could then take on the role of working with Laura as a learner, rather than expecting Talia to do that work.

She also took this stance with her co-workers, recognizing that Race-Work and other experiences meant that she viewed the world through a different lens. This recognition, based on conversations in RaceWork and those such as the one with Talia and Laura, helped her to understand

> how people treat you in your building, especially if they're not as comfortable talking about it as you are . . . That conversation helped me to realize people are at where they're at. And I can't force them, but I can certainly give them resources and let them decide where they want to go from there.

In other words, Morgan acknowledged that her process of "getting it" required her to take on a pedagogical stance with her friends and her colleagues. In conversation with her good friend Laura, she recognized that sometimes what comes across as resistance is a lack of understanding. Morgan acknowledged that she had been there, too. Just as she had changed, so could others. But she could not expect this to happen instantaneously; she recognized "how far my school has to go in even admitting that we have race related issues at our school." Thus, in her work in her building with other teachers, this and other conversations "really made me put the brakes on a little bit and not come in there like 'yeah! Let's do this!' 'Cause they're not at that point." On the first day of RaceWork, Morgan had named her personal goal as "getting to a recognition that schools are a white system set up for white students." Through RaceWork, she better understood her own process of coming to this understanding. Rather than exempting her from responsibility, Morgan recognized how we are all in the process of "getting it." She changed her approach to allow entry points for others who had not spent the time she had in thinking about white supremacy.

Angela perhaps exemplified this understanding of "getting it" as a process most concretely. She had joined RaceWork after years of conflict in her own building:

> . . . because of feeling frustrated and angry and upset because others didn't get it; they just don't get it. I remember last year I used that term all the time when I spoke with a colleague like, "oh my gosh, she doesn't get it," you know? And I thought, I don't want to be that person. I don't want to be that person who's continuously thinking and putting people into a box of "they don't get it." Because really that didn't feel good; it felt kind of arrogant.

Angela had this realization as she read an article in RaceWork. She knew that in her building, in addition to being an outspoken advocate for the needs of English learners, she was a broken record on race and racism. After a year in RaceWork, she knew she needed to approach her colleagues in a different way, rather than being continuously frustrated and angry. At the end of our 1st year, she wrote:

> Conversations that happen in the staff lounge are easier to participate in without all the internal frustration and anger boiling up (probably evident in body language as well) because I simply didn't understand how another person couldn't see what I saw. I am free of the need to criticize others for their lack of insight or understanding of a particular student or group and I can now just participate.

This was apparent to others in the group as well; for Sarah, "it felt a little bit like Angela had stopped at a certain point [in her understanding] and then the class was bringing her through in sort of a graceful way."

Angela came to a different approach to her work, partly through watching how other RaceWork teachers, such as Sarah, approached antiracism. Building on earlier comments about coming to understand that people are on different trajectories in terms of their own learning around race and racism, Angela brought a similar view to how she understood her relationship with the other teachers in RaceWork:

> I wasn't necessarily meeting with like-minded people. I was meeting with people who were all on their own journey, and I needed that. I desperately needed that in order to be able to tone down my own emotional reactions to that element of not getting it.

Angela's statement is important because, as white people, we spend a lot of time trying to figure out who "gets it" and who doesn't—slipping into a trap of being "racism police." But this assumes that there is a final destination, a way in which we can exempt ourselves from white supremacy, and that if we patrol carefully enough, we can stop it all. We can't. Instead, we can approach both ourselves and others pedagogically, teaching and learning in all our interactions. Or, as Morgan put it: "I don't think we'll ever get there 'cause I don't think there's a 'there' to get to."

Beyond the Politics of Language: For a Material Antiracism

RaceWork teachers developed their ability to read racially and to acknowledge—without being mired in guilt or shame—that they were complicit with "it" (white supremacy), but also that they could actively combat it in an ongoing process. After 2 years together, they understood this work more expansively than many common-sense notions or approaches. Frequently, we are hailed to think of antiracism as the ability and imperative to say the right thing at the right time, to not sound racist, to vocally demonstrate our understanding or our knowledge. Antiracism, in this stance, becomes mostly (or solely) about discourse, about the politics of language. Yet in this approach, to return to Leonardo's (2009) critique of No Child Left Behind and its waivers, talking about it (here, racialized disparities) or measuring it stands in for doing or changing. Of course, naming and talking are important, yet, in our learning together, RaceWork teachers ultimately critiqued this stance, despite its prevalence. It wasn't that language wasn't vitally important, but that language seemed to be, too often, all that anyone was being asked to change in order to make their practice function on the side of antiracism.

Charlie, for instance, asked us about the common racial equity program her district was engaging in. We asked what her thoughts on the program were. She replied: "Well, I've kind of had these conversations . . . then you

[said] that was the criticism; they set you up, but they don't really take you any further. And I was like 'all right,' and it just kind of clicked." For Charlie, what "clicked" was the history we learned in RaceWork, starting with our first meeting, and then her own work in figuring out its meaning for her classroom and school. There was so much, she said, that she didn't know. She *worked* to figure more out. Having the language was not enough; she had to apply that language, put it into practice. Nicole echoed this, stating that RaceWork was "a great and safe space to take theory and begin to mesh it, to bring it into practice. There are lots of statistics about teachers going to conferences or PD and how many of them will implement: zero." For Nicole, there was never any question about implementing after RaceWork—the implementation, at least in part, *was* the PD.

As white people, we have been trained to expect rewards for our "correct" antiracist language; we expect to be socially rewarded as the "good white person who gets it," who has been to the training or read a book. Sarah, for instance, critiquing Pete's interjection cited in Chapter 7, said, "this is the judge-y part of me, but when a grown man is professing like he wants a trophy, it's sort of like, 'dude, all right, great. It's not about that.'" Ultimately, rewards in terms of praise or certificates are hollow. Worse, they re-center whiteness, making what is important whether or not we as white people can pass some kind of political correctness test or prove that we've seen the movie or read the blog post or Twitter feed. Saying the right thing at the right time rarely changes racist structures for students and teachers. Instead, we need to focus on material actions. As Sarah said after several years of building restorative justice practices in her school, "I would say 90% of the people really are on the same [page]; they also want to know how to do it differently. . . . They can see that it's not working and that something has to fundamentally shift." Words and understanding are important, of course, but they must not substitute for action.

In some cases, words are not even as important as actions. What we are *doing* and who we *being* are most important in our attempts to enact "getting it." At the end of our 1st year together, Amelia said, "I still just don't know what to say sometimes." This is quite profound, particularly in light of the material antiracist changes Amelia enacted in her classroom and with the equity team. Despite not knowing what to say, Amelia likely influenced students for life, as changes to her grading system resulted in a challenge to a de facto racialized tracking system that impacted college admissions and placement for students of color. Amelia examined her grade books and saw that students of color, on average, had lower grades; upon closer examination, she discovered this was because they had lower scores on formative assessments, such as daily homework. But their grades on summative assessments, such as tests, showed they understood the concepts.

By simply changing the way in which she weighted formative and summative assessments, the grades of students of color in her chemistry class went up, enabling more of them to enroll in AP chemistry and resulting in the highest number of students of color enrolled in an AP course in school history.

Amelia's action of changing how she weighted assessments is a good example of how a small modification can make a big difference. Yet, in school contexts such as Amelia's, where significant building-wide attention is given to racialized discrepancies in discipline and honors enrollments, how one talks about race and racialized differences can feel like the most important thing of all, more important than doing or being with and for students. Even further, this imperative produces a kind of performance that is only relevant for teachers with and for one another. In today's social justice vernacular, we could think of this felt need to say the correct thing as the white teacher equivalent of performing "woke"—saying the right words so as to demonstrate to anyone listening that the speaker understands the justice implications of what they are talking about and is being especially inclusive in their discourse. But such a reality can mean teachers devote more time to how to talk to their colleagues about race and white supremacy than they do to actually shifting practices or policies in their classrooms and schools.

Certainly, developing racial literacy that gives us lenses to see "it" in words and actions is necessary to dismantle this oppressive system. And yet, being able to name it is not enough. Further, we cannot think that we, particularly as white people, are ever finished "getting it." As white people, our pedagogical responsibility is to work with others, both white folks and people of color, to name it *and* to enact material changes to counter it. In the image theatre activity during our first semester together, one group stated that their body-based sculpture attempted to show that there were multiple ways to address white supremacy—under, over, through—but that the path was not always the same or that, even when we perceive resistances, we don't necessarily know how to work with or to break them. Indeed, Zac responded, different forms of oppression have different latches on us. These are hard struggles; we may feel isolated or not even know what we are struggling against. But naming these struggles, even if we don't have a full or complete picture of them, can be a critical part of our anti-oppressive praxis. Most critically, though, it is only part of such engagement. For RaceWork teachers, part of "getting it" meant that those who were concerned only about saying the right thing, even if it was the most inclusive possibility in English, were missing a vital part of their engagement. If one can be unsure of what to say, and yet act in ways that produce antiracist outcomes, such as Amelia's shifts in assessment policies with actual material consequences, then knowing what to say cannot be a prerequisite or even a requirement for engaging in antiracist work.

THE WORK

CHAPTER 9

Approaches and Beliefs

Ladson-Billings insisted that culturally relevant pedagogy is not something one does, but rather something one *is*. We do not *do* critical pedagogy; we *are* critical in our engagement with the word and the world. In this way, Ladson-Billings (2006b) argued that " 'doing' is less important than 'being' . . . Practicing culturally relevant pedagogy is one of the ways of 'being' that will inform ways of 'doing' " (p. 41). An emphasis on being, then, does not leave questions of doing by the wayside. In other words, we are not arguing for a directionless antiracism, nor that teachers should never consider what we are *doing* in the classroom.

Ever since Charlie named the "checklist" problem—teachers' desires for explicit instructions on "what to do"—we have worked to understand what produces and sustains this desire. One sophisticated explanation is Ladson-Billings's (2006b) assertion that we cannot tell someone what to do because they would then do it without full attention to context. In another, Fecho (2004) explained this as the difference between "adapting" and "adopting" curriculum or pedagogical strategies. He argued that far too often schools attempt to *adopt* programs from elsewhere, when what is needed is to *adapt* an initiative or program to the lived realities of their school and classroom contexts.

Teachers want the checklist, but there isn't one. However, this does not mean that there isn't anything the teachers in RaceWork can teach us about "what to do." We've called these lessons "Approaches and Beliefs" because they capture the ways RaceWork teachers came to articulate their own answers to questions of what to do and who to be with and for their students and colleagues. Previous chapters have detailed the ways that teachers in RaceWork were challenged in their buildings, both by other teachers and by structural forces that limited what was possible. Through these struggles, the teachers in RaceWork came to articulate ways of persisting in their antiracist convictions and actions, of enacting antiracism through both doing and being. In this chapter, we work through examples of how RaceWork teachers conceptualized "being" antiracist and the actions—the *doing*—that followed: the ways that RaceWork teachers were continually "moving in," in Sarah's words, in their antiracist work. We explore how RaceWork teachers resisted their and their colleagues' desires for the simplicity of checklists and strategies; this requires pedagogies of complexity based in each teacher's own antiracist approaches and beliefs. As there isn't "one way to do it," we provide examples from each RaceWork teacher.

Desiring and Resisting the Simplicity of Checklists and Strategies

"Teachers want the checklist," the 10 of us reminded each other regularly. This cannot be isolated from the contexts of public education in the United States today. Teachers throughout the United States feel increasingly surveilled in their classrooms, and the very real conditions of many buildings produce requirements for all classroom activities to be "research based" or enacted verbatim following a script or pseudo-scripted curriculum (Crocco & Costigan; 2007; Sleeter, 2008). The idea that teachers could devise their own materials and practices, based on the needs and demands of their subject area and the students with whom they work, is seemingly foreclosed more and more. Thus, when teachers are confronted with more open curricular or pedagogical approaches, we should not be surprised if they resist, as they have been encultured otherwise in their school contexts.

A structural logic in many schools that argues for concepts such as scripted curriculum because so many teachers are new and undercertified is a formidable block to implementing much of the work RaceWork teachers took up in their classrooms. Calling on such public education contexts, Amelia framed the teacher desire for strategies as a response to potential questions: "If somebody asks me, I can say, 'yes, I'm doing it, and here's my proof.'" Amelia theorized that teachers needed a citation for whatever practices they were taking up: They needed a name for what they were doing, something someone else could look up and verify. The pressures for this kind of teaching practice are real, and desires for strategies will likely accelerate at pace with increases in scripting and premade lessons.

We saw this play out when RaceWork teachers worked with their colleagues to address white supremacy. For instance, Amelia and Shannon had this exchange:

AMELIA: A couple people on our Eteam are strategies-focused, and it bugs the heck out of them that we can't come up with— they want to see the Eteam as just strategies and we keep . . .

SHANNON: Strategies for what?

AMELIA: Strategies for classroom management, strategies for, I'd say mostly this year just classroom management.

Charlie had a similar experience in her school with an equity facilitator:

She's come and observed and wanted to try new things with the class, and they're more strategy based, which is great. But at the same time, you know, they're saying this is equitable practice, but it doesn't really explain . . . Equitable or equity is just this buzzword that's being tossed around. . . . They weren't explaining the inequities . . . [and] to make something equitable you have to understand why it was inequitable to begin with.

In this example, while Charlie began by affirming the strategies-focused approach of the facilitator, she was also critical of the ways that work being called "equitable" fell victim to becoming yet another "buzzword" in education, akin to "multicultural" (Casey, 2010); she felt unable to critique the strategies the facilitator was suggesting. While what she found in other PD made sense, "in the back of [her] mind," Charlie was also thinking, "OK, it's not this step process." Similarly, Amelia was critical of those on her equity team who were narrowly focused on strategies, insisting, as in the above example, that concrete classroom management practices were what was needed to address structural racism in their school.

At the same time, Amelia, Charlie, and other RaceWork teachers simultaneously wished we could have reached more solutions in RaceWork. Amelia recognized she was not alone in this dual desire: "I felt like every other teacher [in RaceWork] was struggling with the same things. And that is some comfort—that it's not just me and my kids in my class. But it just felt like nobody had any solutions." Or as Charlie reminded us: "Teachers want things to do, you know; they need something tangible that you can really put toward your classroom."

Thinking through this conundrum, it is important to distinguish between a desire for examples of practices and materials that can be adapted in one's own contexts and a desire for a step-by-step guide. The latter is actually a demand for simplicity; further, step-by-step solutions call for finality and universality. Thinking there are known and easy strategies (e.g., for classroom management) capable of overcoming structural oppressions is yet another example of liberal individualist reductionism. It is a concrete example of desiring simplicity in ways that undermine the sophisticated work of combatting oppression. In the example above, Charlie critiqued such a steps-based approach. She understood that following protocols often leaves little room for understanding things beyond the particular protocol. In other words, what we aren't looking for, we often do not see.

Instead of the step-by-step strategy or protocol, antiracist approaches can come in the form of examples to adapt to meet one's particular needs. While this can be "something tangible," it does not (necessarily) mean something easy. RaceWork provided such examples. As Morgan explained: "To know how other people are approaching these issues in their setting is just invaluable. You don't have to try to reinvent the wheel when you already know it's working for someone else." Morgan took insights gleaned from others in RaceWork and applied them to her own context, most notably in her work to create the first equity team in her district. Her description is rich with contextualizing features: She called attention to others' "settings" and signaled that it was the "approaches" of others that she could take the most from. An approach is not a step-by-step listing, but a description of how to frame engagement.

This means that each teacher, in each context, will have to *work* at antiracism, and that it will take time. Morgan articulated this in her approach to PD that she led in her building. She explained one particular session, where the other teachers

> were all kinda in the same place to talk about their frustrations. And I wanted to give that, let that be valid, to be like "yeah, this is super frustrating that there's not just xyz." It just seemed more important that they kinda grappled with it, without me jumping in right away and saying "well, I've read this and yadda yadda and all that."

Morgan recognized that it could take time for others to understand why there could not be "just xyz" approaches to antiracism in their building. She let those frustrations "be valid" in order for her co-workers/learners to wrestle in their own ways with why this was so. This reflected her own experiences in coming to understand that prescriptive approaches often backfire when they are not adapted to their new context. Put simply: Antiracist approaches demand teacher autonomy. It was not enough to simply explain this; rather, Morgan wanted her co-workers to understand this for themselves. Her pedagogical approach thus offered a rebuttal to the seeming lack of strategies being put forward: She was modeling an approach; her *being* was taking care of the doing.

Such an approach cannot simply be uttered, however, but must be experienced and practiced. As facilitators of RaceWork, we aimed to model the kinds of pedagogies we hoped white teachers would adapt and reinvent for their own contexts. While we can never fully know if we realized this aim, Amelia explained the impact it had on her, saying, "there wasn't like one thing each session; there wasn't like, 'today we're going to talk about this and then at the end of the day you're going to be able to do this in your classroom.' " We never wrote a student learning objective on the board. We did not follow scripts or lessons or use suggested discussion questions for any of the texts or concepts we took up. More importantly, we made adjustments every session (both within and between) to respond to what teachers identified as areas they wanted to engage. Indeed, the entire 2nd year was made up of problem-posing identifications as we went: We decided what we would do month to month to respond to what the teachers wanted to engage more deeply. By never pretending to have checklists or strategies, we were modeling that antiracism work is possible premised on commitments to a tripartite—the personal, local, and structural—understanding of oppression coupled with humanizing pedagogies.

Pedagogies of Complexity: Why There Isn't "One Way to Do It"

Complexity was a recurring theme, especially in our 2nd year together and in our final interviews, with teachers describing nuanced and multiplicious considerations for why they engaged antiracism in their local contexts in the ways they did. There was no one shared way to enact antiracism; each RaceWork teacher's approach was supported by her own beliefs and contexts. In what follows we focus on the complexities of the pedagogical work teachers took on between RaceWork sessions. As demonstrated in these examples, these teachers are *being* pedagogical with their students and colleagues and in their curriculum, yet the realities of contexts (including who each teacher is as a person) led them to approach antiracist work in far-different ways.

Over the time we worked together, Morgan shared stories about how she'd helped her friends and parents trouble their racialized understandings and engage more seriously with what she had been working on at her school. While Morgan, when asked, responded she did not feel she was intentionally teaching her friends and family, she was "glad that we're all in the conversation together about it." Morgan's approach to teaching social justice in her 5th-grade classroom had a similar tenor:

> I don't even feel like I'm necessarily teaching it to my kids. I'm just trying to be real with them about, "this is how things are going on in our world right now. Let's talk about it." And a lot of times I'll just pose a question and let them kinda talk amongst each other. Like this afternoon we were reading an article about the [Boston] Marathon bomber who just got sentenced to death. So we're going to read an article about it and then just let them talk about well, should we have the death penalty? You know, I'm just gonna kinda give them a background, then let them kinda come to their own conclusions about it.

She described her approach to a lesson on the death penalty and domestic terrorism as stemming from wanting to "be real" with her students and giving them space to "talk about it," first providing them with context and direction. Her approach was supported by the ways she took up texts throughout her curriculum: She embraced the practice of asking her students to think about the authors of the texts they read and what kinds of biases or perspectives might be present. While her description might sound like a kind of free-for-all, when we observed her classroom, students were deeply engaged and serious in their approaches to the questions Morgan asked them. She articulated what she wanted her students to be able to do and created spaces for them to do it. In this approach, Morgan allowed her ways of being to take care of the doing.

In some ways, this was easier with her students than with her colleagues. Morgan sometimes found herself feeling that her 5th-graders were more willing and able to engage in deep critical analysis, particularly around race, than her co-workers were. Working with her colleagues to address antiracism was frequently not easy.

> I found myself being frustrated at times. I'm like, "why aren't you getting this?" And I had to [say to myself], "okay, two, three years ago, this is exactly where I was and exactly what I was thinking too." And so I had to bite my tongue and let them have a conversation and not let myself dominate it or correct things like that because I wanted them to kinda get out what they were thinking. But then they also knew that I had been doing all of this work, and they know I'm gonna be our district's equity person, and I didn't also want them to think that I have all the answers either. 'Cause that's what they

were kinda looking at me for, like "what would you do in this situation?" And I'm like, "I don't know these families, these kids; I don't know for sure if this would help or not." And so I'm hoping that through whatever our district does with this equity team will give us some tools, not to solve other people's problems, but to help them through them. But it kinda seemed like, "okay, I'm not getting the answers from the books. What can you tell me the answer is?" And I'm like, "I don't know the answers either."

While it wasn't as easy, Morgan's approach with her co-workers echoed her pedagogical stance with her 5th-graders. When she caught herself positioning her co-workers through a deficit frame, she reoriented her approach to thinking about her own trajectory, understandings, and experiences of learning about race and racism, particularly in the years before RaceWork. Her approach to work with her colleagues and her aims for the equity team was "not to solve other people's problems, but to help them through them." Once again, Morgan centered an approach that placed who she was *being* with and for others ahead of what she was doing. She did not have all of the answers, but she did have ways of orienting and understanding that could support others to engage their world in critical ways and together work toward more humanizing learning.

While also focusing on relationships, Lisa's approach to antiracist practice was entirely different from Morgan's. She began, in our 1st year together, with trying to build relationships with students and their families. Lisa's work to know her students and their families as whole and complex people taught her a lot about the ways that structural oppressions negatively shaped and determined aspects of her students' lives. RaceWork helped her understand how her own race could affect her work with students. She explained her approach in the following way:

> I think about, you know, some of the places that [students'] hurt could come from, and it helped me to remember to back off. Because the hurt could be coming from, not me in particular, but somebody who looked like me—somebody who was, you know, a white lady who treated them poorly or who said something that gave them some kind of mental hurt that they're now projecting onto me. And so [I have been] trying to be as conscious of what I could possibly represent while still trying to maintain their dignity.

Lisa was theorizing citational oppressions: the idea that an act or discourse is oppressive if it cites past oppressions (Kumashiro, 2002). Being a "white lady," for Lisa, might represent a past racial violence, or "hurt," that got in the way of fully connecting with her students. She wanted students to "maintain their dignity" and work through their hurt with her support.

By the time of our final interviews, these new understandings had propelled Lisa to shift the focus of her work from relationships with students and their families to what those new relationships meant for her curriculum—in other words, focusing on using connections (relationships) to help students engage more fully in her course material, French. As she said, students "have to see themselves in my curriculum, and if they don't see themselves, if all they see is me in the curriculum, they're never going to connect to me or the curriculum." To accomplish her aims for shifting her curriculum, she had been working to include far more stories and videos from Africa, Asia, and the Caribbean instead of the traditional European French curriculum that had long been in place in her school. Her notion of "only seeing me" in the curriculum is part of how we can understand the connections that Lisa saw between her early work to have more humanizing relationships with her students and their families and her eventual work to realize those connections in her curriculum. It simply was not enough, for Lisa, to have strong relationships if those relationships were not part of growing engagement and student learning. The point, after all, is not only to have positive relationships with students, but to support their learning. In developing and enacting this understanding, the ways in which Lisa described both herself and her students as well as their relationships with curriculum also grew in complexity.

For Charlie, RaceWork also offered new ways of articulating what she was aiming for in her antiracist work in her building. She told us: "I can be a little more up front about what's really going on [in] the system and why it's so inequitable." This is a skillset. Teachers can grow in their abilities to name and speak powerfully if given resources and opportunities to do so. Those abilities, however, must be directed toward material antiracist pursuits. For Charlie, this led to conducting, and later becoming a trainer for, home visits, as described in Chapter 5. Charlie used home (or home-adjacent) visits to make robust connections between her students' home lives and the classroom. Any location in the student's neighborhood, whether a home, a park bench, or a restaurant, could be a site for learning about students and their families.

Charlie applied her understandings of both students' families and historical inequalities in powerful and sophisticated ways to the work of her classroom:

> The whole equality versus equity thing: you're not going to treat every kid the same because of differences in what they

need from you. I just want to make sure that I'm not doing the expectation game, like "oh, you know, this kid might need a little extra support so I'm going to expect less from him," but [instead] making sure the expectations stay level. And that's something that I'm still—I need to keep fresh in my mind that like, he does need a little extra help for this kid, but expecting the same quality of work. But again . . . part of it is that you might have to switch it from year to year. It's not always going to work for every kid and every classroom.

Charlie affirmed the Kumashiroan (2009) conviction that "No practice is always anti-oppressive" (p. 3). She saw potential ways her responses to struggling students could reinforce oppression, but she also understood herself as needing to constantly balance those risks with specificity and reflexivity in her current work with a student. For Charlie, antiracism wasn't about spending equal time with each student, or having every student working on the same assignment at the same time. Instead, it was about responding in context to unique student needs and ensuring the quality of their work was high. She knew she would need to adapt her own practices and past successes, because "it's not always going to work for every kid and every classroom." In this way, Charlie maintained an intellectually rigorous, anti-oppressive critical pedagogical approach in her classroom. At the same time, for Charlie, there was room in any given classroom to exceed the bounds of what was hegemonically thought possible: room for unpredictability, chaos, and joy that no script or set of stages or strategies could ever fully account for. This reality creates the intellectual work of the pedagogue: the need to adapt and account for the complexities at play in classroom spaces in real time.

Sarah also developed abilities to critically name how disciplinary structures within her school functioned to the detriment of students of color and to adapt practices that were not working. As Dean of students, she began what was to be expanding types of restorative practices. At the end of the 1st year of RaceWork, she told us:

> This idea of restorative measures between teachers and kids: we're gonna track reoccurrences with certain teachers, like how . . . can we decrease the occurrences and compare that data to last year. And it's all subjective. I mean, it's different kids but same teachers, so we'll see.

Mediating conflicts between teachers and students worked so well that the school expanded the practice to not only teacher–student conflicts, but student–student conflicts. A year later, she gave us an update:

> So, this year our referral rate dropped by 150 referrals, which is huge, and I feel like a big part of that was the mediations that we did. So when there was a conflict, we'd be like, "look, here's the deal." We wouldn't ever make [students do this], we'd be like, "you have the option." But nine times out of 10, kids wanted to mediate. They don't want the conflict, you know? They don't want to walk around feeling like, "what's gonna happen?" So they would mediate. And literally we tracked it and there were hardly any, I mean there were some repeats of the same two kids, but hardly ever did the same two kids have another issue.

Sarah's adaptation and reinvention of restorative justice approaches and mediating dropped referrals by more than half in her building. Students spent more time where they were meant to be: in their classrooms.

But dropping referral rates, on its own, is not automatically antiracist. If the decline is produced by lowering expectations for engagement, it is actually perpetuating structural oppression. Sarah was conscious of this risk and approached her role from a pedagogical stance centered on supporting students in developing the skills needed to succeed and stay engaged in their classes. She was thus especially critical of discipline measures where students were removed from class, then sent back without any intervention other than the punishment of being kicked out of class. She questioned:

> Who's teaching them anything? I mean clearly, they're doing things because they're missing some understanding. They don't know how to cope, and we're just kicking them out and then upon reentry, there's nothing, there's no meeting, there's no conversation. This is how we look at it. So [instead] we're teaching them; we're trying to reframe the whole discipline system as teaching. We're teaching them a skill, just like we're teaching them anything else in your subject matter. This is what we're teaching, so we're going to have to teach it over and over and over for some kids.

What does it mean to think of student discipline as just like teaching anything else in a subject matter? For Sarah, this pedagogical orientation reframed notions of "bad behavior" as a fixed trait and became an instance where a teacher's skills at differentiating could be put to use to provide additional support for a student in areas of behavior.

Looking at referral data, she saw that the same students were often sent out of their classrooms for the same types of behaviors: "disrespect or disruption or fighting." Noticing this, the staff could identify "what skill needs to be addressed. And then we pulled a bunch of resources for each skill, so we've got a stock of these worksheets on social and emotional skills to pull out and work with kids when they come in." In other words, they created a curriculum to build skills to address repeated behaviors that get students sent out of the classroom. Using this curriculum went beyond a more abstracted punishment logic, in which a student's very presence in the office is (part of) the punishment for whatever behavior got them sent out of the room, which is supposed to automatically teach the student not to repeat the behavior. But how can we assume this automaticity? For Sarah, such assumptions were why it felt as if the same students got into trouble over and over with the same teachers for the same types of behavior. She reframed this as a pedagogical opening: a space where she could actually work to teach students about how they could learn for themselves more about what they could do to stay engaged in class. And, she knew that they might "have to teach it over and over and over." Yet this approach gave room to respond to discipline in ways that were contextual and premised on learning as what is most important, not on punishment for its own sake.

Sarah connected this to work we took up together in RaceWork on Jansen's (2009) conception of brokenness: "the idea that in our human state we are prone to failure and incompletion, and that as imperfect humans we constantly seek a higher order of living. Brokenness is the realization of imperfection" (p. 269). She put it this way:

> So this idea of vulnerability and brokenness and meeting people at the most human level is something that, it's like constantly—it struck a chord. I didn't realize it would be as impactful. But it's kind of the driving—if I can remember that kind of idea, this is where all this shit breaks down, it's so powerful and impactful. It moves things along, you know? . . . [RaceWork] gave all of us a place to be . . . vulnerable and broken about what our experiences have been, and how things aren't working, and what are we doing, and are we perpetuating things ourselves, you know? It's just a mess of things, so it was a place to feel like you could actually start taking steps.

Jansen's "postconflict pedagogy" centered on the "recognition of likeness" as foundational to building solidarities across difference. He offered a way of reframing deficit-steeped notions for why white people should be invested in antiracist work: not because we feel bad for people of color and our pity drives us to do something to ameliorate it, but because our own humanity is degraded and dehumanized through our experiences in an oppressive social order that brings us into a shared solidarity that can work across difference for justice. Sarah rearticulated this notion for her own work as a way of centering the humanity of those she worked with. Rather than responding to students sent to the Dean's office for behavior as problem students, Sarah's commitments to centering brokenness and vulnerability helped her focus on the skill-building approach that animated her pedagogy as Dean.

Veronica also drew on a concept RaceWork had introduced to help frame her approach to building more antiracist curriculum in her high school. She summed up part of her new approach to world history courses as follows:

> We like to paint certain people to be really evil and certain people really good, but maybe it's not quite that simple. The idea of troubling knowledge, I think from Kumashiro, is the idea that if you don't make the information a little bit harder to grasp, then they're just gonna go on believing everything, so questioning everything is huge.

Troubling knowledge is both a verb and a noun for Kumashiro (2009)—and for Veronica. She wanted her students to engage with work that troubled taken-for-granted assumptions about good and evil and resulted in an intellectual hunger to "question everything." Veronica connected this to her antiracist work in terms of needing to be critical of ways that even initiatives based in good intentions could have oppressive outcomes for students of color.

Veronica said the most important thing she learned in RaceWork was that "you don't have to be a hero to make a difference. I think that's key." Previously, Veronica had seen herself as having been raised in a too-conservative home and school environment to ever be regarded as an expert on social justice teaching. Yet, by the end of our time working together, that's precisely what she had become in her building. And while she didn't feel fully comfortable in that role, she had come to understand she was capable of filling it. She didn't have to "be a hero," but she could "make a difference." Veronica explained her approach:

> But you keep working on stuff, and you keep getting a little bit better and a little bit better. And if you make life better for one kid and one class and you can have real learning in that one class, then it can have an impact.

She saw that teachers could engage students in understanding white supremacy through curricular interventions and anti-oppressive pedagogies and have an impact on students and on their learning. Veronica connected her antiracist commitments to the discipline of social studies in powerful ways and, in so doing, engaged both her students and her co-workers in dialogic pedagogies that worked to trouble knowledge on the side of social justice.

Angela also engaged a dialogic approach to antiracist work with both her students and her colleagues. She had always done so with students, responding to them in real time, based on their interests and work. She knew that she needed to respond "at their appropriate level" when issues of racial injustice arose. For Angela, "a fear of being honest with students has never kept me from doing it." Angela's need to engage racial oppressions was deeply wedded to her sense of what her students deserved and what her responsibilities were to them as their teacher. If she didn't engage questions of justice and equity with her students, if she wasn't "honest" with them, she was "denying" them aspects of their education. Such convictions were also present in her approach to working with colleagues. Part of why Angela was seen as a "broken record" in her building was because of these commitments to being honest, in spite of whatever fears might circulate about the ramifications of naming racial violence at her school. Angela joked with us, saying, "it's hard work teaching, but I also feel that teaching white people about race is as equally difficult as anything." Angela's sense of white antiracism as a process reinforced for her that work on the side of justice was possible from social actors who lacked fully realized or articulated antiracist identities. Even if the work was "equally difficult as anything," it remained inherently possible. Angela's deep concern and respect for her EL students and for her own children of color grounded this work.

Like Angela, Amelia had conflicts with other teachers in her building and was exasperated with their resistance to equity-centered work—as well as their frequent request for "strategies." She flatly told her entire staff in an equity-team-led PD session in her school: "We don't have strategies to give." Yet in telling this story in an interview, she rhetorically nuanced her statement, saying, "the strategy is love your kids. The strategy is really just: love your kids. These are our kids, and we keep talking about them like they aren't. They're in our classrooms; love your kids." Amelia was disturbed by how often other teachers distanced themselves from students, as if they weren't part of the same school community; teachers (both white and of color) rhetorically othered these high school students, calling attention to their own lack of relationship with students. For Amelia, these discoursal moves of talking about students as if they weren't "our kids" meant that other teachers did not seem to focus on their *actual* students. This functioned to deny the students' humanity. She recognized that without a focus on who our students are as people (not their demographic information in a vacuum), any efforts at establishing relationships can be surface-level at best. Thus, "love your kids" can replace "strategies" only if teachers actually know who their students are: their dreams, their habits, their hopes, and so on. When teachers ask for strategies, then, based on Amelia's understanding of such requests, they are asking for ways to not be as invested in who their students are as people. If they know who their students are, and love them for it, the need for "strategies" disappears.

This is not at all to discount Amelia's antiracist strategy of love. Instead, the love Amelia referred to should be thought of in the Freirean (2006) sense, as an "armed love" that equips teachers to fight on the side of their students to create more humanizing conditions within and beyond classrooms. "Love your kids" articulates an approach to work with students, even if it seems overly abstract or decoupled from material practices. Think, for instance, if a teacher's approach to a particular moment in the classroom was always first filtered through the frame of "because I love this student, I'll . . ." This is not a prescription for a particular practice, but rather a reflective engagement in practice that can support anti-oppressive work with students. Indeed, we saw how such an "armed love" equipped Amelia to challenge her school's grading practices and the ways in which her equity team got stuck over and over. This "armed love" also radically shifted the powerful ways in which Amelia articulated herself as a pedagogue.

Nicole has been less present in the pages of this book than have the other RaceWork teachers. Yet it is fitting that we close this chapter with her words, for two reasons. First, Nicole's thinking about teaching often bowled all of us over. Second, she exemplified engagement, community, and commitment. Nicole felt that RaceWork was unlike any other professional space she'd been in. Nicole appreciated "hearing everybody's stories and examples and then I felt like I could contribute to brainstorming on a solution, and for the first time felt like concretely dealing with something that seemed really big and untouchable before." For Nicole, the regular check-ins (storysharing) at the beginning of our sessions functioned as a space where she could "contribute" in ways that represented the first time she felt she was doing work that functioned against structural oppression. Those experiences in RaceWork taught Nicole a powerful lesson about how teachers working with other teachers across buildings and districts could have an impact in ways that would be impossible were they working in isolation.

In our RaceWork sessions, Nicole's contributions included a knack for articulating what we were going after, particularly pedagogically, that created "aha!" moments, resonating in ways that helped us reach group understandings. Over and over, Nicole connected what we were reading to classroom practices and to student needs. After reading Baldwin's (1963) "A Talk to Teachers," for instance, Nicole connected his ideas to our local community, specifically how transportation infrastructure had literally been built on the homes of communities of color. As Baldwin said, society wants citizens who will obey its rules, yet active oppression exists; it is teachers' responsibility to change this, making us as teachers at war with society. This is a tall order, but Nicole continually reminded us it was possible:

> You can do the right work in spite of [conflict], of where you are. . . . Global, personal, or local, if you can start . . . you can just be working with your students and then move out as opportunities present . . . to learn and grow. . . . There are like-minded folks, and there are people and groups out there.

Acknowledging that not everyone had access to "a RaceWork," she said there are reading groups, book clubs, and activist groups that can be "refreshing and healthy and empowering." Nicole reminded us that in spaces like RaceWork we could gather together and be energized for the work.

Being energized to continue the work is important in light of Morgan's comment, shared first in Chapter 8: "I don't think we'll ever get there 'cause I don't think there's a there to get to." This is why when the teachers all asked if we could continue RaceWork for a 2nd year, we did: We weren't finished. Then again, after the 2nd year, we *still* weren't finished (e.g., see Mason, 2016). Being able to observe and interview everyone a year after our last session, we saw that the teachers in RaceWork remain unfinished in their understandings, but also unfinished in their work on the side of antiracism. Every teacher remained engaged in antiracist work a year after RaceWork. Most, in fact, had taken on even more leadership roles in their buildings and districts. As facilitators, we do not take credit for this, but rather are heartened by the example these teachers offer both for us and for others: of possibilities for ever greater transformation on the side of justice and an expansion of who we conceptualize as capable of shaping and leading antiracist interventions.

CHAPTER 10

For the Future of Antiracist Work with Practicing Teachers
From Professional Development to Critical Teacher Learning

RaceWork grew out of our frustrations and commitments. We were frustrated by one-size-fits-all, often mandatory professional development demanding allegiance to particular understandings of race and racism (e.g., a focus on white privilege that frequently leaves little room for more radical analyses of white supremacy). We were frustrated by limited understandings of the work of schools that focus on student achievement measured by narrow metrics, especially on content knowledge as measured by standardized tests. We were frustrated by a lack of spaces for teachers to study deeply and work together to enact antiracist commitments. In short, we were frustrated by how our work as teachers is conceptualized in narrow, technocratic, dehumanizing ways.

Amid these frustrations, we were committed to teacher education and professional development in which content and pedagogy aligned and that was tailored to the needs of teacher-learners. We were committed to working *with* teachers to self-appropriate knowledge and understanding, rather than asking for adherence to prescribed ideas. We were committed to putting ourselves in solidarity with teachers through telling our own stories and sharing our own stuckness, inadequacies, and fears—as well as our break-throughs and successes. We were committed to theory *and* practice. In particular, we were committed to using theory to help teachers explore their own stories and to contextualize the ways their experiences are always situated within structural racial hierarchies. We were committed, as critical pedagogues, to not positioning all white teachers as unthinkingly ignorant, avoidant, or evasive of race and white supremacy, or as Lowenstein (2009) put it: as deficient learners about diversity. We were committed to what has since been called "second-wave whiteness studies" (Jupp, Berry, & Lensmire, 2016). All of this was based on our commitment to an analysis of whiteness as grounded in structural white supremacy (to interdisciplinary critical whiteness studies).

Our collaboration with RaceWork teachers more than affirmed these commitments. These teachers—as well as ourselves—changed personally and professionally; they affected the lives of their colleagues and students in profound ways that could never be captured on a quantitative metric. After our 1st year together, Morgan wrote:

> I am able to be a leader for my school in starting a discussion about race and . . . am no longer concerned that I will upset or ruffle feathers. . . . I am able to be much more honest with what I am observing in my school, classroom, and in myself. . . . Now that fear is gone and in its place is a need to confront what I am seeing and start to discuss ways to change it and myself. I am okay with admitting that I have work that I need to do.

Years later, all of us know our work is still ongoing. We also know that it won't be easy.

We return over and over to the profound wisdom of RaceWork teachers and the ways they internalized RaceWork's tripartite model to work at the personal, local, and structural levels. After a brief look at the genre of professional development, in this final chapter we explore our thoughts on RaceWork as the practice of professional learning that shifted perspectives, centered collaborative relationships, and involved local contexts, as ongoing teacher education, and as paradox. While in many ways, RaceWork was "successful," we argue that this success is hyper-contextualized, that we cannot scale such a model, but must zoom in and reinvent it over and over in different contexts.

Experiencing RaceWork:
Professional Learning Practice

In RaceWork, we specially designed an emergent, yet intentionally sequenced, curriculum based on both the lived experiences of teachers and on sophisticated theoretical and historical work that did not simplify or call upon stereotyped tropes of race or whiteness. Beginning with a nuanced historical and cultural exploration of white racial identities and meanings in a society beset with structural racism (e.g., Roediger, 2007; Thandeka, 2006), we offered space and language for teachers to reflect on historical, institutional, and structural racism and the roles schools and teachers play in both perpetuating and combating white supremacy so that we could work collectively to support each other as RaceWork teachers incorporated and embedded reflexive, antiracist practices and curricula in their classrooms and schools. We engaged white teachers in the terribly difficult, always unfinished work of contesting white supremacy in their classrooms and schools, informed by their own research into their lives as white people, as antiracist agents in their classrooms, and as teachers committed to young people and to more equitable school experiences for all students and particularly those most marginalized.

Rather than step-by-step instructions, RaceWork created space for reflection—and for experiences in talking and thinking from an antiracist stance. Nicole thus explained that after RaceWork, "everything is different, and it's all because of just having an awareness that I didn't have before, so I'm very grateful." RaceWork offered her ways of analyzing and reading things in her school and classroom that she had struggled to name. She called what she gained from RaceWork "awareness," which can be read as constructing the "difference" she now saw in her world. Seeing race everywhere, as multiple teachers in RaceWork said they now did, resulted from time devoted to *explicit* exploration of race and racism. Too often, as educators, we forget that experience can be educative only if we *have* experience(s): If we do not create experiences talking at length about race and racism, for instance, we should not be surprised when we find it difficult to talk about white supremacy and structural oppressions. These experiences, these moments to "practice" as Morgan called them, produced opportunities for RaceWork teachers to rehearse critical ways of *being* in the context of white antiracism, ways of being that would help them resist anti-intellectual pressures for scaling and best practices that limit possibilities for material antiracism in schools and classrooms.

But of course there's more to RaceWork than providing experiences. As we've seen in previous chapters, Veronica regularly contrasted Race-Work with SEED:

> I would say SEED is more geared towards having experiences as opposed to changing things to a certain extent. They never really get into the problems within the school as much as problems, like, broader. So I think that taking everyday steps, trying to improve things bit by bit, that's what's actually going to make a change rather than doing a one-time, one-size-fits-all project to try to solve a massive issue.

In framing the notion of "experience," Veronica hinted at the role of the tripartite approach to antiracism at the center of RaceWork. She saw SEED as falling into the trap of constructing only two levels for antiracist engagement: the personal (having "moments") and the structural ("broader" problems). But for Veronica, "everyday steps" and working "bit by bit" are ultimately more transformative: practices that happen at the level of the local. Importantly, these steps were not prescriptive, but needed to be developed in the moment, drawing on the lives of actual students and teachers.

As mentioned in Chapter 2, the model we created in RaceWork stands in contrast to much of the PD now taking place, which is "increasingly technocratic, top-down" (Kohli, Picower, Martinez, & Ortiz, 2015, p. 7) and most often involves short-term workshops, which tend to be least effective (e.g., see Gulamhussein, 2013; Wei, Darling-Hammond, & Adamson, 2010). Review studies have pointed out the ineffectiveness of much of the PD that is happening now (e.g., Gulamhussein, 2013; Kennedy, 2016; Wei et al., 2010). For instance, PD is often not undertaken with an emphasis on what motivates teachers and how they learn, focusing instead on particular design features or exclusively on content knowledge (e.g., Kennedy, 2016). Even worse, PD is often not intellectually engaging (e.g., Kennedy, 2016) or misaligns content and pedagogy (e.g., see Wilson & Berne, 1999). There tends to be little support for applying PD learning within teachers' work contexts, which makes any learning that does take place feel irrelevant. Further, as PD is often mandatory, it can be less meaningful for teachers: "Mandated PD creates a problem for PD developers, which is analogous to the problem teachers face: *Attendance is mandatory but learning is not*" (Kennedy, 2016, p. 973, emphasis in original). To put it bluntly, "Each year, schools, districts, and the federal government spend millions, if not billions, of dollars on in-service seminars and other forms of professional development that are fragmented, intellectually superficial, and do not take into account what we know about how teachers learn" (Borko, 2004, p. 3).

While we agree with many overarching findings of these reviews, we also disagree with many of their conclusions and recommendations. Most often, teacher PD—and much of the research on it—is situated firmly within our current era of accountability. Accordingly, even much of the literature that comes to similar conclusions as we have does so within the context of experimental conditions, a focus on content knowledge, or links to student achievement measures (e.g., Desimone, 2009; Kennedy, 2016; Wei et al., 2010). A focus on measurement and design is ontologically and epistemologically misaligned with what we believe is needed for white teachers to study and enact antiracism in their classrooms and schools. Indeed, sometimes these reviews even take for granted the accountability regime, without questioning or pushing back: "In this high-stakes era of higher standards and teacher evaluations based in part on student achievement, professional development has to have a laser-light focus on one thing—student learning. However, at present, most professional development misses the mark" (Gulamhussein, 2013, p. 2). Gulamhussein continued: "The overwhelming message of current accountability reforms is that student achievement is what matters most in a school building" (p. 6). In other words, not student *learning*. Not teacher *learning*. Not whether teachers and students are acknowledged and treated as whole human beings.

We suggest that in addition to principles named as characteristic of effective PD in other literature—an extended duration in which learning takes place in community, teachers actively engaging with (not passively listening to) ideas, and support for implementation of learning in daily contexts (e.g., see Desimone, 2009; Gulamhussein, 2013; Randi & Zeichner, 2004; Stein, Smith, & Silver, 1999)—that antiracist PD focus on shifting perspectives, intentionally building community and sharing power in cooperative and dialogical processes, and centering social justice goals within local contexts (see Kohli, Picower, Martinez, & Ortiz, 2015, for similar goals). This moves away from the highly touted focus on subject content to focus on relationships and intellectual engagement in which teachers learn about the ways structuralized white supremacy shapes our daily work environments and the lives of our students.

In designing, conducting, and analyzing our professional development and research, we paid special attention to tensions identified in the research literature on PD but also to social justice approaches to collaborative research and inquiry with teachers. Without an explicit connection between what we are teaching and how we are teaching it, or when the content itself is both critical and culturally relevant but the pedagogy is "banking" or oppressive (see Freire, 2000), PD fails to live out its own stated aims. One-size-fits-all, short-term PD that is anti-pedagogical and deeply anti-intellectual, with little to no connection to teachers' daily work and relationships, actually undermines the work of teaching; it de-professionalizes, and it thwarts any kind of material transformation.

Additionally, while in content-area or grade-level-specific work, it often makes sense for PD to take place within particular grade levels or schools, when examining the ways in which structural violences such as white supremacy are embedded in our schools, it might not make sense to be mandated to sit next to our closest colleagues as well as those who evaluate us, who may or may not share our antiracist commitments and perspectives. Instead, RaceWork has shown us the power of an intentional learning community of teachers from different schools and even districts. We followed Picower's (2007) calls that such work with teachers maintain an explicit focus on social justice, serving as more than a support group but rather being a space where social change agents can both imagine and enact change. We also enacted our social justice commitments by offering RaceWork without charge and providing continuing education credits for participating teachers. The preceding chapters have highlighted the ways in which RaceWork teachers meaningfully engaged antiracism. Here, we want to highlight four characteristics of this professional development: shifting perspectives, centering collaboration through relationships, focusing on contexts, and moving into, regardless of where white teachers are starting from.

Shifting Perspectives

RaceWork shifted the perspective from much of the antiracist PD available for teachers today, which tends to focus heavily on white privilege; this approach also shifts perspectives by calling out structural whiteness as the primary consideration. Through a tripartite model that always considered race, whiteness, and white supremacy at the levels of the personal, local, and structural, RaceWork teachers understood their responsibilities in new ways. Lisa, for instance, wrote at the end of the 1st year:

> I learned a lot about myself as a person and I started to see my lessons and teaching from the perspective of my students . . . the sessions I attended with the other members helped remove an obstacle that I didn't even see was in the way of viewing things through the eyes of my students.

RaceWork helped Lisa to shift perspectives, to understand from a point of view she had not considered. Nicole wrote:

> In my space, which is a very white space, I find myself purposefully talking about race more—mainly my own identity as a white person and explaining how and why I interpret and view texts, situations, words, and actions the way I do.

In ways such as these, RaceWork teachers nuanced their perspective shifts. They recognized that we, as white people, will always experience the world *as white people* and that one of our tasks, then, is to simultaneously understand this reality and to work to de-center whiteness as a frame of reference in our classrooms, schools, and communities. Nicole described her understanding this way:

> I can't arbitrarily teach someone else's perspective, because that would be disingenuous, claim[ing] what isn't ours (imperialism). I can, though, engage with other perspectives as a coach and learner and model how to shift, how to question another's experience, and how to use humble eyes to see how others may interpret the world.

This is a fundamental shift in perspective, one not solely about content knowledge and having nothing to do with metrics. It is a perspective with which "accountability" has no language to reckon.

Centering Collaborative Relationships

A second way that the accountability regime cannot make sense of Race-Work is that it is not possible to quantify relationships, yet working in collaborative relationship over time was crucial to what we learned and did together. Amelia wrote after year 1:

> I really thrive by being a part of an intellectual, committed, passionate, and encouraging group of people. I cannot tell you how absolutely refreshing it is to come here every month, and yes, even though we complain about teacher-stuff, we genuinely care about kids and want to better ourselves for our kids. I absolutely wouldn't be able to do this work on my own, so having facilitators and a framework around which this work is centered has helped me tremendously.

Sarah's written comments echoed this sentiment:

> This community of people has kept me in a problem-solving mode rather than a "this problem is too big and I can't do anything about it" mindset. I've felt supported by the group and by Shannon and Zac. I see the group as a think-tank for approaching different problems.

A sense of responsibility (rather than accountability) to one another made for a dialogic and critical space in which not only the co-facilitators were understood as having knowledge, but all teacher-learners and learner-teachers were recognized as engaged in creating knowledge and meaning. As one teacher put it: "I knew there were other people trying really great things, and that made me want to work harder on my own project." In interviews, we were struck by how frequently teachers noted that suggestions from other teachers in the group had made a significant impact on their work—such as revising grading practices—or how a particular teacher had been inspiring or helped the work feel less lonely. Throughout the school year, then, teachers in this small-group program built collaborative relationships with each other that were both personally supportive and integral to implementing antiracist actions in their local schools and classrooms.

This is important because, as Veronica put it, "Teaching is a job but also who you are. You need personal renewal with teaching that you can't always get at your school or your job." Nicole echoed that we needed each other because "the movement and change we want can't happen without trust." This trust is what we built in RaceWork; trust is a primary component of what RaceWork teachers enacted in their buildings—with colleagues and with students.

Involving Local Contexts

A third way in which an accountability regime cannot make sense of RaceWork is its grounding in local contexts—including those that were *not* shared among the eight teachers, as they came from different districts. RaceWork extended well beyond the basement room in which we met one Saturday morning a month. We brought our own local contexts to that room, found and shared resources from our communities, and returned this work to separate local contexts. RaceWork teachers did not confine their learning to Saturday mornings. For instance, Nicole brought a poster she had created in RaceWork back to her school and shared it with others. She said:

> With my principal, I've talked about how I feel certain traditional units and structures are oppressive and how I want to break through those models . . . and he was excited and supportive of my work, saying he was proud of me and thrilled that I was taking an active role in affecting change in the school.

While each teacher designed and implemented her own change, there was cross-fertilization among them, drawing on resources that we provided. All of this centered the localized needs of teachers and their students.

We also note that given the prevalence of white supremacy, surprisingly little literature (Hyland, 2005; Jupp, 2013; Lawrence & Tatum, 1997; Michael, 2015; Pennington, Brock, & Ndura, 2012; Picower, 2012; Schniedewind, 2005) exists on how white *practicing* teachers enact antiracist commitments after engaging in extended PD. Lawrence and Tatum (1997), for instance, found that over half of the suburban white teachers in a voluntary, semester-long antiracist PD course subsequently undertook antiracist actions in interpersonal interactions, curriculum, and/or institutional support services for students of color; likewise, five teachers who had group discussions on race and racism following a school-district PD diversity course then actively supported students of color, educated all students about stereotyping, addressed white privilege, and challenged institutional racism (Schniedewind, 2005). We need more of these accounts to support antiracist white teachers as they navigate the fraught landscapes of actually making concrete antiracist changes in their school settings. Charlie identified the importance of this work in her interview at the end of the 2nd year. Feeling a lack of support in her building, she also said "this is where our work together really helped too. It's frustrating because I know it's a systemic thing but also it made me feel a little bit better that it's not all my fault."

There is thus very little research literature with which RaceWork can dialogue, particularly in working explicitly with white teachers.[1] Perhaps even situating this work as professional *development* is part of the problem, as this terminology echoes paradigms that we explicitly rejected in RaceWork. After reviewing PD literature across fields (e.g., business, health, teaching), Webster-Wright (2009) argued that the term PD is

> part of a discourse that focuses on the professional as deficient and in need of developing and directing rather than on a professional engaged in self-directed learning. This discourse, and the professional context of control and standardization that perpetuates it, are rarely questioned in research or commentary about PD. Second, the focus of much research and practice in PD is atomistic, considering the professional and learning context as separate though related. Consequently, research often examines a specific factor: the PD activity and its outcomes, the context for learning, the learner and his or her preferences, or professional knowledge per se. Research is required that views the learner, context, and learning as inextricably interrelated rather than acknowledged as related, yet studied separately. (p. 712)

In other words, Webster-Wright argued, "implicit in most current PD literature is an objectivist epistemology that views knowledge as a transferable

---

1. Note also that a growing body of work on critical PD (e.g., Kohli, 2019; Navarro, 2018; Picower, 2015; Pour-Khorshid, 2016) focuses primarily on teacher-led PD work/critical praxis of teachers of color, often through teacher inquiry or critical study and action groups.

object" (p. 713). We thus follow Webster-Wright in suggesting a focus on *learning* rather than development. Perhaps we might even follow Britzman (1991) in terming what we have done in RaceWork the *practice* of professional learning.

Moving Into, Regardless of Where Teachers Are Starting From

Naming our antiracist work *practice* also means we can worry less about emphasizing where white teachers are starting from. Sarah's theorization regarding what RaceWork had taught her about engaging white people in antiracist work in schools is instructive:

> You don't have to have any kind of prerequisite, like experience or understanding. Or you didn't have to have grown up in a certain area or have certain parents to care about it and to move forward, to move into it. I'm saying forward, but it's more like to move into it. I feel like it's really the only way that anything is going to start to change is if white educators start to do exactly what we did: face into something that you're like, "uh this seems wrong; let's figure it out."

If we rely on preconceived notions of who is "supposed" to engage in antiracist work and whether they have the kinds of past experiences seemingly required for such engagement, we construct barriers to engaging in antiracism. Sometimes this can take the form of asking the impossible: asking white people if they know what it "feels like" to be a person of color in a white supremacist social context. The answer of course is no. But such a request is impossible if we drill down into what is actually being asked. We would struggle to articulate fully, for instance, what it feels like to be our siblings, people we have shared much of our socialization with. I can never fully *know* what it feels like to be someone else. But that is not what antiracism asks of us.

For Sarah, this is why there can't be "prerequisites" to engaging in antiracist work. Instead, we need to create spaces for white teachers to "move into" antiracist work. (This echoes Jansen's [2009] language to move toward and Milner's [2010] reminder to "start where you are, but don't stay there," an African proverb introduced to him in his first semester of doctoral studies.) Sarah distinguished between moving forward and moving into. At first she wanted to call what we did in RaceWork moving forward, but then corrected herself. Instead, she gestured at "moving into" in ways that evidence the kinds of approaches she was taking to antiracist work. Her stance was similar to Kumashiro's (2009) insistence that we are always already responding (which can also take the form of *not* responding) to oppressions in our schools and classrooms. The trouble is that too often our lack of attention to those oppressions, and to the ways our practices can reinforce them, reproduces the same old marginalizations and discriminations. "Moving into" is a powerful notion in the context of white teachers engaging antiracism more fully in their work. Injustice and inequity are already present within our schools; the need is to engage what is already happening, not to learn about it abstractly before responding. The challenge is to "face it," and Sarah saw RaceWork as supporting her in doing just that. The idea of "moving into" enacting antiracism means that we are constantly engaging in praxis. This is also part of the work of what we believe teacher education should be, as teacher education doesn't—or shouldn't—end when teachers get a diploma or certification.

RaceWork as Teacher Education

As we have mentioned, RaceWork teachers, in interviews, our monthly sessions, and conversations they had with others, called RaceWork a class, but a class unlike other classes. As Amelia said, "it was never hard to get there." For us as facilitators, RaceWork felt both like and unlike our regular university courses. It was like them in that we met in a university classroom—and one in which we had both taught (and thus knew the code in order to access the room on Saturday mornings). We had readings and assignments; we asked teachers to do things between our sessions. As in our "official" classrooms, we centered discussion, community building, and shared knowledge construction. It was unlike a class in that there were no grades, no formal assignments, and no official sanction for our work together.

Yet RaceWork teachers were serious about their own work and about our collective work together; they were committed to the engaged learning that was happening when we met and between our sessions. Learning was meaningful. For us, then, this was teacher education: It is what our classrooms feel and sound like when they come closest to our beliefs about teaching and learning and our hopes for what the emancipatory space of education or a classroom can be. This type of education is what it means to be an antiracist white teacher. It is ongoing but need not be exhaustive. As Angela wrote, "these three hours, once a month, for the past year have been a life changer." Further, this teacher education expanded into the space of P–12 schools, in the many ways detailed throughout this book.

Again, we return to an understanding of teaching that goes well beyond our current accountability regime. As Freire (1998) wrote, teachers must

> exercise their right to demand and fight for permanent and ongoing teacher preparation—a preparation that is based in the experience of living the dialectical tensions between theory and practice. Teachers must think about practice in terms of developing more effective means of practice, must think about practice and begin to recognize the theory inherent in it, must evaluate practice as a means of theoretical development and not merely as an instrument to punish teachers. (p. 7)

This is a challenge in a time when theory is denigrated and learning and teaching reduced to standardized metrics. RaceWork, in our time and space, is paradoxical.

RaceWork as a Paradoxical Model

Our monthly Saturday morning meetings were in many ways what we had hoped: Teachers recognized concrete manifestations of white supremacy and worked in material ways to combat them. Over 2 years, we built a critical community of white people supporting one another in the daunting yet inherently possible work of combating white supremacy in schools. These teachers took up equity leadership positions, vocally supported students of color, revised curriculum, and more. Yet RaceWork is a paradoxical model for antiracist work in education for the following reasons:

- We centered our thinking in research outside the field of education, drawing, for instance on the nonfiction writing of Baldwin, on Lipsitz as a professor of Ethnic Studies, and on the psychoanalytic work of Unitarian-Universalist minister Thandeka. Further, that we asked teachers to read dense texts cuts against the anti-intellectualism so prevalent in the field of education. We did not draw much on research studies that used experimental methods or large-scale data sets. This is not "best practice" in our field.

- Second, in this kind of work, students of color are often positioned as the "problem." In RaceWork we positioned white supremacy as the problem, asking the question of how our own white, racialized identities impact who we are as teachers and who we are with our students. At the same time, this is paradoxical in that it runs the risk of re-centering whiteness.

- Third, RaceWork is paradoxical in that these teachers did it for themselves, yet the consequences were not solely for themselves. While we heard frequently about their own personal change, more significant were the changes in their classrooms and buildings.

- Fourth, RaceWork demonstrated that there is no checklist to "fix racism" even as it is our responsibility as white people to address the ongoing legacies of centuries of white supremacy, in collaboration with peoples of color and Indigenous peoples. As Veronica said, prior to RaceWork, she was "feeling enlightened but certainly not competent—[there is] so much to know, so much to do wrong. [I was] thinking that there was still a right way [but now I know] there is no checklist."

- Last, but perhaps most significant, RaceWork is paradoxical because it is not replicable. We formed a small, intimate group from schools in the metro area in which we lived, worked, taught, and researched; our work, both collectively and individually, was hyper-contextual, situated within actual building politics, curriculum, and geography, as well as in our own stories and histories and bodies. No other group can ever *be* this group; while there is plenty to adapt for other needs and contexts, there is nothing to adopt from RaceWork.

Scaling Up and Zooming In: Shrinking the Terrain of Antiracist Professional Learning

These paradoxes are intimately intertwined with a critique of scaling. In the field of education, when we determine that something is "successful," we aim to decontextualize and scale up. This results in an emphasis on "best practices," a "scientific knowledge base" of teaching, or a "What Works Clearinghouse" touted as the gold standard for our work as teachers and researchers. But this desire to scale is neoliberal and anti-intellectual. Further, assuming that best practices are real means denying the concrete realities of students' and teachers' actual lives and contexts. Instead, we argue, antiracist work in education must be hyper-contextual. We cannot import it or export it wholescale. The practices that enacted antiracist change at Morgan's school are not the same as those in Veronica's school, even as both teachers revised social studies curriculum to be more inclusive and antiracist. Their contexts are different; students are different; building politics and leadership are different. Indeed, what "worked" in Amelia's practice—what radically altered the racial composition of AP chemistry courses—was endangered in subsequent years by "best practices" requiring standardized grading practices across the school. In sum, what we have learned from RaceWork is that rather than emphasizing "what works," we would do better to have many more models so that teachers can learn from others and make practice relevant to *their* schools, classrooms, and students, intellectual work that teachers are uniquely positioned to carry out in ways no other social actors can. In other words, "scaling up" should actually mean zooming in to the level of the local.

This also means reframing what we mean by success. As we read written versions of the work of teachers such as Morgan and Amelia, we were struck by how professional, antiracist, and impressive they appeared. We have, after all, written a book about them! But this book also hyper-contextualizes these practices, situating them not as "best practices," but in the mess, fear, ambiguity, and confusion these teachers experienced *even as* they enacted these changes. At times, to these teachers, what they were doing did *not* feel professional or impressive in practice—it even sometimes felt just barely antiracist in the face of the vastness of white supremacy.

Another reason, then, that we need more models is that the "success stories" we often hear about are people who literally, or sometimes figuratively, gave their lives for antiracism: John Brown, Violet Liuzzo, Morris Dees, and more. The portraits we see in movies such as *Dangerous Minds* are fantasy fiction; they do not reflect the daily lived realities of teachers and students. Snippeting stories such as those from Morgan and Amelia, as we've done in writing and in presentations, may make them sound valiant and extraordinary also. But, as Morgan and Amelia live their own lives, they just feel ordinary. Further, when compared with the enormity of the structures, practices, and discourses we are up against, starting a district equity team or changing grading policies feels like a molecule against an ocean.

Our shared fear, ambiguity, and confusion is likely because we sense—no, we *know*—this. As Morgan said in our informal evaluation of year 1: "I am still concerned that I and the school are not doing enough; we have a long ways to go." We know that at the same time we are enacting antiracist practices, we are re-inscribing white supremacy because of our own experience and generations of this thinking and action. As facilitators, we felt this too; we worry about not doing enough, getting it wrong, misunderstanding. Indeed, in her journal reflection after our sixth Saturday together, Shannon wrote, "I feel a little inadequate to do this work sometimes, because I don't have easy answers, even as I know that there are no easy answers." We know we will make mistakes, as white people always do (e.g., see Allen, 1974). Amelia wrote at the end of year 1 that

> I know that I am part of the problem and the solution. I don't see myself as an activist or a charismatic community organizer,

so I think for me I just need to keep on working on my own classroom and personal pedagogy, and trying to influence as many colleagues or school decisions as I can.

Nothing we do seems to possibly compare to the exemplars we see or have in our heads. But this is also precisely the point of the community-building we have attempted in RaceWork: Individually, these efforts are tiny. Collectively, they are enormous. One person can't dismantle white supremacy, but the collection of disparate actions and thinking *can*, even if not in our lifetimes. In the meantime, sustained efforts in pursuit of antiracism make an absolute difference in the lives of newly enrolled AP chemistry students or an individual Black student who has been continually sent out of the classroom.

Thus, we argue that we need *more* examples of localized, unique, and hyper-contextual antiracist work, not less. We need to study their particulars. We argue that localized, intentional forms of professional development—more appropriately called critical teacher learning—around antiracism and whiteness with white practicing teachers, like RaceWork, can do more to combat structural white supremacy in schools than PD settings in which interpersonal relationships with colleagues or supervisors are threatened. While we resist the hegemonic notion of "safe space" as a prerequisite for learning or critical conversations about race, perhaps our greatest insight that others can adapt is to build cohorts of teachers from different schools to come together to learn with each other.

These cohorts must be, like RaceWork, hyper-contextual and emergent. Their approaches to contesting white supremacy must mobilize teachers to self-appropriate, for themselves, the knowledge, skills, and resources they need. In RaceWork, we did not ask teachers to arrive at the same conclusions regarding white racial identity, structural racism, and oppression; we did not provide formulas, slogans, or "correct" ways of being antiracist. Thus, as Charlie kept reminding us, "there are no checklists, even if I or others keep wanting them." There is no step-by-step formula for creating antiracist, anti-oppressive classrooms and schools. Realizing this, we must then reorient antiracist professional development for practicing teachers away from reliance on "seven essential steps" or "achievement triangles." We must also recognize that this open-endedness and the enormity of the challenge of dismantling white supremacy in schools may not be as gratifying as a certificate of completion or a 10-point plan to follow. But justice work in schools is never finished; we can never articulate all the various ways teachers can work against oppression in schools. Instead, we return to the Freirean (2006) notion of "reinvention."

Returning to Reinvention

White supremacy is bigger than any one white person, bigger than any particular school, district, or even state. Work in schools will never be enough, on its own, to end centuries of white domination; our responses are of necessity and condition limited. We thus follow Freire (2006) in insisting, "it is true that education is not the ultimate lever for social transformation, but without it transformation cannot occur" (p. 69). To do so, we must continually reinvent antiracist practices and perspectives in ourselves, our schools, and our contexts.

In RaceWork, we reexamined our grade books for racially biased policies. We worked to close the discipline gap. We brought in new texts and histories to engage our students' cultures in more authentic ways. We worked with colleagues to shift practices that worked in opposition to racial equity. We organized with others, joining (and even creating) equity and leadership teams. We taught others and ourselves. We became "experts" in our schools and pedagogical communities. And we grew, as pedagogues and as people.

This work is ongoing; it is always unfinished, always in the process of being revealed. We continue to ask critical questions of our practices and our contexts, because we recognize that we are not done growing, done learning, or done acting in hopeful ways premised on our love for humanization through education. Paulo Freire, one of our intellectual heroes, always insisted on the need for teachers to be humble in their work on and with the world.

But this is a tough concept to actually embody. After all, as teachers (and perhaps even more so, as teacher educators) we are supposed to be the experts, the more knowledgeable others, the certified professionals with the credentials. Yet our RaceWork group resisted any such stance, instead expressing discomfort with being positioned as racial equity experts. This humility, this unwillingness to name ourselves as finished or expert, is perhaps the most powerful learning from our time in RaceWork. This kind of humility is required to understand why there cannot ever be *one* answer, why we can never say "always do this, and you will get the socially just results you crave."

In a conversation with Macedo toward the end of his life, Freire said, "Donaldo, I don't want to be imported or exported. It is impossible to export pedagogical practices without reinventing them. Please tell your fellow American educators not to import me. Ask them to re-create and rewrite my ideas" (Freire, 1998, p. xi). Freire worried that his work would become seen as "best practice," as an "effective method" of literacy instruction rather than the deeply personal and pedagogical work he'd described. Instead, he asked those of us who take up his ideas not to merely do what he did, but rather to "reinvent" his ideas—to bring to bear our own experiences with those of our co-learners and co-teachers to build a practice that brings the ideas to life in ways that connect to the lived experience(s) of those engaged in the educative act. It is in this spirit of Freirean reinvention that we hope the ideas of this book are used.

In this spirit, we took the collective knowledge and experience we recorded and theorized over 2 years of work together and the subsequent years, turning it into something else, this book, reinventing 2 years of conversations and classroom activities into a collection of writing. The specific lessons and ideas we've produced in RaceWork are not the most important results of our work. Nor, despite how incredibly proud we are when telling others about them, are the concrete examples of antiracism these eight teachers enacted in their classrooms and schools. Instead, to us, the most important result of our work is the model we can offer for white people, working with other white people and in interracial collaboration, to take up this work in powerful ways. The power of our group rests in how we have been with each other, who we are in that space, and how that being can inform what we do and how we act both inside and outside of classrooms.

It will take many acts of reinvention, many pedagogically oriented interventions, to build spaces similar to the one we created together over 2 years. Yet it is precisely this challenge, that it will never be the same, that fills us with possibility and hope. So we hope that the readers of this book can also use these ideas in ways that make sense for you and for those you are working with. Change and transform these ideas, make meaning together with people who share a commitment to being together in humanizing ways, and know that others are doing the same.

As we have stated, there is no way to present on these two-dimensional pages the power and possibility that RaceWork has been for us as teachers, facilitators, learners, scholars, and researchers. On those Saturday mornings, we jointly created a space to learn and laugh and grow with each other. Together, we built opportunities to work with others to better understand the ways that white supremacy and structural oppression impact our work in classrooms and schools and then to begin to undo them. As facilitators, we are forever indebted to this group and its model of the power of an affirming and critical group of practicing educators. RaceWork has strengthened our faith and belief in the liberatory potential of schools and classrooms immeasurably. It has given us newfound evidence for the possibilities of white antiracism.

In this text, we of course have been unable to recreate or re-present our group—but we always knew that was not the point. As we made the commitment to each other to get smarter about race and equity with our colleagues, we hope that this book helps others to do so as well, to *be* different in the world, to collectively build anti-oppressive pedagogical spaces from the stance that antiracism is not a static identity; it is not something someone *is*. It is a practice, a way of being in the world. As a practice, it will always have multiple possible and worthy variations. And thus this book reminds and protects this point: *There is no best way to do it*. There are endless possibilities for how we can engage this work, and thus endless possibilities to act on our world in just, humanizing ways.

To reinvent in the Freirean sense requires that we learn together, that we imagine together, that we dare together, that we together defy "best practices" or the ways we are commonly positioned. Darder (2002) put it this way:

> Reinvention is an act of empowerment that can be accomplished only when teachers truly recognize themselves as subjects of history and as ethically responsible for their practice. Reinvention is seldom permitted to students or their teachers in public schools. There, reproduction is more sought after, leading to "teacher-proof" methods and the standardization of knowledge. These are antithetical to the creativity inherent in reinvention, for reinvention entails imagination. Unfortunately, imagination is often a suspect or prohibited quality in public schools. (p. 151)

Our antiracist work is thus even more challenging: Not only are we confronting centuries of engrained white supremacy in ourselves, our schools, our policies, our laws, our practices, and our histories, we are challenging notions of what schools are even about or what our work as teachers is. Freire (1998) wrote:

> The task of the teacher, who is also a learner, is both joyful and rigorous. It demands seriousness and scientific, physical, emotional, and affective preparation. It is a task that requires that those who commit themselves to teaching develop a certain love not only of others but also of the very process implied in teaching. It is impossible to teach without the courage to love, with the courage to try a thousand times before giving up. In short, it is impossible to teach without a forged, invented, and well-thought-out capacity to love. (p. 3)

This is daunting. In RaceWork, we found comfort in Freire's words in his dialogue with Horton: "I *always* am in the beginning, as you" (Horton

& Freire, 1990, p. 55). Freire emphasized that we "cannot wait to create tomorrow, but we have to start creating" (p. 55); we begin over and over again. RaceWork was one such beginning, and we invite many others to reinvent and re-begin as well. As one RaceWork teacher wrote anonymously at the end of our 2nd year together: "This work is never done and there are many ways to approach it." We are thus, even here at the end, once again and always *beginning*.

Appendix A
What We Read

First Semester: Building a Foundation

October 2012, Structural Whiteness

Lipsitz, G. (1995). The possessive investment in whiteness: Racialized social democracy and the "white" problem in American Studies. *American Quarterly*, 47(3), 369–387.

Mayer, J. (1997). Barriers to organization between anti-racist white people. Retrieved from www.cwsworkshop.org/pdfs/CARC/Challenging_White_SJ/3_Barriers.PDF

Wong, N. (2002). When I was growing up. In C. L. Moraga & G. E. Anzaldúa (Eds.), *This bridge called my back: Writings by radical women of color* (3rd ed., pp. 5–6). Berkeley, CA: Third Woman Press.

November 2012, Institutional Whiteness and Structural White Supremacy in Schools

Delpit, L. (1996/2006). The silenced dialogue: Power and pedagogy in educating other people's children. In L. Delpit, *Other people's children: Cultural conflict in the classroom* (pp. 21–47). New York, NY: The New Press.

Lensmire, T. J., McManimon, S. K., Tierney, J. D., Lee-Nichols, M. E., Casey, Z. A., Lensmire, A., & Davis, B. M. (Midwest Critical Whiteness Collective). (2013). McIntosh as synecdoche: How teacher education's focus on white privilege undermines antiracism. *Harvard Educational Review*, 83(3), 410–431.

Thandeka. (1999). Why anti-racism will fail. Retrieved from revthandeka.org/assets/why_anti_racism_will_fail.pdf

December 2012, White Racial Identities (and Cultural Norms)

Casey, Z. A. (n.d.) "Am I an Indian Killer?" Unpublished essay.

Morrison, T. (1983). Recitatif. In A. Baraka & A. Baraka (Eds.), *Confirmation: An anthology of African American women* (pp. 201–227). New York, NY: Morrow.

Okun, T. White supremacy culture. Retrieved from www.cwsworkshop.org/PARC_site_B/dr-culture.html.

Thandeka. (1999). Abuse. In Thandeka, *Learning to be white: Money, race and God in America* (pp. 20–41). New York, NY: Continuum.

Second Semester:
Goal-Setting for Our Own Contexts/Pedagogical Spaces

January 2013, Whiteness in Contexts of Schools

Baldwin, J. (1963). A talk to teachers. Retrieved from richgibson.com/talkto teachers.htm

Jansen, J. D. (2008). Bearing whiteness: A pedagogy of compassion in a time of troubles. *Education as Change, 12*(2), 59–84.

Leonardo, Z. (2009). Race and the war on schools in an era of accountability. In Z. Leonardo, *Race, whiteness, and education* (pp. 127–142). New York, NY: Routledge.

Milner, H. R. (2003). Reflection and race in cultural contexts: History, meanings, and methods in teaching. *Theory into Practice, 42*(3), 173–180.

February 2013, Inquiring Into Our Own Practices in Schools

Darder, A. (2011). The establishment of liberatory alliances with people of color: What must be understood. In A. Darder, *A dissident voice: Essays on culture, pedagogy, and power* (pp. 80–91). New York, NY: Peter Lang.

Fecho, B. (2004). Hopelessness and possibility. In B. Fecho, *"Is this English?": Race, language, and culture in the classroom* (pp. 12–25). New York, NY: Teachers College Press.

March 2013, Our Work as Educators

Freire, P. (1998). Sixth letter: On the relationship between the educator and the learners. In P. Freire, *Teachers as cultural workers: Letters to those who dare to teach* (pp. 55–62). Boulder, CO: Westview.

Kumashiro, K. K. (2002). Theories and practices of anti-oppressive education. In K. K. Kumashiro, *Troubling Education: Queer activism and antioppressive pedagogy* (pp. 31–71). New York, NY: RoutledgeFalmer.

May 2013, Each Teacher Chose to Receive a Copy Of Either

Grineski, S., Landsman, J., & Simmons, R. (Eds.). (2013). *Talking about race: Alleviating the fear*. Sterling, VA: Stylus.

Pollock, M. (Ed.). (2008). *Everyday antiracism: Getting real about race in school*. New York, NY: The New Press.

Second Year: What Do We Need for Further Action?

September 2013, Exploring Other Models of Antiracist Work

(draft of) Casey, Z. A. (2016). The impossibility of whiteness: On white privilege and race treason. In Z. A. Casey, *A pedagogy of anticapitalist antiracism: Whiteness, neoliberalism, and resistance in education*. Albany: State University of New York Press.

October 2013, Having Conversations with Colleagues

Briscoe, F., Arriaza, G., & Henze, R. C. (2009). Becoming effective in using critical language awareness. In F. Briscoe, G. Arriaza, & R. C. Henze, *The power of talk: How words change our lives* (pp. 35–47). Thousand Oaks, CA: Corwin.

November 2013, Intersectionality

Frankenberg, R. (1993). Epilogue: Racism, antiracism, and the meaning of whiteness. In R. Frankenberg, *White women, race matters: The social construction of whiteness* (pp. 236–243). Minneapolis: University of Minnesota Press.
Local newspaper article and op-eds on racial equity work in local school district.

December 2013, Working in Our School Contexts

Gillborn, D. (2008). Developing antiracist school policy. In M. Pollock (Ed.), *Everyday antiracism: Getting real about race in school* (pp. 246–251). New York, NY: The New Press.
McIntyre, A. (2008). Engaging diverse groups of colleagues in conversation. In M. Pollock (Ed.), *Everyday antiracism: Getting real about race in school* (pp. 279–281). New York, NY: The New Press.
Pollock, M. (2008). Complete list of everyday antiracist strategies. In M. Pollock (Ed.), *Everyday antiracism: Getting real about race in school* (pp. 343–348). New York, NY: The New Press.

January/February 2014, Being an Expert and Being a Beginner

Excerpts (pp. 56–67 and 128–131) from Horton, M., and Freire, P. (1990). *We make the road by walking: Conversations on education and social change*. Philadelphia, PA: Temple University Press.

March 2014

Ladson-Billings, G. (2006). From the achievement gap to the education debt: Understanding achievement in U.S. schools. *Educational Researcher*, 35(7), 3–12.

Appendix B
Intertwined Research

Methodological Choices, Processes, and Approaches

From the very beginning, research was central to this project in two ways: First, we embedded a research study into the project and brought RaceWork teachers into this understanding on our 1st day. Second, RaceWork teachers themselves engaged in research, coming up with a question relevant to their own teaching locations, gathering data, making a change, and then repeating—in other words, a form of action research, weaving together questions, stories, learning, and action.

For us, knowing that we wanted to learn with these teachers and to understand and theorize what would happen in our work together, Race-Work was simultaneously a pedagogical space and a research project. We approached this research project in the same way that we do our teaching: as praxis. A "praxis-oriented" approach to research is critical and empowering, "openly committed to critiquing the status quo and building a more just society" (Lather, 1986, p. 258); it intertwines research methodology with "our theoretical concerns and commitments" (p. 258), and, we argue, with our pedagogical commitments as well. This requires self-reflection on the part of all involved, as well as a "give-and-take, a mutual negotiation of meaning and power. It operates at two primary points in emancipatory empirical research: the junctures between researcher and researched and between data and theory" (p. 263).

Patel (2016) reframed research from (traditional) ownership of knowledge by researchers to answerability. Situating both education (particularly schooling) and research in the ongoing system of settler colonialism, Patel argued that educational researchers are responsible to these trajectories of oppression (including their ontologies and actions) and to working to dismantle them (including understanding the roots of qualitative research in histories of colonialism). As researchers, we are part of an exchange, a conversation that responds not only to the present, but to what has come before. She thus argued that "research is a fundamentally relational project—relational to ways of knowing, who can know, and to place" (p. 48); this relationship makes us responsible, or as she put it, answerable: to learning, to knowledge, and to context. This means understanding "learning as a constant becoming and unbecoming, a constant inquiry and coordinate-taking, which sounds a lot like what research is supposed to be" (p. 77). In RaceWork, as both educators and researchers, we worked to be answerable to the learning of these teachers and their students, to histories of racialized oppression that continue to the present, to local contexts, and to working to dismantle white supremacy.

While we had strategies for generating data, our interest in researching RaceWork was not about the how of research. At various times, we called our work "practitioner inquiry" (as we were in some ways studying our own practices as teachers) or case study, following Stake's (1995) conceptions (case study as "the study of the particularity and complexity of a single case, coming to understand its activity within important circumstances" [p. xi] in which a researcher finds methods that work "for one's style and circumstances" [p. xii]). Stake argued that case study researchers "draw from understandings deep within us, understandings whose derivation may be some hidden mix of personal experience, scholarship, assertions of other researchers" (p. 12), that "there is much art and much intuitive processing to the search for meaning" (p. 72). He also wrote about the shared responsibilities and intentions of research and teaching: "The intention of research is to inform, to sophisticate, to assist the increase of competence and maturity, to socialize, and to liberate. These are also the responsibilities of the teacher" (pp. 91–92).

Despite a frequent demand in educational research to demonstrate methods, squeezing into already-defined methods boxes is antithetical to our practices and commitments, to research as praxis, and to answerability. Practically, then, this stance aligns us with Weaver and Snaza's (2016) arguments against methodocentrism: "the belief that particular, pre-formed methods can guarantee the validity of an intellectual investigation into the world by factoring out the vicissitudes of the observer's entanglement with the world" (p. 1056). They argued not that educational research has no need for methods ("rigorous, philosophically grounded approaches to problems in the world" [p. 1055]), but that insisting upon selecting methods from those already existing and before approaching a study is "an avoidance that ultimately produces bad science" (p. 1056). Instead, they argued for a "science of embeddedness" that centers listening and co-construction of knowledge. In other words, predetermining or preplanning methods moves the focus from engagement with the world and instead centers the methods themselves.

While the work of such scholars exemplifies why we are thus reluctant to name our research methods, we did have processes and systematic means of generating and analyzing data. Shannon took detailed field notes in each session and also during our facilitation debriefing sessions. Zac also took field notes. We audio recorded each monthly session and kept copies of syllabi and session plans. We each wrote ongoing analytic memos capturing our thoughts after sessions and our planning work. Throughout the 2 years, we formally and informally asked RaceWork teachers to evaluate our work together through (anonymous) surveys and written evaluations, conversations, and writing prompts. We collected all of these, along with artifacts from our sessions (such as posters teachers made, handouts, discussion prompts, presentation slides, and photographs of our work) and observations when we visited RaceWork teachers' classrooms. We interviewed each teacher at the end of the 1st year and again a year after we had ended our joint work and transcribed each interview; like our other work, these interviews were pedagogical spaces.

Zac began data analysis through inductively coding the teacher interviews. Our analysis focused on understanding RaceWork teachers' learning and enactment of antiracist pedagogies; we drew on coded data, on interpretation directly from our experiences, and on what teachers reported. We put this analysis into conversation with critical literatures in the fields of critical whiteness studies (Delgado & Stefancic, 1997; Du Bois, 1935/1992; Dyer, 1988; Jacobson, 1998; Lipsitz, 1995; Morrison, 1992; Roediger, 2007); critical pedagogy (Casey, 2011, 2016; Casey, Lozenski, & McManimon, 2013; Freire, 2000, 2006; hooks, 1994; Shor, 1987); and second-wave white teacher identity studies (Jupp, Berry, & Lensmire, 2016; Lensmire et al., 2013). This analysis forms the bulk of this book.

Personally and professionally, we cannot disentangle the concerns and processes of theory, method, research, and pedagogy. This was even more so as our research project intertwined with the action research of these teachers. In this intertwining, what happens can be (was) both unpredictable and potentially transformative in multiple spaces. In "Research as Praxis," Lather (1986) wrote:

> For praxis to be possible, not only must theory illuminate the lived experience of progressive social groups; it must also be illuminated by their struggles. Theory adequate to the task of changing the world must be open-ended, nondogmatic,

informing, and grounded in the circumstances of everyday life; and, moreover, it must be premised on a deep respect for the intellectual and political capacities of the dispossessed. (p. 262)

Our work throughout the last years has been to ask questions and to share stories in attempts to get smarter together. This is our theory, our method, our research, and our pedagogy.

References

Allen, R. (1974/1983). *Reluctant reformers: Racism and social reform movements in the United States*. Washington, DC: Howard University Press.
Althusser, L. (2008). *On ideology*. London, UK: Verso.
Applebaum, B. (2011). *Being white, being good: White complicity, white moral responsibility, and social justice pedagogy*. Lanham, MD: Lexington Books.
Arao, B., & Clemens, K. (2013). From safe spaces to brave spaces: A new way to frame dialogue around diversity and social justice. In L. Landreman (Ed.), *The art of effective facilitation: Reflections from social justice educators* (pp. 135–150). Sterling, VA: Stylus.
Baldwin, J. (1963/1985). A talk to teachers. In J. Baldwin, *The price of the ticket: Collected nonfiction 1948–1985* (pp. 325–332). New York, NY: St. Martin's/Marek.
Baldwin, J. (1985). *The price of the ticket: Collected nonfiction 1948–1985*. New York, NY: St. Martin's/Marek.
Bell, D. A. (1980). Brown v. Board of Education and the interest-convergence dilemma. *Harvard Law Review*, 93(3), 518–533.
Boal, A. (1985). *Theatre of the oppressed*. New York, NY: Theatre Communications Group.
Boal, A. (2002). *Games for actors and non-actors* (2nd ed., A. Jackson, Trans.). London, UK: Routledge.
Bonilla-Silva, E. (2003). *Racism without racists: Color-blind racism and the persistence of racial inequality in the United States*. Lanham, MD: Rowman & Littlefield Publishers.
Borko, H. (2004). Professional development and teacher learning: Mapping the terrain. *Educational Researcher*, 33(8), 3–15.
Briscoe, F., Arriaza, G., & Henze, R. C. (2009). *The power of talk: How words change our lives*. Thousand Oaks, CA: Corwin.
Britzman, D. (1991). *Practice makes practice: A critical study of learning to teach*. Albany, NY: State University of New York Press.
Carter, P. L. (2006). Straddling boundaries: Identity, culture, and school. *Sociology of Education*, 79, 304–328.
Carter, P. L. (2010). Race and cultural flexibility among students in different multiracial schools. *Teachers College Record*, 112(6), 1529–1574.

Casey, Z. A. (2010). Remembering to be radical in teacher education: Defanged multicultural education. *The Journal of Multiculturalism in Education, 6*(1), 1–19.

Casey, Z. A. (2011). The fight in my classroom: A story of intersectionality in practitioner research. *i.e.: inquiry in education, 2*(1), Article 3.

Casey, Z. A. (2016). *A pedagogy of anticapitalist antiracism: Whiteness, neoliberalism, and resistance in education.* Albany: State University of New York Press.

Casey, Z. A. (2017). Making the inherently inefficient (more) efficient: Neoliberalism as "aim" in teacher education. *Teacher Education & Practice, 30*(2), 314–316.

Casey, Z. A., Lozenski, B. D., & McManimon, S. K. (2013). From neoliberal policy to neoliberal pedagogy: Racializing and historicizing classroom management. *Journal of Pedagogy, 4*(1), 36–58.

Challenging White Supremacy Workshop. (n.d.). Available at www.cwsworkshop.org

Crenshaw, K. (1989). Demarginalizing the intersection of race and sex: A Black feminist critique of antidiscrimination doctrine, feminist theory and antiracist politics. *The University of Chicago Legal Forum, 140*, 139–167.

Crocco, M. S., & Costigan, A. T. (2007). The narrowing of curriculum and pedagogy in the age of accountability: Urban educators speak out. *Urban Education, 42*(6), 512–535.

Darder, A. (2011). *A dissident voice: Essays on culture, pedagogy, and power.* New York, NY: Peter Lang.

Delgado, R., & Stefancic, J. (Eds.) (1997). *Critical white studies: Looking behind the mirror.* Philadelphia, PA: Temple University Press.

Delgado, R., & Stefancic, J. (2014). *Critical race theory: An introduction* (2nd ed.). New York, NY: NYU Press.

Delpit L. (1996/2006). The silenced dialogue: Power & pedagogy in educating other people's children. In L. Delpit, *Other people's children: Cultural conflict in the classroom.* New York, NY: The New Press.

Delpit, L. (2006). *Other people's children: Cultural conflict in the classroom.* New York, NY: The New Press.

Delpit, L. (2012). *"Multiplication is for white people": Raising expectations for other people's children.* New York, NY: The New Press.

Demby, G., & Meraji, S. M. (2016, May). Can we talk about whiteness? *Code Switch: Race and Identity, Remixed* podcast, episode 1. Retrieved from www.npr.org/sections/codeswitch/2016/05/31/479733094/the-code-switch-podcast-episode-1-can-we-talk-about-whiteness

Denzin, N. K. (2010/2016). *The qualitative manifesto: A call to arms.* New York, NY: Routledge.

Desimone, L. M. (2009). Improving impact studies of teachers' professional development: Toward better conceptualizations and measures. *Educational Researcher, 38*(3), 181–199.

Dewey, J. (1897/2010). My pedagogic creed. *School Journal, 54*, 77–80. Retrieved from dewey.pragmatism.org/creed.htm

DiAngelo, R. (2018). *White fragility: Why it's so hard for white people to talk about racism.* Boston, MA: Beacon Press.

Dinkelman, T. (2003). Self-study in teacher education: A means and ends tool for promoting reflective teaching. *Journal of Teacher Education, 54*(1), 6–18.

Du Bois, W. E. B. (1920/1999). *Darkwater: Voices from within the veil.* Mineola, NY: Dover Publications.
Du Bois, W. E. B. (1935/1992). *Black reconstruction in America.* New York, NY: The Free Press.
Dyer, R. (1988). White. *Screen, 29*(4), 44–64.
Ellsworth, E. (1989). Why doesn't this feel empowering? Working through the repressive myths of critical pedagogy. *Harvard Educational Review, 59*(3), 297–324.
Ellsworth, E. (1997). *Teaching positions: Difference, pedagogy, and the power of address.* New York, NY: Teachers College Press.
Fecho, B. (2004). *"Is this English?": Race, language, and culture in the classroom.* New York, NY: Teachers College Press.
Fine, M. (2018). *Just research in contentious times: Widening the methodological imagination.* New York, NY: Teachers College Press.
Frankenberg, R. (1993). *White women, race matters: The social construction of whiteness.* Minneapolis: University of Minnesota Press.
Freire, P. (2000). *Pedagogy of the oppressed.* New York, NY: Continuum.
Freire, P. (2006). *Teachers as cultural workers: Letters to those who dare teach.* New York, NY: Westview Press.
Gay, G., & Howard, T. (2000). Multicultural education for the 21st century. *Teacher Educator, 36*(1), 1–16.
Gillborn, D. (2008). Developing antiracist school policy. In M. Pollock (Ed.), *Everyday antiracism: Getting real about race in school* (pp. 246–251). New York, NY: The New Press.
Glaser, B. G., & Strauss, A. L. (1967). *The discovery of grounded theory: Strategies for qualitative research.* Chicago, IL: Aldine Publishers.
González, N., Moll, L. C., & Amanti, C. (Eds.) (2005). *Funds of knowledge: Theorizing practices in households, communities, and classrooms.* Mahwah, NJ: Lawrence Erlbaum Associates.
Gramsci, A. (1971). *Selections from the prison notebooks.* New York, NY: International Publishers.
Grineski, S., Landsman, J., & Simmons, R. (Eds.). (2013). *Talking about race: Alleviating the fear.* Sterling, VA: Stylus.
Gulamhussein, A. (2013). *Teaching the teachers: Effective professional development in an era of high stakes accountability.* Alexandria, VA: Center for Public Education.
Hampl, P. (1999). *I could tell you stories: Sojourns in the land of memory.* New York, NY: W. W. Norton & Company.
Hardiman R., Jackson, B. W., & Griffin P. (2013). Conceptual foundations. In M. Adams, W. J. Blumenfeld, C. Castañeda, H. W. Hackman, M. L. Peters, & X. Zúñiga (Eds.), *Readings for diversity and social justice* (3rd ed.) (pp. 26–35). New York, NY: Routledge.
Harris, C. I. (1993). Whiteness as property. *Harvard Law Review, 106*(8), 1709–1791.
Helms, J. E. (Ed.). (1990). *Black and White racial identity: Theory, research, and practice.* Westport, CT: Greenwood Press.
Henry J. Kaiser Family Foundation. (2018). Poverty rate by race/ethnicity. Retrieved from www.kff.org/other/state-indicator/poverty-rate-by-raceethnicity/?data

View=1&currentTimeframe=0&sortModel=%7B%22colId%22:%22Location%22,%22sort%22:%22asc%22%7D

hooks, b. (1994). *Teaching to transgress: Education as the practice of freedom.* New York, NY: Routledge.

hooks, b. (1995). *Killing rage, ending racism.* New York, NY: Henry Holt and Company.

hooks, b. (2003). *Teaching community: A pedagogy of hope.* New York, NY: Routledge.

hooks, b. (2013). *Writing beyond race: Living theory and practice.* New York, NY: Routledge.

Horton, M., & Freire, P. (1990). *We make the road by walking: Conversations on education and social change.* Philadelphia, PA: Temple University Press.

Howard, G. R. (2006). *We can't teach what we don't know.* New York, NY: Teachers College Press.

Hyland, N. E. (2005). Being a good teacher of black students? White teachers and unintentional racism. *Curriculum Inquiry, 35*(4), 429–459.

Jacobson, M. F. (1998). *Whiteness of a different color: European immigrants and the alchemy of race.* Cambridge, MA: Harvard University Press.

Jansen, J. D. (2008). Bearing whiteness: A pedagogy of compassion in a time of troubles. *Education as Change, 12*(2), 59–84.

Jansen, J. D. (2009). *Knowledge in the blood: Confronting race and the apartheid past.* Stanford, CA: Stanford University Press.

Jensen, R. (2005). *The heart of whiteness: Confronting race, racism, and white privilege.* San Francisco, CA: City Lights Books.

Jupp, J. C. (2013). *Becoming teachers of inner-city students: Life histories and teacher stories of committed white teachers.* Rotterdam, The Netherlands: Sense Publishers.

Jupp, J. C., Berry, T. R., & Lensmire, T. J. (2016). Second-wave white teacher identity studies: A review of white teacher identity literatures from 2004 through 2014. *Review of Educational Research, 86*(4), 1151–1191.

Kennedy, M. M. (2016). How does professional development improve teaching? *Review of Educational Research, 86*(4), 945–980.

Kincheloe, J. L. (2008). *Critical pedagogy primer.* New York, NY: Peter Lang.

Kohli, R. (2019). Lessons for teacher education: The role of critical professional development in teacher of Color retention. *Journal of Teacher Education, 70*(1), 39–50.

Kohli, R., Picower, B., Martinez, A., & Ortiz, N. (2015). Critical professional development: Centering the social justice needs of teachers. *International Journal of Critical Pedagogy, 6*(2), 7–24.

Kumashiro, K. K. (2000). Toward a theory of anti-oppressive education. *Review of Educational Research, 70*(1), 25–53.

Kumashiro, K. K. (2002). *Troubling education: Queer activism and antioppresssive pedagogy.* New York, NY: Routledge Falmer.

Kumashiro, K. K. (2009). *Against common sense: Teaching and learning toward social justice.* New York, NY: Routledge.

Ladson-Billings, G. (1995). Toward a theory of culturally relevant pedagogy. *American Educational Research Journal, 32*(3), 465–491.

Ladson-Billings, G. (2006a). From the achievement gap to the education debt: Understanding achievement in U.S. schools. *Educational Researcher*, 35(7), 3–12.

Ladson-Billings, G. (2006b). "Yes, but how do we do it?": Practicing culturally relevant pedagogy. In J. Landsman & C. W. Lewis (Eds.), *White teachers/diverse classrooms* (pp. 29–42). Sterling, VA: Stylus.

Lather, P. (1986). Research as praxis. *Harvard Educational Review*, 56(3), 257–277.

Lawrence, S. M., & Tatum, B. D. (1997). Teachers in transition: The impact of antiracist professional development on classroom practice. *Teachers College Record*, 99, 162–178.

Lensmire, A. (2012). *White urban teachers: Stories of fear, violence, and desire*. Lanham, MD: Rowman & Littlefield Education.

Lensmire, T. J., McManimon, S. K., Tierney, J. D., Lee-Nichols, M. E., Casey, Z. A., Lensmire, A., & Davis, B. M. (Midwest Critical Whiteness Collective). (2013). McIntosh as synecdoche: How teacher education's focus on white privilege undermines antiracism. *Harvard Educational Review*, 83(3), 410–431.

Leonardo, Z. (2004). The color of supremacy: Beyond the discourse of "white privilege." *Educational Philosophy and Theory*, 36(2), 137–152.

Leonardo, Z. (2009). *Race, whiteness, and education*. New York, NY: Routledge.

Lipsitz, G. (1995). The possessive investment in whiteness: Racialized social democracy and the "white" problem in American Studies. *American Quarterly*, 47(3), 369–387.

Lipsitz, G. (2006). *The possessive investment in whiteness: How white people profit from identity politics*. Philadelphia, PA: Temple University Press.

Loughran, J. (2007). Researching teacher education practices: Responding to the challenges, demands, and expectations of self-study. *Journal of Teacher Education*, 58(1), 12–20.

Lowenstein, K. L. (2009). The work of multicultural teacher education: Reconceptualizing white teacher candidates as learners. *Review of Educational Research*, 79(1), 163–196.

Macedo, D., & Freire, A. M. A. (1998). Foreword. In P. Freire, *Teachers as cultural workers: Letters to those who dare to teach* (pp. ix–xix). New York, NY: Westview Press.

Marx, K. (1852/1963). *The eighteenth Brumaire of Louis Bonaparte, with explanatory notes*. New York, NY: International Publishers.

Mason, A. M. (2016). Taking time, breaking codes: Moments in white teacher candidates' exploration of racism and teacher identity. *International Journal of Qualitative Studies in Education*, 29(8), 1045–1058.

Mayer, J. (1997). Barriers to organization between anti-racist white people. Available at www.cwsworkshop.org/resources/ARAgenda.html

McIntosh, P. (1988). White privilege and male privilege: A personal account of coming to see correspondences through work in women's studies (Working Paper 189). Wellesley, MA: Wellesley Center for Research on Women.

McIntosh, P. (2008). White privilege: Unpacking the invisible knapsack. In P. Rothenberg (Ed.), *White privilege: Essential readings on the other side of racism* (pp. 123–127). New York, NY: Worth.

McIntyre, A. (1997). *Making meaning of whiteness: Exploring the racial identity of white teachers*. Albany: State University of New York Press.

McIntyre, A. (2008). Engaging diverse groups of colleagues in conversation. In M. Pollock (Ed.), *Everyday antiracism: Getting real about race in school* (pp. 279–281). New York, NY: The New Press.

McManimon, S. K. (2018). Canons and contestation, fairy tales and trickster tales: Educational storytelling as intellectual work. *Storytelling, Self, Society, 14*(2), article 3.

McManimon, S. K., & Casey, Z. A. (2018). (Re)beginning and becoming: Antiracism and professional development with white practicing teachers. *Teaching Education, 29*(4), 395–406. doi.org/10.1080/10476210.2018.1506429

McManimon, S. K., Casey, Z. A., & Berchini, C. (2018). *Whiteness at the table: Racism, antiracism, and identity in education.* Lanham, MD: Lexington Books.

Merriam, S. (1998). *Qualitative research and case study applications in education.* San Francisco: Jossey-Bass.

Michael, A. (2015). *Raising race questions: Whiteness and inquiry in education.* New York, NY: Teachers College Press.

Mills, C. W. (1959). *The sociological imagination.* London, UK: Oxford University Press.

Milner, H. R. (2003). Reflection and race in cultural contexts: History, meanings, and methods in teaching. *Theory into Practice, 42*(3), 173–180.

Milner, H. R. (2010). *Start where you are, but don't stay there: Understanding diversity, opportunity gaps, and teaching in today's classrooms.* Cambridge, MA: Harvard Education Press.

Morrison, T. (1983). Recitatif. In A. Baraka & A. Baraka (Eds.), *Confirmation: An anthology of African American women* (pp. 201–227). New York, NY: Morrow.

Morrison, T. (1992). *Playing in the dark: Whiteness and the literary imagination.* New York, NY: Vintage Books.

National Center for Education Information. (2005, August 18). *Profile of teachers in the U.S. 2005* [Press release]. Retrieved from www.ncei.com/POT05PRESSREL3.htm

Navarro, O. (2018). We can't do this alone: Validating and inspiring social justice teaching through a community of transformative praxis. *Curriculum Inquiry, 48*(3), 335–358.

Nieto, S., & McDonough, K. (2011). Placing equity front and center revisited. In A. F. Ball & C. A. Tyson (Eds.), *Studying diversity in teacher education* (pp. 363–384). Lanham, MD: Rowman & Littlefield.

Okun, T. (n.d.). White supremacy culture. Available at www.cwsworkshop.org/resources/ARAgenda.html

Omi, M., & Winant, H. (1994). *Racial formation in the United States: From the 1960s to the 1990s* (2nd ed). New York, NY: Routledge.

Paris, D. (2012). Culturally sustaining pedagogy: A needed change in stance, terminology, and practice. *Educational Researcher, 41*(3), 93–97.

Paris, D., & Alim, H. S. (2014). What are we seeking to sustain through culturally sustaining pedagogy? A loving critique forward. *Harvard Educational Review, 84*(1), 85–100.

Patel, L. (2016). *Decolonizing educational research: From ownership to answerability.* New York, NY: Routledge.

Payne, R. (2005). *A framework for understanding poverty* (4th ed.). Highlands, TX: aha! Process.
Payne, R. K. (2009). Poverty does not restrict a student's ability to learn. *The Phi Delta Kappan, 90*(5), 371–372.
Pennington, J. L., Brock, C. H., & Ndura, E. (2012). Unraveling the threads of white teachers' conceptions of caring: Repositioning white privilege. *Urban Education, 47*(4), 743–775.
Picower, B. (2007). Supporting new educators to teach for social justice: The critical inquiry project model. *Penn GSE Perspectives on Urban Education, 5*(1), 22.
Picower, B. (2009). The unexamined Whiteness of teaching: How White teachers maintain and enact dominant racial ideologies. *Race Ethnicity and Education, 12*(2), 197–215.
Picower, B. (2012). *Practice what you teach: Social justice education in the classroom and the streets.* New York, NY: Routledge.
Picower, B. (2015). Nothing about us without us: Teacher-driven critical professional development. *Radical Pedagogy, 12*(1).
Pollock, M. (2004). *Colormute: Race talk dilemmas in an American school.* Princeton, NJ: Princeton University Press.
Pollock, M. (Ed.). (2008). *Everyday antiracism: Getting real about race in school.* New York, NY: The New Press.
Pour-Khorshid, F. (2016). H.E.L.L.A.: Collective *testimonio* that speak to the healing, empowerment, love, liberation, and action embodied by social justice educators of color. *Association of Mexican American Educators Journal, 10*(2).
Randi, J., & Zeichner, K. M. (2004). New visions of teacher professional development. In M. A. Smylie & D. Miretzky (Eds.), *Developing the teacher workforce* (pp. 180–227). Chicago, IL: University of Chicago Press.
Rankine, C. (2016). The condition of black life is one of mourning. In J. Ward (Ed.), *The fire this time: A new generation speaks about race* (pp. 145–155). New York, NY: Scribner.
Roediger, D. R. (2007). *The wages of whiteness: Race and the making of the American working class.* New York, NY: Verso.
Rogers, C. (1989/1957). Personal thoughts on teaching and learning. In H. Kirschenbaum & V. L. Henderson, *The Carl Rogers reader* (pp. 301–304). Boston, MA: Houghton Mifflin.
Schniedewind, N. (2005). "There ain't no white people here!": The transforming impact of teachers' racial consciousness on students and schools. *Equity & Excellence in Education, 38*, 280–289.
Shor, I. (Ed). (1987). *Freire for the classroom: A sourcebook for liberatory teaching.* Portsmouth, NH: Boynton/Cooke Publishers.
Silko, L. M. (1977). *Ceremony.* New York, NY: Penguin Books.
Singleton, G. E., & Linton, C. (2006). *Courageous conversations about race: A field guide for achieving equity in schools.* Thousand Oaks, CA: Corwin Press.
Sleeter, C. E. (1996). *Multicultural education as social activism.* Albany: State University of New York Press.
Sleeter, C. (2008). Equity, democracy, and neoliberal assaults on teacher education. *Teaching and Teacher Education, 24*(8), 1947–1957.

Sleeter, C. E. (2016). Learning to work while white to challenge racism in higher education. In N. M. Joseph, C. Haynes, & F. Cobb (Eds). *Interrogating whiteness and relinquishing power* (pp. 13–26). New York, NY: Peter Lang.

Stake, R. E. (1995). *The art of case study research*. Thousand Oaks, CA: Sage Publications.

Steele, C. (2010). *Whistling Vivaldi: How stereotypes affect us and what we can do*. New York, NY: W. W. Norton & Company.

Stein, M. K., Smith, M. S., & Silver, E. A. (1999). The development of professional developers: Learning to assist teachers in new settings in new ways. *Harvard Educational Review, 69*(3), 237–269.

Tatum, B. D. (1997). *"Why are all the Black kids sitting together in the cafeteria?" and other conversations about race*. New York, NY: Basic Books.

Thandeka. (2006). *Learning to be White: Money, race, and God in America*. New York, NY: Continuum International Group.

Thandeka. (1999). Why anti-racism will fail. Retrieved from revthandeka.org/assets/why_anti-racism_will_fail.pdf

Thompson, B., & Tyagi, S. (1996). *Names we call home: Autobiography on racial identity*. New York, NY: Routledge.

Trainor, J. S. (2005). "My ancestors didn't own slaves": Understanding white talk about race. *Research in the Teaching of English, 40*, 140–167.

Valenzuela, A. (2008). Uncovering internalized oppression. In M. Pollock (Ed.), *Everyday antiracism: Getting real about race in school* (pp. 50–55). New York, NY: The New Press.

Watkins, W. H. (2001). *The white architects of Black education: Ideology and power in America, 1985–1954*. New York, NY: Teachers College Press.

Weaver, J. A., & Snaza, N. (2016). Against methodocentrism in educational research. *Educational Philosophy and Theory, 49*(11), 1055–1065.

Webster-Wright, A. (2009). Reframing professional development through understanding authentic professional learning. *Review of Educational Research, 79*(2), 702–739.

Wei, R. C., Darling-Hammond, L., & Hammond, F. (2010). Professional development in the United States: Trends and challenges. Dallas, TX: National Staff Development Council.

Weis, L., & Fine, M. (2012). Critical bifocality and circuits of privilege: Expanding critical ethnographic theory and design. *Harvard Educational Review, 82*(2), 173–201.

Wilson, S. M., & Berne, J. (1999). Teacher learning and acquisition of professional knowledge: An examination of research on contemporary professional development. *Review of Research in Education, 24*, 173–209.

Winkler, E. N. (2009). Children are not colorblind: How young children learn race. *PACE, 3*(3), 1–8.

Wise, T. J. (2008). *White like me: Reflections on race from a privileged son*. Brooklyn, NY: Soft Skull Press.

Wong, N. (2002). When I was growing up. In C. L. Moraga & G. E. Anzaldúa (Eds.), *This bridge called my back: Writings by radical women of color* (3rd ed., pp. 5–6). Berkeley, CA: Third Woman Press.

Yancy, G. (2009). Engaging whiteness and the practice of freedom: The creation of subversive academic spaces. In M. del Guadalupe Davidson & G. Yancy (Eds.), *Critical perspectives on bell hooks* (pp. 34–67). New York, NY: Routledge.

Index

accountability: need for, 71; neoliberal, 54, 109, 198–99; in RaceWork, redefined, 196–205; relational, 20, 52–53, 63–64, 83–84, 97, 109–13, 201–202; in schools, 76, 86
achievement gap. *See* educational debt
action research projects, 55–56, 59–60, 219
action. *See* antiracist, practices; praxis
anti-oppressive education, 37–38, 49–62, 68, 108, 187
antiracist: pedagogies, 10–11, 12–13, 117; practices, 43–44, 70, 175–76, 179–93, 210
asset-based approach, to teachers, 141, 144, 158–61
autonomy, teacher, 182–83
avoidance. *See* defense mechanisms

Baldwin, James, 28, 31–32, 193
becoming, as teachers, 19–20, 100–103, 160, 169–74, 193, 210. *See also* learning, as process
being vs. doing, 101, 175, 179, 212
best practices, critique of, 19, 151, 207–208
Beyond Diversity. *See* Courageous Conversations
binary, good and bad white people, 42, 61, 62, 156, 168, 171, 175
Boal, Augusto. *See* image theatre
brokenness, 31, 154, 189

caring, 69, 79, 90, 116–17
colorblindness, 3, 32, 39
colormuteness, 40–41
community, importance of, 80–84. *See also* accountability, relational
complicity, 166–69
confession, 40, 59, 136, 156–58
conflict, with colleagues, 75, 90–92, 98, 125–44
conversations, difficult, 58, 60–61, 149, 154–55, 170–73
co-teaching, 52, 62–63
Courageous Conversations, 47–48, 71, 143n
crisis, 38, 50. *See also* Kumashiro, Kevin
critical pedagogy. *See* anti-oppressive education
critical teacher learning, 196–205
critical whiteness studies, 24–25
cultural norms, 35, 36, 150, 153, 155, 173
culturally relevant/sustaining pedagogies, 7, 87–89, 101, 160, 179
curricular changes, 70, 72, 89, 184, 186

defense mechanisms, 47, 55, 74, 127–31, 132, 164
deficit thinking/orientation, of families, 140; of students, 41, 88–89; of teachers, 48, 103, 159, 184–85, 189, 195–96, 203

233

Delpit, Lisa, 33–34, 43
discipline gap. *See* school, discipline

easy answers (desire for), 121–22. *See also* teachers, checklist desire
education, purposes of, 31, 49–50, 193. *See also* anti-oppressive education
educational debt, 41, 59
emotion: brokenness, 189; confidence, 60, 90–91, 99, 142; discomfort, 142–43; frustration, 72, 91, 139, 168, 173–74, 182, 184, 195; guilt, 154; hope, 82–83; inadequacy, 208; isolation, 80–84, 171, 203; shame, 35, 154–55. *See also* fear
equity team, school or district: desire for action, 68–69; feelings toward: 141–42, 170–71; leadership of, 78, 91, 96, 143; professional development in, 138, 149
expectations, for students, 114, 153, 159–60, 187, 188
expert: people of color as, 42; RaceWork teachers positioned as, 20, 123, 142, 190; teacher as, 51, 169, 210–11

families. *See* relationships, with students' families
fear, 67–84, 100, 113, 126–28, 137, 196; of being called racist, 77–80; of getting antiracism wrong, 68–70; of harming relationships, 74–77; of not doing enough, 71–73; as productive, 80–84
finished. *See* becoming
framing, 41
Freire, Paulo, on: peoples' needs, 51; humanity, 82, 101, 160; love, 108, 192; pedagogy, 124, 158, 205–206, 212–13; reinvention, 210–11
funds of knowledge, 10, 118, 160

"getting it," 163–76

good and bad white people. *See* binary
growth, 86

hidden curriculum, 117, 168
home visits, 120, 186

identity: complexity of, 9, 13–14; racialized processes, 36; white racial 9, 34–36, 200. *See also* binary, good and bad white people; intersectionality
image theatre, 58, 176
intentions, 117, 140, 153, 168, 190
intersectionality, 13–14, 49n

Jansen, Jonathan, 30–31, 189

knowledge, as not enough, 37; as solution, 48
Kumashiro, Kevin: against common sense, 37–38; on learning, 50, 142–43, 190; on oppression and schools, 68, 88, 185, 187, 204–205

Ladson-Billings, Gloria, 7, 19, 41, 87–88, 101, 179
language: police, 58, 60, 61; racist and antiracist, 38–43, 48, 75, 93–94, 174–76. *See also* colorblindness; colormuteness; framing; white privilege; white talk
Lather, Patti, 219, 221
learning: as process, 169–72; beliefs on, 46, 49–50, 58, 85, 108, 142–44, 220; embodied, 58–59; self-appropriated, 10, 50, 122, 144, 209; teachers as, 92, 97–100, 114, 122. *See also* accountability, relational; anti-oppressive education; critical teacher learning
love, 108, 113, 191–92, 212

Midwest Critical Whiteness Collective, 5, 8, 40, 148
Minneapolis/St. Paul, 3–4

Morrison, Toni, 13, 29, 36

No Child Left Behind, 32–33, 174

Obama, Barack, 2–3
opportunity gap. See educational debt
oppression, internalized, 34

paradox, 206–209
Patel, Leigh, 219–20
Payne, Ruby. See poverty, cultural
pedagogy: banking, 47, 124, 199; defined, 12–13; in practice, 46–64, 133–34; problem-posing, 183. See also education, purposes of
"postracial" society, 3, 39
poverty: cultural, 150–51. See social class
praxis, defined, 158, 175; research and, 219, 221–22
privilege. See white privilege
professional development: challenges of, 7, 53, 71, 86, 175, 198–99, 203–204; characteristics of, 47–49, 199, 203; effects of, 202–203; teachers of color and, 203n. See also critical teacher learning

race: stage theory, 34, 48, 152; treason, 40n; and young children, 168–69
RaceWork: curriculum, 9, 23–44, 45–64; goals, 8–11, 51, 54–55, 86–87; facilitation of, 11, 45–64, 51, 183; origins, 5–8; pedagogy of, 183–93, 212; participants from different schools/districts, 53–54, 81, 112–13, 157, 199–200, 202, 209; theoretical approach, 24, 30, 48, 149–50, 152; tripartite model, 18, 24–27, 55
RaceWork teachers: Amelia, 14, 68–69, 74, 78–79, 82–83, 96–97, 100, 102, 109, 113–14, 121, 127–28, 130, 132, 137–38, 141–42, 149, 152–53, 164, 165, 169, 170–71, 175–76, 180–81, 183, 191–92, 201, 205, 208–209; Angela, 1, 14–15, 54, 59, 60, 74, 91–92, 98, 111, 123, 128–29, 139, 142, 150–51, 156–57, 173–74, 191, 205; Charlie, 7, 15, 60, 71, 73, 81–82, 94, 99, 112, 119–21, 134–35, 139–40, 144, 151–52, 156, 158, 159–60, 174–75, 181, 186–87, 203; Lisa, 15, 77, 81, 88–90, 95, 110–11, 116–17, 132, 169, 185–86, 200; Morgan, 15–16, 60, 76–77, 83, 91, 93–94, 99–100, 112, 119, 121–22, 126–27, 130–31, 133–34, 143–44, 164–65, 168–69, 171–73, 174, 182–85, 196, 208; Nicole, 2, 16, 48, 79, 97–98, 109, 110, 118, 129–30, 136, 154, 165, 167–68, 175, 192–93, 197, 200–201, 202; Sarah, 16–17, 54, 69, 72–73, 74–75, 79, 85, 90–91, 100–101, 111–12, 114–16, 118–19, 122–23, 130, 132–33, 138–39, 153–54, 156, 157, 166, 173, 175, 187–90, 201, 204; Veronica, 17, 23, 70, 72, 80, 95–96, 103, 112, 136–37, 141, 157, 167, 170, 190–91, 197, 202, 207
racial fluency or literacy, 93–97, 163–66, 176
racism, liberal individualist conception of, 125–41, 157, 182
reflective practice, 32, 37, 85, 158, 192, 197
reinvention, 210–13
relationships, 107–24, 125–44, 201–202, 220; with colleagues, 121–23, 125–44, 170–71, 172–73, 184–85, 191, 192; interpersonal, 94–96, 171–72, 183–84; with students, 113–18, 131–35, 167–68, 185–87, 191–92; with students' families, 59, 88–90, 95, 114, 118–21, 123, 139–40. See also accountability; relational

research, approach to, 219–22
resistance, to addressing racism, 77, 128, 159, 170, 172, 176
restorative justice, 17, 74–75, 79, 115–16, 122, 175, 187–88. *See also* school discipline

safe space, critique of, 54, 95, 209
scaling, 207–208
school: culture, 76–77; safety, 150
school discipline: changes to, 74–75, 78, 114–16, 119, 187–89; expectations and norms, 153–55, 167–68; policy, 72–73, 137–39; practices, 126–27, 133–34, 166, 169
school-to-prison pipeline, 73
second-wave whiteness studies, 148–50, 196, 221
Seeking Educational Equity and Diversity (SEED), 47–48, 136–37, 141, 157, 167, 197
segregation, 136
social class: and race: 28, 33, 147, 150–51; of students, 73, 92, 97–98, 122, 139
sociopolitical consciousness, 87–93
South Africa, 30–31
stereotype threat, 79
stories, 35–36, 52–53, 59, 61–62
storysharing, 52–53
strategies. *See* teachers, desiring checklist

talk. *See* language
teacher education, 32, 159–60, 205–206
teachers: checklist desire, 7, 158, 169, 170, 180–83, 191–92, 207; as learners, 38, 169. *See also* becoming, as teachers
Thandeka, 35, 42, 154
tokenizing, 70

white fragility, 155
white privilege: analysis of, 134–35, 147–61, 171–72; defined, 13; as framework, 6, 40, 59; resistance to, 27; as stopping point, 99, 136, 164
white racial identities. *See* identity, white racial
white supremacy, defined, 2n, 4–5, 12, 31, 46
white talk, 39–40
white-Black binary, 13, 29
whiteness: centering/de-centering, 152, 165, 175, 200, 206, 210; and communication, 33–34; creation of, 13, 27, 28–30, 35, 57; and economics, 28–30; hegemonic, 152–55; as invisible, 4, 29, 33, 39; and law, 28–29; learning of, 59; and schools, 30–34; and U.S. citizenship, 28–29. *See also* cultural norms

www.ingramcontent.com/pod-product-compliance
Lightning Source LLC
Chambersburg PA
CBHW020649230426
43665CB00008B/366